Romanticism and Contemporary Criticism

Romanticism and Contemporary Criticism

Edited by
MORRIS EAVES and
MICHAEL FISCHER

Cornell University Press

ITHACA AND LONDON

First published 1986 by Cornell University Press.

International Standard Book Number (cloth) 0-8014-1795-3
International Standard Book Number (paper) 0-8014-9352-8
Library of Congress Catalog Card Number 85-19472
Printed in the United States of America
Librarians: Library of Congress cataloging information
appears on the last page of the book.

The paper in this book is acid-free and meets the guidelines for
permanence and durability of the Committee on Production Guidelines
for Book Longevity of the Council on Library Resources.

To

DASHIELL EAVES
JOSHUA FISCHER
OBADIAH EAVES
SARAH FISCHER
whose exuberance is beauty

Contents

Preface   9

NORTHROP FRYE
The Survival of Eros in Poetry   15
Questions and Answers   29

W. J. T. MITCHELL
Visible Language: Blake's Wond'rous Art of Writing   46
Questions and Answers   86

J. HILLIS MILLER
On Edge: The Crossways of Contemporary Criticism   96
Postscript: 1984   111
Questions and Answers   118

M. H. ABRAMS
Construing and Deconstructing   127
Questions and Answers   158

STANLEY CAVELL
In Quest of the Ordinary: Texts of Recovery   183
Appendix: Poe's Imp   214
Questions and Answers   225

Notes on Contributors   241
Index   243

Preface

The present book began with the simple observation that English Romanticism is important to contemporary literary theory. The first product of this observation was "The Romantic Self," a course that we taught at the University of New Mexico in 1982–1983. In the course we examined how some major critics and philosophers approach critical theory as students of nineteenth-century literature. Contributors to this volume were selected from that group because they represent significant attempts to apply Romanticism to contemporary theoretical issues. Their indebtedness to Romanticism has not meant agreement with Romantic writers: in this context, Romanticism deserves credit not for answering questions but for asking them in their fundamental— provocative and disturbing—forms. The critics represented here not only define Romanticism in different ways but also use it to underwrite strikingly different theories of literature.

The relevance of Romanticism is especially clear in the work of Northrop Frye, whom M. H. Abrams has justly called "the most innovative, learned, and important literary theorist of my generation." Frye finds "the keys to poetic thought" (*The Stubborn Structure*) in Blake. Extending a line of thought begun in *A Study of English Romanticism* (1969), "The Survival of Eros in Poetry" explores the background of Romanticism by tracing the emergence and transformation of a major element in the history of postclassical poetry. In a wide-ranging question-and-answer session Frye identifies himself as a Romantic critic and comments for the first time in print on deconstruction and other critical trends.

9

Romanticism and deconstruction also meet (and cross) in W. J. T. Mitchell's "Visible Language: Blake's Wond'rous Art of Writing," which takes up the relation of poetry and painting, writing and printing, criticism and politics. Though indebted to contemporary criticism, Mitchell revises its assumptions, finding in Blake an antidote to what he sees as nihilistic tendencies in deconstruction. In his question-and-answer session Mitchell discusses Blake's place in the poststructuralist environment and the role that Romanticism might play in future literary theory.

Romanticism invites rather than cures deconstruction in J. Hillis Miller's "On Edge: The Crossways of Contemporary Criticism," which treats Wordsworth's "A Slumber Did My Spirit Seal," one of the so-called Lucy poems, as a parable of "the relation of metaphysics and the deconstruction of metaphysics." In his question-and-answer session Miller distinguishes deconstruction from the New Criticism and replies to several of its critics, including Walter Jackson Bate.

Miller's deconstruction reappears, this time as an illustration of the deconstructive method, in Abrams' "Construing and Deconstructing." Abrams places Miller's interpretation of Wordsworth in the broader contexts of philosophical skepticism and Jacques Derrida's writings. (In a postscript to "On Edge," Miller responds to Abrams' arguments.) Abrams in his question-and-answer session comments on key issues raised by deconstruction, Frye's archetypal criticism, critical pluralism, and Abrams' own work on Romanticism.

Going to works by Coleridge, Heidegger, Wisdom, Wordsworth, and Poe, Stanley Cavell's "In Quest of the Ordinary: Texts of Recovery" searches out connections between Romanticism and a crisis of knowledge brought on by skepticism. "The ordinary" is also the main topic of Cavell's question-and-answer session, which relates his own thought to a philosophical tradition that for him includes Emerson and Thoreau as well as the later Wittgenstein and J. L. Austin.

Numerous supporters from the University of New Mexico helped us: F. Chris Garcia, dean of the College of Arts and Sciences; Hamlin Hill, chairman of the Department of English; McAllister Hull, Jr., provost; Joel Jones, associate provost for academic affairs; Charlene A. McDermott, dean of graduate studies; and the office of the president.

The sets of questions and answers that follow each essay began as three-hour classroom sessions focusing on the work of each contributor, including the essays published here. Credit for the demanding lines of questioning pursued in and out of class belongs entirely to the undergraduate and graduate students of "The Romantic Self," 1982–1983, who made intellectual rigor seem natural for a time. Though we hope that the published result retains some of the life of the original occasions, the final versions, based on tapes of those sessions, have been extensively edited by us and reworked by the contributors. Georgia Eaves and Marta Field spent many hours turning barely audible cassettes into typed pages. And finally, we especially thank Georgia Eaves and Kim Fischer for taking so much time from their own work to help us with ours.

MORRIS EAVES AND MICHAEL FISCHER

Albuquerque, New Mexico

Romanticism and Contemporary Criticism

The Survival of
Eros in Poetry

Every society is characterized by concern, a term so broad that it is practically equivalent to conscious awareness itself, or at least to the awareness that life is serious, on both its individual and its social sides. The verbal expression of such concern is, in modern times, mainly conceptual and theoretical, taking the form of political, religious, psychological doctrines. Before the rise of conceptual language, however, such verbal expression most naturally took the form of stories, stories tending to explain or identify the gods, the structure of authority in the society, the legendary history, and the like. It is obvious that a great many societies had two categories of stories, one "sacred" or particularly serious and important, telling the society what it essentially needed to know, and one more relaxed and secular, stories told for entertainment or mere sociability.

Our own culture, by which I mean essentially the culture of Western Europe from the beginning of the Christian era to the present day, along with its descendants in the New World and elsewhere, was characterized, for many centuries, by a group of sacrosanct stories derived from the Bible. These stories had consolidated into a mythology, a reasonably coherent account of the relations of God to man from creation to, in the future, the end of the world; and the metaphors within the mythology had taken the form of a cosmology. Like most mythologies of concern, its primary function was to illuminate and rationalize the structure of authority, both spiritual and temporal, within its society. Although its cosmology, in some respects, was admitted to be metaphorical, still most of it enjoyed the prestige of a science for a long time. But the cosmology remained essentially related to the sense of concern about human duties and destiny that had inspired it, and it was not really a proto-science.

This cosmos of authority envisaged a universe on four main levels. At the top was heaven in the sense of the place of the presence of God. The word "top" is a metaphor, but it was so pervasive a metaphor that it got into practically every type of reference to God, who was invariably thought of as "up there." This God was a Creator, the creation myth of the Bible being an artificial creation myth in which the universe is made by a divine sky-father, in contrast to others where it is brought into being by an earth-mother. Such a God could have created only a perfect world, with no sin or death in it: this perfect world is described in the Book of Genesis in its first chapter, and in the story of Adam and Eve in the Garden of Eden. An alienation myth or fall is necessary to account for the difference between this originally perfect world and the one we are now in. The latter forms a third level, also part of the order of nature, and below it is the demonic world or hell—again a metaphorical "down," but an inescapable metaphor. There are, then, a divine presence above nature, a demonic world below nature, and two levels of the order of nature itself, or the created world.

The third or "fallen" world is the one we are born into, and animals and plants seem to be relatively well adjusted to it, but man is not. His natural home is the perfect world God originally created for him and intended him to live in. Nothing remains of this world physically except the stars in their courses, along with the legends concerning the stars, that they are made of quintessence, that they move in perfect circles about the earth, that they give out an inaudible music. Otherwise, the original home of man is no longer a place, but may to some degree be achieved as a state of mind. Man's primary duty, in fact, is to move upward on the scale of being, coming as close to his original state as possible. Many things are "natural" to man that are not natural to any other organism: the wearing of clothes, the being in a state of social discipline, the practice of religion and law, the possession of consciousness. Everything good for man in religion, law, and education has for its end his promotion from the lower to the higher level of nature. Man's pilgrimage is a purgatorial one, whether an actual doctrine of purgatory is involved or not.

If we take such a period as the Elizabethan age in English literature, we can soon see how impossible it is to understand, in many crucial aspects, without realizing that for Spenser, Sidney, Shakespeare, and their contemporaries there are two levels of nature, an upper level of human nature, where nature and art are much the same thing, and a lower level of physical nature, from which man's essential humanity feels alienated. Thus Sidney says that nature's (i.e., lower nature's) world is brazen, in contrast to the poet's golden world, and that (on the higher level) art is a "second nature." In *King Lear* the nature whom Edmund accepts as his goddess is lower nature; what Lear's own references to nature are concerned with is an order of nature that Edmund has shut out of his mind. Such a conception of nature, it is obvious, is one that throws a very heavy emphasis on the aspect of nature called *natura naturata*, nature as a structure or system.

This emphasis derives from the biblical horror of nature-worship, that is, of finding anything numinous in nature to adore. This is primarily what the Bible means by idolatry, and the corollary of its condemning of idolatry is the principle that man is to turn away from nature and seek his God through human institutions. Nature was of course created along with man, and the traces of its original perfection may still be seen in it, but whatever we find to admire in it must be instantly referred back to its Creator. Everything God has created possesses two impulses: an impulse to die or decay, which is inevitable in a fallen world, and an impulse to return to its Creator, something that only man can do consciously.

Not that man can set out to do such a thing of his own volition. In this cosmos all the initiative comes from above, the initiative that in human life is known as grace. Even a revolutionary thinker in this period, such as Milton, could not think of liberty as anything that man can achieve for himself or even wishes to achieve. Liberty is good for man because God wants him to have it, but without grace no man wants it. There is a current of love flowing from God to man, and it is man's duty to accept that love and communicate it to his neighbor. That is Christian love in its pure form of *agape* or charity. Whatever springs from the sexual instinct is mainly something that belongs to the behavior of a gregarious animal.

All of this represents a very considerable divergence from the tradition of Classical literature, starting with Plato and continuing through Virgil and Ovid, which assigns a powerful impetus in human life to Eros, the energy of a love rooted in the sexual instinct, which can be a destructive passion or an ennobling power. It is profoundly significant for the central question in literary criticism of the social function of the arts, that poets from the medieval period on simply inserted Eros into their cosmos, as something the religious and philosophical authorities had left out, and ought not to have left out.

There is no need to rehearse in detail the familiar story of courtly love in medieval poetry. Influenced largely by Virgil and Ovid, the

poets worked out an elaborate correspondence between sexual love and
Christian *agape*. One might be living one's life carelessly, in complete
freedom from the perturbations of love; then the God of Love, Eros or
Cupid, would suddenly strike, and from then on one was Love's abject
slave, supplicating the favor (usually) of a mistress. Sometimes, as in
Dante, the cult of Eros is sublimated, in other words assimilated to
the Christian one. It is Eros who inspires Dante with his *vita nuova* that
started from his first sight of Beatrice, but Beatrice in the *Paradiso* is
an agent of divine grace. In another great medieval epic, however, *The
Romaunt of the Rose*, the climax of the poem is a clearly sexual allegory,
and in Petrarch, who did far more than Dante to popularize the theme,
at least in English literature, love for Laura is rooted in Eros throughout,
even though again it is sublimated, involving no sexual contact and
easily surviving her death.

In these sublimated forms the love of a mistress becomes a parallel
quest to the purgatorial one: it is what inspires a hero to great deeds
and a poet to great words. A poet who attempts poetry without experiencing the power of Eros is conventionally assumed to be a rather
poor creature. Sublimation usually means that the mistress is an inspiring object but not a sexual one; love poetry, however, covers the whole
spectrum from idealism to bawdiness. What is essential, normally, is
a long period of frustration during which the mistress is proud, dis-
dainful, cruel, and the like. Lovers who die or go mad through such
frustration are the saints and martyrs of the God of Love: in Chaucer's
Legend of Good Women, meaning women good by Eros' standards, we
find Helen of Troy, Cleopatra, and Dido. The question has been raised
of whether Romeo's suicide would, in the minds of Shakespeare's audience, involve him in damnation. Most of the audience would recognize
that Romeo has his own religion, which does not conflict with Christianity but nevertheless goes its own way: when Romeo speaks of "my
bosom's lord" he means the God of Love, and he dies a martyr in the
odor of erotic sanctity.

Although the main sources of such love poetry are Classical, there
are certain biblical allusions that reinforce it and help to assimilate it
to other types of poetry. The Song of Songs, whatever the commentators
had done to it, still remained a great monument of poetry inspired by
sexual love, and there the bride is described as "a garden enclosed, a
fountain sealed." The imagery of trees and water reminds us of the
Garden of Eden, and there too the love of Adam and Eve before the
Fall remains a pattern of sexual union, even though not everyone shared
Milton's view that sexual intercourse as we know it took place before
the Fall. Let us glance at a familiar lyric of Campion:

There is a garden in her face,
Where roses and white lilies grow;
   A heav'nly paradise is that place,
Wherein all pleasant fruits do flow.
   There cherries grow which none may buy
   Till cherry-ripe themselves do cry . . .

   Her eyes like angels watch them still;
Her brows like bended bows do stand,
   Threat'ning with piercing frowns to kill
All that attempt with eye or hand
   Those sacred cherries to come nigh,
   Till cherry-ripe themselves do cry.

The theme of forbidden fruit is associated with sex; the biblical image of the angels forbidding entrance to Eden after the Fall is assimilated to the lady's disdain; echoes of the garden of the Hesperides mingle with the memories of Eden suggested by such words as "paradise" and "sacred." Similarly with Fulke Greville:

Caelica, I overnight was finely used,
Lodged in the midst of paradise, your heart;
Kind thoughts had charge I might not be refused,
Of every fruit and flower I had part.

But curious knowledge, blown with busy flame,
The sweetest fruits had in down shadows hidden,
And for it found mine eyes had seen the same,
I from my paradise was straight forbidden.

The "heart" is invariably a respectable suburban address: if the lover moves into the downtown business section other complications arise. More accurately, the theme of forbidden knowledge is given an even more explicitly sexual connotation than it has in Genesis.

Another association involved here is that between the mistress's body and the garden itself. If we look carefully at the imagery of *Paradise Lost*, we can see how subtly but constantly Milton associates the Garden of Eden with the body of Eve. Marvell's well-known poem "The Garden" describes a union first of the body and then of the soul of the narrator with the garden, and then goes on to make the paradoxical point that the garden itself was the only mistress that Adam needed, the creation of Eve being the beginning of the loss of paradise. A different aspect of the same kind of identification appears in Bartholomew Griffin's *Fidessa* sequence:

> Fair is my love that feeds among the lilies,
> The lilies growing in that pleasant garden
> Where Cupid's mount, that well belovèd hill is,
> And where that little god himself is warden.

The first line contains an echo of the Song of Songs, but "Cupid's mount" can hardly be anything but the *mons veneris*. The same imagery, according to most Spenserian scholars, appears in the Gardens of Adonis episode of *The Faerie Queene*, where the gardens are also referred to as a paradise. In a very long poem called *Loves Martyr* by Robert Chester, best known now because a group of rather better poets, including Shakespeare, wrote pendants to it (Shakespeare's contribution was the poem called "The Phoenix and the Turtle"), a conventional feature of such poems, the detailed description of the heroine's body, is provided. In case our attention relaxes, the author places in the margin the feature of the lady's anatomy he is talking about: we begin with "Hair," "Brow," "Eyes" and the like, and finally work our way down to "Bellie." Just as we are beginning to get a flicker of interest in this dreary poem, the next stanza has in the margin merely "Nota," and the stanza itself talks about the four rivers of Eden. If the author had been a distinguished poet, we might assign this to a quirky originality, but when he is Robert Chester we can be sure that nothing but straight convention is involved.

Shakespeare's "Phoenix and the Turtle" is a different matter: there the biblical metaphor of two people becoming "one flesh" in marriage is applied, in an erotic context, to the union in "death," which can mean sexual union, of a red bird and a white bird on St. Valentine's Day. Some of the paradoxes resulting from two things becoming the same thing almost read like parodies of the Nicene creed on the persons and substance of the Trinity. Donne uses the same kind of imagery, especially in "The Canonization" (the title means that the narrator and his mistress have become saints in Eros' calendar):

> The phoenix riddle hath more wit
> By us; we two being one, are it.
> So to one neutral thing both sexes fit,
> We die and rise the same, and prove
> Mysterious by this love.

And, of course, the same biblical paradisal imagery, the same identification of God-created garden and the body of his bride (or virgin-
mother) could occur in a straightforward Christian poem with no courtly
love overtones at all. Thus in Henry Vaughan's "Regeneration":

> With that, some cried, Away; straight I
>   Obey'd, and led
> Full East, a fair, fresh field could spy
>   Some call'd it, Jacob's Bed;
>
> A Virgin-soil, which no
>   Rude feet ere trod,
> Where (since he stepped there) only go
>   Prophets, and friends of God.

The epigraph to this poem is again the passage in the Song of Songs
that includes the reference to the enclosed garden and the sealed fountain.

   The points I have been making up to now are not particularly novel;
my purpose in making them is to bring out certain aspects of historical
criticism that are less frequently discussed. One is the status of allusions
to Classical mythology. From the very strict orthodox point of view,
all the resemblances between Classical and biblical stories and images
result from the activity of the devils, who seized control of the Classical
oracles (Cowley, for example, speaks of "the fiend Apollo") and instilled
demonic parodies of the sacred myths into the minds of the heathen.
Such demonic parodies may be called negative analogies. But there are
other Classical myths that can be regarded as positive analogies, as
moving, from the poet's point of view, in counterpoint to the sacred
texts. It was a commonplace in the Renaissance period that many of
the Classical myths, especially those in Ovid's *Metamorphoses*, could be
used contrapuntally in this way. Thus Giles Fletcher:

> Who doth not see drown'd in Deucalions name
> (When earth his men, and sea had lost his shore)
> Old Noah; and in Nisus' lock, the fame
> Of Sampson yet alive; and long before
> In Phaethon's, mine own fall I deplore:
>   But he that conquer'd hell, to fetch again
>   His virgin widow, by a serpent slain,
> Another Orpheus was than dreaming poets feign.

   The story of the worldwide deluge in Ovid, which Deucalion and
Pyrrha alone survived, is a positive analogy of the story of Noah in

21

Genesis; the story of "Nisus' injur'd hair," as Pope calls it, has resemblances to the Samson saga; the story of the fall of Phaethon is an analogy of the fall of man; the descent of Orpheus to hell to reclaim his bride Eurydice is an analogy of the harrowing of hell by Jesus and his rescue of his bride the Church. The final phrase about "dreaming poets" is an example of the traditional ingratitude of Christian poets who levy such tribute on the Classical writers while officially denouncing the truth of their stories. Similarly, in the first Canto of the *Paradiso*, Dante uses the Classical images of Marsyas, who was flayed alive for challenging Apollo to a contest in flute-playing (the Olympians were notoriously poor losers, but Apollo had not even the excuse of losing), and of Glaucus, who ate some miraculous grass that turned him into a sea-god. The images are exquisitely precise: Marsyas stands for the divesting of the garment of flesh in paradise and Glaucus for the plunge into a new and unknown element. But the touch of grotesquerie in the same images still keeps a hint of negative analogy or demonic parody.

To understand this more clearly we may turn to the passage in *Paradise Regained* in which Satan suggests that Jesus, if he does not want earthly power of any kind, might become one of the great Athenian philosophers. Here Jesus, in a passage which has troubled many of Milton's commentators, rejects the whole of the Classical tradition as worthless. Its taproot is the theology and culture of hell described in Book II of *Paradise Lost*, and Jesus must reject every atom of it if he is to proceed with his ministry. But having rightly rejected it in the right context, he thereby redeems it, at any rate for his followers. In the Nativity Ode all the heathen gods are put to flight by the rising sun of the Incarnation. Our own sympathies are divided: nobody wants Moloch back, and he will always be a demonic parody, but we have more sympathy with the "parting Genius" who is "with sighing sent" from his habitation. Milton can use Moloch only as a devil, but the "Genius" is a positive analogy of a Christian guardian angel, and appears as such in "Lycidas," "Arcades," "Comus," and "Il Penseroso."

The cult of Eros in medieval and later poetry, then, is a special case of imaginative conquest by Classical poetic mythology, sometimes in the teeth of religious opposition, but steadily increasing the range and power of poetry in the Western world. As society became more complex and sophisticated, other types of analogies grew up: in Protestant England, for example, Jewish or Catholic imagery could be used either as types or as aesthetic analogies of what would be acceptable to authority. In Milton's "Il Penseroso" the narrator, choosing to live in the melancholy tonality, so to speak, for the rest of his life, speaks of dwelling among cloisters, stained glass, Gothic architecture, organ music, and finally a hermitage. All these were deprecated in strictly Puritan circles, but in a mood-poem, where aesthetic feelings are so important, they are acceptable as aesthetic analogies. It is probable, but not absolutely necessary, that the nun who is the muse of this poem is more of a Classical vestal virgin than a Christian nun. The poem closes with a phrase that delicately indicates the analogical nature of its imagery, specifically in the passage about becoming a hermit:

> Till old experience do attain
> To something like prophetic strain.

To anticipate a little, a poet with strong Christian commitments might use Classical imagery as analogical to Christian themes, but he would do so, presumably, with the assumption that the Christian theme was primary and the Classical one peripheral. Thus Francis Thompson, in *Assumpta Maria*:

> I am the four Rivers' Fountain
> Watering Paradise of old;
> Cloud down-raining the Just One am,
> Danae of the Shower of Gold.

The same imaginative link between the Virgin Mary and the story of Danae is made by Ezra Pound, in the fourth Canto, but this time there is no sense of the greater reality of one story than of the other: they are simply two themes in poetic counterpoint:

> upon the gilded tower in Ecbatan
> Lay the god's bride, lay ever, waiting the golden rain . . .
> Across the Adige, by Stefano, Madonna in hortulo,
> as Cavalcanti had seen her.

Cavalcanti has a poem which tells us that the miraculous cures ascribed to a picture of the Virgin were the result of the fact that the model for the Virgin was his mistress: a further secularizing piece of counterpoint.

The general principle this argument is leading to may be expressed as follows. In the earlier stages of a culture, there is usually a dominating myth of concern which controls the arts. In the Middle Ages, for example, the ecclesiastical authorities who were the main patrons of painting prescribed the subjects to be painted and the way they were to be treated, stated which saints were bearded and which clean-shaven, which ones barefooted and which shod, and insisted on certain conventions, such as clothing the Madonna in blue. As painting grew more complex and its patronage widened, the artist became increasingly aware of technical discoveries to be made in the art of painting itself, which might command his loyalties no matter what his patrons wanted. By the time we reach the *Salon des refusés* of the French Impressionists, we have gone a long way in this direction. The principle is more easily illustrated by science. Galileo and Bruno felt a commitment to the scientific conception of a heliocentric solar system even when the anxieties of the time demanded a geocentric one. Darwin and Huxley, opposing Bishop Wilberforce on the question of evolution and creation, were committed in the same sense. Today the authority of science is generally recognized, even though the lethal dangers of our time indicate that the conflict of science and social concern is a two-way street, that concern still has its own case, and that there can be such a thing as socially irresponsible science.

But society is much less willing to grant literature or the other arts any degree of inner authority of this kind. Certain Marxist regimes, such as Stalinist Russia with its "social realism" and the so-called Gang-of-Four group in China, deny such authority as a matter of dogma and insist that the arts, including literature, must be hitched to the bandwagon of ideology. In theory, of course, there is no ideology, merely the natural creativity of workers released from the constraints of other ideologies, but it would take a fairly gullible observer to accept that. There have been some startling outbreaks of hysteria in the democracies, too, that indicate similar feelings there, even when not expressed in government action. In the period that we have been looking at, there were certainly tensions between the anxieties of the prevailing social concern and the poet's loyalty to his own craft, though their expression was necessarily very oblique. In the thirteenth-century French romance *Aucassin and Nicolette*, for example, Aucassin is warned that his uncompromising pursuit of his lady may place him in danger of hell fire. He replies that hell is clearly the only place to go, because everything that makes life worth living seems headed for it, whereas nobody cares about heaven except for a few old crocks who are fit for nothing else. For all the gossamer-light humor, there were contemporaries of the *Aucassin* poet who would have said the same thing in grim earnest. An even more familiar example is the "Retractation" at the end of Chaucer's *Canterbury Tales*, where the poet repudiates those of his tales "that sownen into synne," a phrase that takes his Friar and Summoner at their own valuation. There is a strong aroma of "sign here" about the Retractation, but if it is a voluntary composition of Chaucer's it merely demonstrates the conflict of concern and craftsmanship within the same mind, a conflict that has raged in many great poetic minds before and later. Tasso and Tolstoy are obvious examples.

It seems to me that the question of the authority of poetry within a culture, which is much the same thing as the question of the social function of poetry, is a central problem of critical theory. It is obvious that such authority has no direct or simple connection with content. Most literary critics would recognize a core of authority in the essential visions of Pound or D. H. Lawrence, while admitting freely that they talked a good deal of nonsense as well. As W. H. Auden apostrophizes Yeats: "You were silly like us; your gift survived it all." But what constitutes a "gift"? If we accept the poet's own answer, the ability to write well, we are simply going around in circles.

Around the latter part of the eighteenth century, or about the time of Rousseau, the older cosmos of authority began to break down. What was at issue, as far as literature was concerned, was not the objectively true but the rhetorically convincing: within literature, the word "truth" is a term in rhetoric and means what carries one along in emotional agreement. The cosmos of authority could not outlive the authority that supported it; and the American Revolution, the French Revolution, and the later Industrial Revolution were cracking up the authority on all sides. Let us look first at the metaphorical association of the presence of God with the upper heavens. After Newton's time, it was no longer believed that the stars were made of an imperishable substance, that they moved in perfect circles, or that they symbolized the underlying harmony of the universe. A universe held together with gravitation suggests a mechanism, not a design, and within literature there is a sharp difference between the two. In Romantic thought the superiority of the organism to the mechanism is a central principle: there being no visible organism in the skies, the upper world becomes increasingly a symbol of alienation, as it still is, for the most part, in science fiction.

More central to our present argument is the poetic treatment of Eros, which from this period on begins to acquire a larger reference. Human sexuality comes to be seen increasingly as an aspect of the neglected *natura naturans*, nature as a vast reservoir of life and reproductive power. Such nature is indissolubly linked to man: man is, therefore, as much a child of nature as he is of God. And so another cosmos began to grow up in poetry, with much the same set of levels as before, but, in effect, the older world stood on its head. At the top was empty space, filled by an emotionally meaningless world of stars. This world suggested nothing to the human imagination except the

25

involuntary and mechanical: hence the sky-god in Romantic and much later poetry, Blake's Urizen, Shelley's Jupiter, Hardy's Immanent Will, becomes a source of tyranny. Below this is the world we live in; below that again is a nature, huge, mysterious, morally ambivalent, an otherness that is still an essential part of our own identity. In more optimistic writers, this "nature" is what man needs to complete his own being, a wise and benevolent teacher, as normally in Wordsworth. Elsewhere it is a sinister image, predatory, ruthless, and totally indifferent to human values, but man is inescapably attached to it nonetheless.

In the older construct, the two levels of nature were arranged so as to put the ordinary world we are all born into—or thrown into, according to some—metaphorically below an ideal or paradisal world where man was, at one time, fully integrated with his natural surroundings. In the newer Romantic construct the world of ordinary experience sits on top of a world in which man rediscovers his integration with nature but does not necessarily find this discovery beneficial. Some writers in the Rousseau orbit associated the natural with the rational, and assumed that a natural society would also be a rational one: it is this attitude that changed the word "artificial" from a term of approval to a deprecatory one. In Shelley a relation of sexual love normally includes the reintegration of nature with humanity: thus in *Epipsychidion*:

> Let us become the overhanging day,
> The living soul of this Elysian isle,
> Conscious, inseparable, one.

Such an integration with nature as environment would have been impossible for, say, Donne, with his conviction that there is nothing paradisal outside the regenerate human mind. Elsewhere the sense of otherness in nature is associated with its size and strength: the feeling of awe that produced the "sublime" in Romantic and preromantic aesthetics. I have elsewhere spoken of the curious "drunken boat" construct in nineteenth-century thought, where the world of experience seems to float precariously on something immensely powerful that both supports it and threatens it. Examples are the world as will in Schopenhauer, the world of unconscious impulse in Freud, the world of the excluded proletariat in Marx, the world of evolutionary development in Darwin and the social applications of Darwinism. In some of these constructs the lower world contains only monsters of the deep; in others there is a submarine Atlantis to be reached.

It is particularly the latter group who revive the ancient theme of the quest of descent, which had been kept alive because of the prestige

26

of Virgil's *Aeneid* and the extraordinary vision of its sixth book, but which in Christian constructs was usually demonized. With the Romantic period there begins that inner quest to something oracular in the depths of the mind which has developed, among other things, the technique of fantasy. In De Quincey, for example, particularly in the great mail-coach essay, there is, first, a long, diffuse, and digressive piece of reminiscent writing, as though the author were scanning the ground for clues; this suddenly tightens up into a moment of intense action, except that the action is not performed but observed by him, and after that it funnels into the dream-world in a descending spiral. The dream-world is, like all the levels of the Romantic cosmos, morally ambivalent: the *Confessions* ends with two sections, one on the pleasures and the other on the pains of opium, the good and the bad trips, after which there is a succession of visions representing the fact that the greatest intensity of the imagination is to be found at the bottom rather than the top of experience, as in the Classical oracles, which were also assisted by drugs or narcotics. In the mail-coach essay the experience described dramatizes to the writer the essential weakness of human consciousness as based on observation, and hence on the lack of a crucial spontaneity where action is needed. Perhaps, De Quincey concludes, the central thing that dreams are trying to tell us is that man's rational and observing consciousness is his original sin:

> Upon the secret mirror of our dreams such a trial is darkly projected, perhaps, to every one of us. That dream, so familiar to childhood, of meeting a lion, and, through languishing prostration in hope and the energies of hope, that constant sequel of lying down before the lion, publishes the secret frailty of human nature—reveals its deep-seated falsehood to itself—records its abysmal treachery. Perhaps not one of us escapes that dream; perhaps, as by some sorrowful doom of man, that dream repeats for every one of us, through every generation, the original temptation in Eden.

We are reminded of the fact that the *Confessions* ends with a line from the end of *Paradise Lost* about the angels expelling man from Eden, and, by anticipation, of the dream of Finnegan, or rather of HCE, in Joyce, with its feelings of primordial guilt as the unreached source of the dream pilgrimage itself. For modern literature the essential link between man and nature seems to be the sexual one, and the great battle between sexuality and self-consciousness, or what Lawrence called sex in the head, is so prevalent a theme in literature now as to suggest that the integration of Eros is close to the center of whatever new cosmos will replace the Romantic one.

I spoke at the beginning of concern as one of the essential elements of all civilization. It seems to me that there is primary concern and secondary concern. Primary concern is based on what can be expressed only in the baldest and biggest of platitudes: the sense that life is better than death, happiness better than misery, freedom better than slavery. Secondary concern has to do with the structure and source of authority in society, with religious belief and political loyalties, with the desire of the privileged to keep their privileges and of the nonprivileged to get along as well as they can in that situation. I think the present age, with its threats of nuclear warfare and environmental pollution, is an age in which secondary concerns are rapidly dissolving. Down to the Romantic period, and for many poets later than that, the cosmos within which most writers worked was either the cosmos of authority already described, or the cosmos of revolt, which we said was essentially the same kind of structure upside down. As the sixteenth-century Anabaptist theologian Hans Denck remarked, after publishing a list of antithetical statements culled from scripture: "Whoever leaves an antithesis without resolving it lacks the ground of truth."

Occasionally one discovers a writer who is not satisfied to inhabit his world unconsciously, or by instinct, or whatever the right term is. Thus Poe's *Eureka* is an essay on speculative cosmology which sounds as though it were using scientific or philosophical language, but which Poe himself says at the beginning he wishes to be considered as a poetic product. Paul Valéry's note on *Eureka* remarks that cosmology is primarily a *literary* art: it is based, not on the scientific or philosophical ideas of its time, but on metaphorical analogies to them that appeal to poets. The purpose of such cosmologies is to give us some notion of the kind of context within which literature is operating, the imaginative counterpart of the worlds explored by intellect and sensation. Since then a good many such speculative cosmologies have emerged, some disguised as historical or scientific treatises, and eventually, one hopes, we shall have a clearer notion of what kind of world our creative writers are living in.

Such a world is dominated by forces that were originally gods, Eros, Prometheus, Cybele (perhaps the closest approach to Graves's white goddess) and others. In consequence some modern writers have accepted a polytheistic outlook: Hölderlin did, and Ezra Pound often talked as though he did. But it is only a nervous habit that keeps us calling such forces gods: they are states of the human mind with metaphorical identities in nature. More important, they are the shaping powers of poetry, the authentic muses. In Greek myth the muses bore the names of literary genres and were in the aggregate daughters of memory, that is, of literary convention. In our day they bear names like Anxiety, Absurdity, and Alienation, and they are the daughters of Frustration; but their power is as great as ever, and their cultural achievements could be as impressive as ever.

QUESTIONS AND ANSWERS

Question: "The Survival of Eros in Poetry" is typical of your work in its focus on Christian metaphors and beliefs. I want to ask a question that might help me understand the relation between metaphors in art and beliefs in religion. In the conclusion to his review of your book *The Great Code* and Robert Alter's *The Art of Biblical Narrative* for *The Georgia Review*, Herbert Levine remarked that "the Christian notion of original sin, claiming that man cannot fulfill his destiny without divine help, simply expresses (in Frye's liberated view) man's fear of his own freedom. The ex-Christian Frye, who has apparently passed beyond good and evil, imagines us as self-delighting, self-enlightening beings capable of our own redemption. The liberal Jew [Robert Alter] imagines no redemption whatsoever, only the difficult task of living in history." Did you write *The Great Code* as an ex-Christian, and do you agree with Levine's judgment?

Answer: Well, I don't know this audience very well, so I can't express my opinion of those sentences in a language that I think is appropriate to them. The United Church of Canada, of which I am an ordained clergyman, would be surprised to hear that I am an ex-Christian. I think that the answer to the reviewer's puzzlement is simply that all my life I have learned my views of Christianity more or less from Blake, who would never split the efforts of man from the efforts of God. He would say that God works only through man, and that only when the divine and the human become identified is man himself created and genuinely alive. And certainly mere man, or natural man, can do nothing about it by himself—and to that extent the conception of original sin is quite valid. The reviewer has accepted it and so have I. It doesn't mean, however, that you are going to call an objective God down out of the sky to help man in his state of original sin. The God that will help not only works through the man but is the man.

Question: That way of explaining original sin seems similar to your explanation of the passage about the fall of man being reenacted in dreams from De Quincey's mail-coach essay, which you use to show a change in metaphorical constructs brought about by Romanticism. That passage comes at the end of the description of the running down

29

of the two trapped people by the mail coach. The scene has the quality of a nightmare, but I can't see a connection between that kind of dream and the fall of man. Could you put that together for me, please?

Answer: De Quincey is one of the great pioneers of a principle which we largely take for granted today. He was one of the first people to understand the spiritual world in metaphorical terms. Dante uses categories of time and space: the inferno is underneath the surface of the world, and the people there know the future, not the present. Purgatory is a mountain on the opposite side of the spiritual world, and paradise is in the stars. These are all to some degree metaphorical constructs that suggest that the real drama of the spiritual life of man is going on elsewhere: real eternal life is after death, and souls are saved across the world in purgatory.

Ever since the Romantic period, we've become increasingly aware that all the drama and spectacle of heaven and hell is enacted inside the human mind. I remember some years ago a manic depressive who was caught by the BBC—this is the kind of thing that could only happen on the BBC—and asked on the radio what it was like to be a manic depressive. His answer contained one thing which struck me; he said, "It's no good arguing with me about heaven and hell. I've been there." One of the earliest statements of that realization is in the passage where De Quincey proposes that in every dream, every night, the original sin that brings about the fall of man is reenacted. The drama is within our consciousness the whole time and never leaves us.

Original sin is not being born with the capacity to murder and rape. Original sin is essentially inertia, the feeling of helplessness—that beyond a certain point we can't go. It is that nightmare feeling of being stuck with our feet in concrete which De Quincey seizes on as the psychological essence of the doctrine.

Question: The key to the explanations of your own Christianity and of the passage from De Quincey's essay seems to be metaphor. How do you define it?

Answer: The grammatical form of metaphor is *a is b*—Joseph is a fruitful bough and Issachar is a strong ass—although it is extremely obvious to any sane person that *a* is not *b* at all. So what is the point of saying that *a* is *b* and making it the cornerstone of poetic expression when *a* is not *b*? I suggest that the function of metaphor is the opening of a channel of verbal energy between the subjective world and the objective world, which is easiest and most natural at a period of society when the subjective and objective worlds are not clearly distinguished.

Question: Do you agree then with Paul Tillich that symbols, which in clusters become myth, are the highest possible articulation of experience and belief, and that using words metaphorically is superior to using them literally?

Answer: I certainly do agree with Tillich on that point, but I would make a slight alteration in your phrasing. People who say the Bible is literally true, for example, usually mean that here in a book is a stack of words which is related by correspondence to certain events in the spiritual and historical world outside. Now it seems to me that one should read the Bible literally, but one should remember that the literal meaning is in fact the metaphorical meaning, that it is the symbolic meaning, because the structure of words cannot be literally anything but a structure of words. So the things that bind the structure of words together—the metaphors, the images, the symbols, and the like—are the bedrock of the reading of anything.

Question: In *The Great Code* you describe three phases of language—metaphoric, metonymic, and descriptive—and allude to a fourth phase that you seem to believe we might be entering. Can you describe the fourth phase?

Answer: In *The Great Code* I spoke of the origin of thought in metaphor, the sense of an undifferentiated energy flowing between personality and nature. The essential unit of this phase is the god. That phase is displaced by more abstract language, in particular the dialectical language of Plato, which I connect with metonymy: *a* is *put for b*. Then, the distinctively modern form of expression is close, accurate description, in which the verbal structure *a* is *like b*, the body of phenomena that is being described. These phases perhaps give you the keys to the immanent language that the Romantic poet wants in connecting man with nature, the transcendental language that the theologian and metaphysician want in connecting man with the world of ideas, and the descriptive language that the scientist wants in getting a clear account of things in words. A fourth stage, which I mention as a future possibility, would unite these three and perhaps do other things by uniting them. But one of the functions of poetry, as I see it, is to keep alive the metaphorical habit of mind and to make sure that its significance remains obvious to all receptive people.

Question: The marvelous capacity of your system for categorizing suggests the possibility of a metacriticism that would categorize other critical theories. Can you categorize your own system?

Answer: I rather gave up categorizing forms of criticism after I published the *Anatomy*. Increasingly since then I've felt that bringing critical theories in is really a job for somebody else, preferably somebody younger. I can only pursue my own course at this point. I can't see myself in perspective.

31

Question: Would it make sense to describe your critical theory as Romantic?

Answer: Oh, it's entirely Romantic, yes. I see the Romantic movement as the first great step in clarifying the role of criticism and bringing in a conception of creativity that could unify the mental elements in the creative process. While Samuel Johnson's criticism is an unmatchable instance of its type, it is also the kind of criticism that follows literature at a certain distance, commenting on it and thereby mediating between works of literature and the reading public. For all his limitations, Johnson was an extraordinary critic who is right nine times out of ten, but his kind of criticism does not go on to study what literature is doing in the world. But Coleridge's criticism—for all the blither—does give me some sense of that, and some sense of the autonomy of the creative person. A critic like Addison will say that the artist has to meet the standards of taste established in his day, whereas the Romantics are more apt to say that if the standards of taste in my day don't like what I'm doing, so much the worse for the standards of taste. That's rather a difficult axiom to live by, but Blake survived for seventy years.

Question: You compared your Christianity to Blake's. Is your theory of literature different in any way from Blake's?

Answer: It probably doesn't differ very much, because I've learned everything I know from Blake. At the same time, I do live in a later age among different social phenomena, and I'm an academic, which means I'm much fuzzier around the edges, much less certain of my certainties, than he was.

Question: Does your identity as a Romantic critic affect your teaching?

Answer: Teaching is a very difficult art. One of the first things to remember is that you are not the source of the student's knowledge. That is, teaching is not a matter of conveying information from somebody who has got it to somebody who has not got it. The teacher has to try to transform himself into a kind of transparent medium for whatever he is teaching. If he's lucky, there may come a point at which the entire classroom is pervaded by the spirit of the subject—of Blake, or Shakespeare, or romance. And then the relationship between teacher and student, which in itself is a somewhat embarrassing relationship, disappears, and you are all united in the same vision.

Question: You said that you can't see yourself in perspective. But you do go so far as to characterize your theory as Romantic, and your description of Romantic criticism seems to suggest, at least implicitly, that Romanticism made it possible for critical theory to progress. Has critical theory progressed?

Answer: The most I could say is that it can and should progress.

Question: Doesn't your comparison of Johnson to Coleridge imply that criticism progressed from neoclassicism to Romanticism?

Answer: I think that Romanticism brought in some essential things that we need for a coherent criticism, and one can trace certain new ideas about criticism—including some twentieth-century ideas—back to Romanticism. At present, the fact that there are various schools of critical theory indicates that it's still a relatively immature discipline. I believe, however, that the materials are being collected which will permit criticism to improve and expand, and that there's a fair chance that it will.

Question: If conflicting schools of thought are a sign of immaturity in a discipline, then do you conclude that metaphysics, philosophy, and theology are immature disciplines?

Answer: You are quite right in picking me up on that. I was expressing myself rather carelessly. I think there are different criteria in the different disciplines, and that there is a sense in which science tries to escape from controversy. I don't mean that a subject like genetics can ever be noncontroversial, but that the authority that science appeals to, the authority of established facts and repeatable experiments and certain methods of proof of validity, is a way of trying to get away from controversy to a body of evidence beyond controversy. At the same time, philosophical and theological and undoubtedly humanistic studies as well are existential. They are too deeply rooted in immediate human concerns ever to avoid the collision of different schools and modes of agreement.

When I spoke of the immaturity of criticism, I was thinking specifically of the number of false antitheses that flood the critical journals. Most of the major critics of our time are, I think, in fairly solid agreement about the value of literature. Their differences are differences in methodology and techniques of approach, but those will always be there.

Question: When you say that criticism is in a sort of prescientific state, are you suggesting that it's in roughly the same prescientific state that it was in when you wrote the *Anatomy*? Has the *Anatomy* helped to make criticism more scientific? With the proper historical perspective, might we see the roots of systematic criticism in the work that you have done in these decades?

Answer: When I said in the *Anatomy* that criticism is a branch of social science, that attracted a great deal of adverse comment because of the strength of the rather provincial prejudice of humanists against social scientists as "those fellows over there who can't write." But if you read through the program of an MLA meeting, you'll find it in many respects almost indistinguishable from a meeting of social scientists. To that extent certain changes have taken place which would probably have taken place if the *Anatomy* had not been written. I have some hopes, however, that in a few minds changes have taken place with a bit more clarity because it was written.

While, as I say, I believe that criticism can and should improve and become more comprehensible as a whole as it goes on, it happens that I have no worries about my own place in it. If posterity doesn't like me, the hell with posterity—I won't be living in it anyway. And while I'm a little disappointed that there is still so much clutter and confusion in critical theory, at the same time I am interested and even exhilarated by the variety of things that do appear, and by the number of approaches to the study of literary documents that would have been inconceivable half a century ago.

Question: You've said that literature may recur and expand but may not progress, while criticism may progress. What accounts for the difference?

Answer: The title of Hazlitt's essay "Why the Arts Are Not Progressive" lays down one of the central conditions with which the literary critic has to work. There is nothing in literature corresponding to the accumulation of knowledge within a science. The literary tendency is to produce the masterpiece, and that remains *sui generis*—something that can be seen in a context but cannot be compared in value with anything else. So, as long as the human mind remains what it is, it is not really possible to have literature in the future which will be on the whole better than the literature that we already have. On the other hand, I think criticism is close enough to a social science to have different conditions underneath it—conditions that make progress possible. Of course, saying that criticism can progress and ought to progress is like saying that we can be wise and good and ought to be. Saying it isn't going to make us wiser or better—and criticism will probably be floundering as wildly in 2083 as it is in 1983, but still one has the hope. The work of criticism as I see it is to understand the place of the creative imagination in society—to see what it's doing and why society can't get along without it.

Question: Concerning the potentially scientific nature of criticism, it seems that in the physical sciences there is a self-motivating impetus toward system. You don't have to urge the physical sciences to be systematic or to develop broad hypotheses. That just happens. But in criticism, judging from what you called the clutter and confusion in literary theory, the natural tendency seems to be a resistance to system.

Might that resistance have something to do with the nature of criticism or of literature?

Answer: The difference does have to do with the nature of the disciplines. But we need to distinguish the sciences, which are one thing, from arts and skills, which are another. The practice of medicine—of meeting a patient, diagnosing what is wrong, and prescribing accordingly—has to have a considerable amount of art or skill in it, however scientific its basis. That is also true of a great many forms of critical contact with literature, and many of those critical contacts are attempts to formulate the experience that one has had in making the contact. They are really forms of psychological criticism, and that's all right, except that there are no words for the direct experience of literature. I once had a student who, after a performance of *King Lear*, walked the streets until the sun came up and it was time to go to breakfast. It seems to me that that is a perfectly valid response to *King Lear*, but there's no sense trying to put it into words.

We have criticism simply because the direct experience of literature is never adequate. We build up the analogical structure of criticism as a means of compensating us for the fact that we do not enter directly into the work of literature, for the same reason that we cannot eat our food until it has to some extent been cooked and processed. I think it's that sensitivity to the central importance of experience that makes people distrust any form of systematization. You build up what you hope will be a critical palace like the Alhambra, and people stand back to look at it and say "Look at that jail." All the psychological overtones of a *system* as a spiderweb that might catch and hold you if you're not careful seem to me superstitions.

Question: If literary criticism is a systematic, even scientific, discipline, how narrow are its boundaries? Is the language of linguistics, for example, an encroachment on a language of criticism that comes—as you say it should—from literature itself? Is textual linguistics, which attempts to study scientifically all discourse, part of criticism or criticism part of textual linguistics?

Answer: I'd have to look at instances. Of course there are no rigid boundaries. Back in my younger days, a literary critic could carry on quite happily with the subject of literature without even being aware that there was such a subject as linguistics. Those days are gone. You can no longer study literary criticism without immediately realizing that linguistics is another area of what you're doing. With the gradual breaking down of barriers—which, after all, were never established as matters of theory, only of practice and of the limitations of the human mind—we can begin to enter a period in which literary criticism becomes an aspect of the whole study of words, the function of words in human society and its relation to the conscious mind.

But when a discipline is trying to find its boundaries it does tend to break up into a variety of technical approaches. In the dissolving of boundaries, if there are occasional acts of looting and raiding—if Chomsky's linguistics takes over certain techniques of criticism or Derrida's deconstruction takes over certain others—that again is not a thing that harrows me particularly, because it's the machinery of a very complicated discipline trying to function as best it can. But I would certainly like to see a more coherent theory of poetics built up in the center of literary criticism. I dislike the notion of shifting the center of the study of literature from literature to something else.

Question: Then what is your view of Marxist and Freudian literary criticism?

Answer: I want the study of literature to arise from the actual conditions and modes of expression that are within literature itself. That is why I am opposed to any construct—Marxist, Freudian, Thomist, or whatever—that is going to annex literature and simply explain literature in its own terminology. What happens in that case may be illuminating for Marxists, Freudians, and Thomists, but it does nothing for the subject of literary criticism.

Question: You are saying then that the critic's responsibility is to criticize an art in its own context rather than to force upon it social concerns which may not belong to it?

Answer: The last part of your question is practically a definition of bad criticism. The first part of your question is connected with another: What makes some literature endure? And if literature endures because it is good, what makes it good? I have never been able to answer that question, although it is the most natural kind of question to ask. The fallacy in most ways of putting such questions is that the standard is the audience's response: what the critic has rather than what the work he is studying has. I have been saying all through my critical career that the old metaphor of the critic as judge is totally wrong. The critic does not judge literature, he studies it and tries to understand it and thereby understand its social functions, but if he is up against something the size of Shakespeare, the critic is the one getting judged. The best he can offer is none too good. In some lectures on Shakespeare earlier this year, I said that for the nineteenth century the central play of Shakespeare was *Hamlet*, because it dramatized the conflict between experience and structures of thought about experience, which was the nineteenth century's preoccupation. The twentieth century, with its existential absurdity and anguish contemplating nothingness and the like, found that *King Lear* was the central play of Shakespeare, and the twenty-first century will almost certainly find the central play of Shakespeare to be *Antony and Cleopatra*, because it deals with the grotesque dislocation between the fate and fortunes of world history and the private lives of two or three highly spotlighted people in the middle. But these are not reflections that make the plays of Shakespeare good. The plays of Shakespeare are the standard: they illuminate the preoccupations and diseases of *our* time. It is in that direction that one has to direct questions about the greatness of literature.

A critic conditioned by a certain time and place will make value judgments against certain works. But these value judgments don't prove to be immortal, and the next age may discover that what he said was bad wasn't bad at all. A critic is to be judged as a critic primarily by the authors he has understood. That is, T. S. Eliot is to be judged by what he has said about Dante and about Marvell and about Dryden, but on Blake and Thomas Gray and D. H. Lawrence, Eliot is just in the position of somebody saying "I pass." If you open F. R. Leavis anywhere, you will find appreciative references to D. H. Lawrence and sneers at Joyce. Well, what Leavis says about Lawrence is genuine criticism, because he understands Lawrence. What he says about Joyce is rubbish, and we have to wait for somebody else to deal with him.

Question: But doesn't the act of theorizing about literature entail implicit value judgments?

Answer: I would certainly express a lot of value judgments about my own theory and fewer about other people's theories, but I do not say that value judgments have no place in literary criticism. What I say is that they are an expression of certain social attitudes, that social attitudes are subject to change, and consequently, that the study of literature always has the power of veto over any value judgment.

You may develop a passion for a poet at the age of ten, and at the age of twenty you may outgrow him, or you may stay with him for the rest of your life. But value judgments are like happiness in life. The American Constitution talks about the pursuit of happiness, but that's bad grammar. You can't pursue happiness: you pursue the course of your life and if you're lucky it may produce happiness from time to time. Similarly, you pursue the study of literature and from time to time these value judgments keep popping up as a kind of emotional response to what you are studying. So I'm not calling for the abolition of value judgments but merely for their rigid subordination to the study of criticism generally. I'm constantly being told that when I select one writer to talk about rather than another I'm implying a value judgment.

Of course I am. And that is where value judgments belong, in the preliminary area of original hunch. They may remain at the original level or they may be qualified, but they must always be regarded as subject to change.

Question: Concerning factional disputes in literary theory, do you see poststructuralist criticism as a direct attack on Romantic critical theory?

Answer: It may look like that, but these are eddies in the general swirl. Around the time of T. E. Hulme an antiromantic movement caught the early Eliot and the early Pound, but that movement turned out to be actually a development of Romanticism itself. Similarly, it seems to me, Derrida's analysis of Rousseau is an eddy in a current which eventually brings one of the world's first and greatest Romantics into focus with regard to his social function as a writer. The action and counteraction, thesis and antithesis, in criticism are probably a necessary part of the process—something that ought to be seen wherever possible in the light of an expanding totality.

Question: Would you disagree with Dame Helen Gardner that some contemporary schools of criticism threaten to destroy the imagination?

Answer: Nothing like that is going to destroy the imagination. Anything that could destroy the human imagination would have to be infinitely more powerful and infinitely more evil than any of the critics with whom I am personally acquainted.

Question: Are you suggesting that deconstruction differs from other criticism in matters of technique or methodology but isn't really different in its view of literature?

Answer: I don't think that in the long run deconstruction will seem different in its view of literature. It may seem to be different for a while, but wherever you have deconstruction, you also have construction. Wherever you have somebody analyzing the metaphorical structure of Rousseau, you will have somebody else wondering what the metaphorical construct in itself means by being there. The two methods of approach, it seems to me, are complementary rather than antithetical.

Question: A deconstructionist is like a microbiologist, then, while the constructionist is like an ecologist—both part of the same field of study?

Answer: That's more or less what I would feel, yes.

Question: When faced with gloomy local possibilities, you often seem to look for a broad optimistic view that will outshine the gloom. I wonder if you have an optimistic view of language to outshine the gloomy view of language being highly advertised by poststructuralists.

Answer: I have often been told that I'm optimistic and I usually reply by saying that there are two kinds of people: those who in the face of a new social phenomenon point out its dangers and those who point out its opportunities. Once when somebody took me for a ride in British Columbia, I saw on the highway a sign saying "Watch for falling rocks," and then we turned the corner and saw another sign saying "Prepare to meet thy God." I realized then that the impulse to warn is very deeply imbedded in human nature. I don't need to worry about it: there's always somebody there to tell you what the results of an all-out nuclear war will be. Our own age is an extremely apocalyptic one, and there are always two aspects to an apocalypse: the vision we finally get when it clears away, and the sun and moon turning to blood before that happens.

Question: You've been accused of optimism by Harold Bloom in particular: he says that you exaggerate the cheerfulness with which poets share archetypes, and that the actual process of displacing archetypes is much more anxious and dark than you've made it out to be. Do you care to comment?

Answer: Oh, sure. The creation of literature is a process of human nature, and nothing that involves human nature is going to be devoid of anxiety and darkness. It is the job of the critic, when he reaches a point of anxiety and darkness, to fish out his flashlight and see what is happening in that dark corner.

Question: As far as those "dark corners" of human nature are concerned, haven't you been accused of allowing criticism to avoid human nature and society by drawing a line around literature? To put it another way, do works of literature have meaning beyond the myth that unifies them, or does criticism stop at identifying the myth?

Answer: Yes, the meaning goes beyond that identification simply because identifying the mythical construct is a matter of putting it into a literary context. The literary context extends from the individual work into a study of all the aspects of literature that are in the least like that particular work. That study of context takes you out, in its turn, to the frontiers of literature as a means of working within society. So there is really no end to the directions in which you can go from that identification. If you identify the myth behind *King Lear*, the next step, or at least one next step, is to see it as being tragedy, and that leads you to thinking about the role of tragedy in literature. Consequently, the study doesn't tend to detach what you're reading from its social context; it's quite the opposite. The function of criticism is to try to find out enough about literature to determine the nature of its social autonomy and its social authority. And that in a way is parallel to the clarifying of the limits of the authority and autonomy of the sciences.

Question: What kinds of connections do you see between literature and society in this century?

Answer: It seems to me that literature has been increasingly over the last century or so a fact of social, moral, and political significance, although to my knowledge there is very little critical theory that explains very coherently just what that social, moral, and political significance is. But if we look at, say, literature in Russia over the last fifty or sixty years, what we most cherish is the work of people who are banned by the Soviet government. And over here we have cases like Ezra Pound and the people who were hounded by the McCarthy hearings in the fifties, so that there is obviously a very great tension between the sense of social concern and the feeling of loyalty to one's own art which is characteristic of genuine writers.

Of course the sense of social concern, by the time it gets expressed, has filtered down into some pretty crude categories. The McCarthy hearings in the United States and the flatbottomed bureaucracy of Russia do not represent the actual concerns of those societies by a long, long way. Nevertheless, the tension does remain, and in consequence it puts a rather sharper light on the social function of literature. Compare the Galileo and Giordano Bruno crises in science: you can't judge the Christian church by its attitude toward Bruno, which involved a specific aspect of the church in a remarkably jittery time. But the tension itself highlighted the conflicting claims of social concern and loyalty to a discipline of increasing coherence.

Question: Galileo, Bruno, and the McCarthy hearings are negative examples of the connection between social and vocational responsibilities. What positive social obligations does a writer have?

Answer: The positive obligations are the ones that arise from his loyalty to his own art. As I've said, the old doctrine of the muse means that the writer has a very limited choice in what he writes. He writes out what takes shape in his mind. That's his muse. And if he is not faithful to that, he is not faithful to what makes him a writer. His positive obligation is to remain loyal to his muse, however horrified society may pretend to be as a result.

Question: Milton believed that in order to write great poems, you have to make yourself as pure a vessel as possible—and pure for Milton clearly meant morally pure. Do you believe that great art can ever come from the mind of a racist or antisemite?

Answer: Yes. I think great art can arise in any kind of mind. An example is the French novelist Céline, who was a fascist and an antisemite and generally a most reprehensible person, but whose novels nevertheless have a kind of intensity that interests people in that field. I can't get through him myself, but I know there are other people who can and do. The whole history of literature is strewn with neurotics and people with wrecked lives who nevertheless saw with the most tremendous power. There are the Goethes who see life steadily, see it whole, and bring a great sanity to bear on whatever they see, and there are the Rimbauds, the Hölderlins, and the Nietzsches who smash their lives up but rescue fragments of the smash that have an even greater intensity. Just as God is no respecter of persons, so literature is no respecter of persons either. Any kind of person may come through as a person of unforgettable insight.

Question: In *The Critical Path* you say that no writer's work is inherently revolutionary or reactionary and that any writer's work "may be potentially useful to anybody in any way." Are you sure that Hitler's *Mein Kampf* would become something besides programmatic anti-semitism in a different social context?

Answer: I'm not saying that any critical power can turn *Mein Kampf* into a good book. I was really repeating what Milton says in *Areopagitica*: that a wise man will make better use of an idle pamphlet than a fool will make of holy scripture. Consequently, the reactionary or revolutionary tendencies within an age, after that age has passed, become things for the critic to observe in any way he can. A better example than *Mein Kampf* is, again, the fiction of Céline. People regard his power of imagination as something worth investigating. It is the critical use made of him that is really decisive. The actual tendency in the author's own life fades out when its social context has gone by.

Question: While you're discussing the social context of literature, would you explain the balance between what you call concern and freedom?

Answer: Man being a social being, there is an interplay between his social concern and his individual freedom. The freedom of a society depends entirely on the degree of genuine individuality that it permits, because there are many essential aspects of freedom that only the individual can really experience. I would even say there is no such thing as social freedom as such. However important it is to get legislation properly worked out, social freedom still remains an approximate and potential thing, and the actual experience of freedom is that of the individual. Either the sense of concern which binds society together or the sense of freedom which makes individuals individual can of course break its connection with the other. When that happens social concern freezes into intolerance and bigotry and unreflective dogmatism, while freedom freezes into nihilistic skepticism. Obviously both of those extremes are undesirable.

Question: What is the position of education with respect to concern and freedom?

41

Answer: One very important role of education is to determine the relationship between them. Social concern comes from a desire to integrate society, and by itself that desire would go in a totalitarian direction. It would proscribe the expression of disciplined belief and would compel the whole of society to believe the same things—or to say it believed them, which in that kind of atmosphere would be much the same thing. On the other hand, the myth of freedom, if it works without any awareness of its social function, ends in a kind of directionless anarchy in which people have no standards beyond the ones that have been suggested by their own subconscious. That is why I think that education has a crucial function in society. A scientist has a loyalty to the conditions of his science and a loyalty to the particular research that he is doing, but, at the same time, in an age like ours he can hardly work without the awareness that science has a social function and is an expression of social will to that extent. It's not so hard to see that in science, though it's perhaps a little harder in literature where, for instance, a poet has a loyalty to his own means of expression within literature and at the same time has a social function.

Question: Why do you say that the myth of concern precedes the myth of freedom?

Answer: Because all of us belong to something before we are anything: I was conditioned to be a twentieth-century Canadian middle-class intellectual nine months before I appeared on earth. In the process of acting out the social conditioning we have acquired, we come to understand something of the strength and the unity of the social concerns around us, and we take part in those. But then gradually an individuation process—the growth of the genuine individual, not the ego—takes place in us as well. The genuine individual takes his concerns from society and reabsorbs them in his own individual way. The question often raised in criticism about whether analyzing a work of art will kill it is connected with this process. Every work of literature has to die and to be reborn in the individual studying it. It doesn't just stay out there; it becomes part of him or her. Without that death and resurrection, there is no genuine possession of literature. When it is possessed, then what I call the myth of freedom is being formed.

Question: Why do you call the myth of freedom a myth? Is that meant to suggest that the criteria of detachment, objectivity, and the like are illusions?

Answer: I would certainly want to keep well away from the vulgar use of myth to mean that which is not really true. Myth to me always means primarily *mythos*, that is, story or narrative. In early societies these stories are stories in a fairly restricted sense. As time goes on they become more flexible narratives, so that you can get a type of mythos which is essentially a description of a lifestyle. You could, I think, define the mythos of the Middle Ages or Marxist Russia or democratic America in certain recognizable verbal terms. It wouldn't be a story in the restricted sense, but it would be a narrative in the sense that it would see society as going in a certain direction and moving toward a certain vision, as in the quest themes of romance.

Question: When you define the myth of freedom in isolation from the myth of concern, you say that it would be totally incoherent, valuing detachment in and of itself. But can't we imagine science as an isolated myth of freedom without any myth of concern to attach it to a culture? In fact, don't we imagine science that way all the time in the nightmares of science fiction?

Answer: The myth of freedom by itself would minimize the sense of social concern and therefore ultimately would minimize the sense of social function. A poet or a novelist working hard to express what he sees in the world in his own terms would still resent very much being told that what he was doing had no relevance to society. In science that problem hardly exists psychologically. Certainly in fields like nuclear physics or in genetics the immediate relevance of the science to the concerns of society is pretty obvious. In societies that have pushed the myth of concern as far as it will go—the European Middle Ages in certain respects, China during the Cultural Revolution, and the Soviet Union—the arts have been made to serve as instruments of the social and political program. In the past there were efforts in this country to say that certain things are American and certain things un-American, but those voices of concern were never representative voices. The representative voice of concern spoke for democracy and certain rights of the individual.

It's difficult to define the conception of freedom by itself because it really can't exist by itself. It always has a social context of some kind, and it exists to diversify and make more flexible that context. It's misleading in some respects even to use the word "freedom," because the ability to set yourself free to play the piano or tennis or to paint pictures or anything of that kind is made possible by a repetition of habit and practice, so that genuine freedom and genuine necessity become the same thing. If you're still exercising your free will as to whether to play the right notes on the piano, you still don't know how to play the piano. For a painter like Cézanne, who is said to have cleaned his brushes after every stroke, it is clear that what he wanted to do and what he had to do were the same thing. On that level there isn't very much argument about relevance to the needs of society.

Question: Freedom of will is usually opposed to necessity, and yet you say that what artists want to do and what they have to do ultimately become the same thing. Could you clarify that?

Answer: If a person says "I want to do what I like, that is what freedom means to me," he will very soon discover that what he likes to do involves certain impulses in him that are pushing him around. So we start with the conception of freedom in the child's mind as what he wants to do, which is up against its antithesis, what society will allow him to do, and we generally work out a kind of uneasy compromise: the feeling of freedom is what we want to do minus whatever society will let us do. But the word "want" in that case refers to something which is pushing the mind around, usually undeveloped impulses within the mind that are demanding expression but are not understood.

There are two kinds of repetition, habit and practice. One kind of repetition is inorganic: you keep on doing the same thing over and over because you are too dumb to think of doing anything else. Naturally, that goes nowhere. The other kind is the accumulating repetition that builds up some kind of skill. If you play the piano or tennis or chess, there is a great deal of repetition in the practice that makes you skillful. But if you want to play the piano, what you are really saying is that you wish to be set free to play the piano. If you have arrived at that pitch of freedom, then, as I said, you'll find that the notes that you want to play and the notes that you have to play are exactly the same notes. If you are playing so that in a sense you cannot play the wrong notes, then you are really free to play. What a painter wants to do is paint his picture. What he has to do to paint the picture that he wants to paint is to put this stroke there and that stroke there and so on. The freedom and the necessity are simply aspects of the same activity.

Question: Are you dissociating free will from choice?

Answer: I don't see anything wrong with associating free will with choice. The issue of freedom, of course, is bound up not simply with the act of choosing but with a perception of the possible consequences of choosing, and that is where the question of awareness comes in. To my mind, the free person is primarily in a state like that of the freedom called academic freedom. I sometimes think there is no genuine freedom except academic freedom, where the resources of human knowledge are open for people to assimilate as they best can. Then they are faced with the tactical difficulties of working in a society made up of people who hate the very idea of freedom and can't stand having it anywhere near them. In situations like that the question of choice may come up, but choice in relation to freedom seems to me to have a great deal to do with the tactical maneuvering of the free individual in a hostile world.

Question: There appears to be an astounding amount of reading behind everything you write. What kind of preparation do you actually do?

Answer: Someone asked me how I find time to read everything I read. I said it's simple—I don't. It's very seldom that I do any program of reading before embarking on a piece of writing except when I'm writing about something specific; when you write about Blake, you read Blake. Otherwise, my reading is rather random and is largely confined to primary sources. That is not arrogance on my part, just self-preservation.

I do find that I often am attracted to subjects that would kill a younger, unestablished writer with stage fright. The thought of leaping into a field like the Bible and trying to write a general popular introduction which would still make sense as literary criticism is rather petrifying when one thinks about it. And therefore I think about it as little as possible. When you write such a book you know that the actual scholars in that field will react much as the sons of Jacob reacted to the rape of Dinah. It means simply that you have to draw on everything you have read, because it is a corollary of my own view of literature that any verbal document may be potentially useful, and that what counts is not so much the amount and variety of what you've read as the intensity with which you have read it. As Henry James said in giving advice to a young novelist, "Don't worry about getting enough experience to write novels, just try to be the kind of person on whom nothing is lost." I'm an omnivorous reader in the sense that I can read almost anything in words—as Charles Lamb said, "I can read anything that I call a book"—and one never knows when that is going to come in handy.

W. J. T. MITCHELL

Visible Language: Blake's
Wond'rous Art of Writing

All agree that it is an admirable invention: To paint speech, and
speak to the eyes, and by tracing out characters in different forms to
give colour and body to thoughts.
> —Alexander Cruden,
> *Concordance to the Old and New Testament* (1738)

But to show still clearer that it was nature and necessity, not choice
and artifice, which gave birth and continuance to these several species
of hieroglyphic writing, we shall now take a view of the rise and
progress of its sister-art, the art of speech; and having set them together
and compared them, we shall see with pleasure how great a lustre
they mutually reflect upon one another; for as St. Austin elegantly
expresses it, *Signa sint VERBA VISIBILIA: verba, SIGNA AUDIBILIA.*
> —William Warburton,
> *The Divine Legation of Moses* (1740)

"Visible language" is a phrase that has primarily a metaphorical
meaning for both art historians and literary critics. In painting we
construe "visible language" in the idiom of Joshua Reynolds or Ernst
Gombrich, as the body of conventional syntactic and semantic techniques available to a pictorial artist. Reynolds called these techniques
"the language of art," and Gombrich has provided the outlines of a
"linguistics of the image" that would describe its syntax (schematisms)
and its semantics (iconography).[1] In literature, conversely, the notion

[1] See Discourse V of Reynolds' *Discourses on Art* (1797): "This first degree of proficiency
is, in painting, what grammar is in literature. . . . The power of drawing, modelling, and
using colours, is very properly called the Language of the art." Quoted from the Robert
Wark edition (New Haven, 1975), p. 26. Gombrich discusses the "linguistics of the visual
image" in *Art and Illusion* (Princeton, 1956), p. 9.

of "visible language" imports the discourse of painting and seeing into our understanding of verbal expression: it tempts us to give terms like "imitation," "imagination," "form," and "figuration" a strong graphic, iconic sense and to conceive of texts as images in a wide variety of ways.[2] If there is a linguistics of the image, there is also an "iconology of the text" which deals with such matters as the representation of objects, the description of scenes, the construction of figures, likenesses, and allegorical images, and the shaping of texts into determinate formal patterns. An iconology of the text must also consider the problem of reader response, the claim that some readers visualize and that some texts encourage or discourage mental imaging.

Both of these procedures—the "linguistics of the image" and the "iconology of the text"—involve a metaphorical treatment of one of the terms in the phrase "visible language." The treatment of vision and painting in the lingo of linguistics, even in a strong sense like Bishop Berkeley's "visual language" of sight, is commonly understood to be metaphoric.[3] Similarly, the "icons" we find in verbal expressions, whether formal or semantic, are (we suppose) not to be understood literally as pictures or visual spectacles. They are only likenesses of real graphic or visual images—doubly attenuated "images of images" or what I have elsewhere called "hypericons."[4]

But suppose we were to take *both* the terms of "visible language" literally? We would encounter, I suggest, the point at which seeing and speaking, painting and printing converge in the medium called "writing." We would grasp the logic that made it possible to change the name of *The Journal of Typographical Research* to the simpler, more evocative *Visible Language*. "Writing," as Plato suggested in the *Phaedrus*, "is very like painting," and painting, in turn, is very like the first form of writing, the pictogram. The history of writing is regularly told as a story of progress from primitive picture-writing and gestural sign-language to hieroglyphics to alphabetic writing "proper."[5] Writing is thus the medium in which the interaction of image and text, pictorial and verbal expression, adumbrated in the tropes of *ut pictura poesis* and the "sisterhood" of the arts, seems to be a literal possibility. Writing

---

[2]See *The Princeton Encyclopedia of Poetry and Poetics* (Princeton, 1974) s.v. "Imagery." For further discussion of the notion of "text as image," see my "Spatial Form in Literature," in *The Language of Images*, ed. W. J. T. Mitchell (Chicago, 1980), and "What Is an Image?" *New Literary History* 15:3 (Spring, 1984), 503–37.

[3]See Berkeley, *The Theory of Vision or Visual Language* (1733).

[4]In *Iconology: Image, Text, Ideology* (Chicago, 1986).

[5]See, for instance, I. J. Gelb's *A Study of Writing* (Chicago, 1952; rev. ed. 1963), which characterizes "writing in its evolution from the earliest stages of *semasiography*, in which pictures convey the desired meaning, to the later stage of *phonography*, in which writing expresses language" (p. 190).

makes language (in the literal sense) visible (in the literal sense); it is, as Bishop Warburton noted, not just a supplement to speech, but a "sister art" to the spoken word, an art of both language and vision.

There is no use pretending that I come innocently from the sister arts to the topic of writing. We live in an era obsessed with "textuality," when "writing" is a buzz-word that is not likely to be confused with the sort of writing promoted by textbooks in composition. We even have what sometimes looks like a "science of writing," a "grammatology" that concerns itself not only with the graphic representation of speech, but with all marks, traces, and signs in whatever medium.[6] This science includes an interpretive method for deconstructing the complex ruses of writing and for tracing the play of differences that both generates and frustrates the possibility of communication and meaning. What I propose to do in the following pages is to come at the topic of writing from the standpoint of what it seems to exclude or displace. In a sense, of course, this is almost a parody of deconstructive strategies, and I suppose one could think of this as an essay written about and "for" Blake, and "against" Derrida, as long as one understands its "Blake" as a complexly de-centered authority figure, and its "Derrida" as a dialectical background rather than an opponent.

What is it that writing and grammatology exclude or displace? Nothing more or less than the *image*—the picture, likeness, or simulacrum— and the *iconology* that aspires to be its science. If "differance" is the key term of grammatology, "similitude" is the central notion of iconology. If writing is the medium of absence and artifice, the image is the medium of presence and nature, sometimes cozening us with illusion, sometimes with powerful recollection and sensory immediacy. Writing is caught between two othernesses, voice and vision, the speaking and the seeing subject. Derrida mainly speaks of the struggle of writing with voice, but the addition of vision and image reveals the writer's dilemma on another flank. How do we say what we see, and how can we make the reader see?

The familiar answer of poets, rhetoricians, and even philosophers has been this: we construct a "visible language," a form that combines sight and sound, picture and speech—that "makes us see" with vivid examples, theatrical gestures, clear descriptions, and striking figures. If we are a painter-poet like William Blake we may even construct a "composite art" of word and image that plays upon all the senses of "visible language" simultaneously. But alongside this tradition of

[6]Although Jacques Derrida is usually regarded as the founder of grammatology, it may be worth noting that the first book to employ the notion systematically was I. J. Gelb's *A Study of Writing*, cited above.

accommodating language to vision is a countertradition, equally powerful, that expresses a deep ambivalence about the lure of visibility. This tradition urges a respect for the generic boundaries between the arts of eye and ear, space and time, image and word. And its theory of language is characteristically oriented around an aesthetic of invisibility, a conviction that "the deep truth is imageless," and that language is the best available medium for evoking that unseeable, unpicturable essence.

Both these traditions were alive and well in Blake's time, but I think it is fair to say that the latter, antipictorialist position is the dominant one among the major, canonical Romantic poets. For all the talk of "imagination" in theories of Romantic poetry, it seems clear that images, pictures, and visual perception were highly problematic issues for many Romantic writers. "Imagination," for the Romantics, is regularly contrasted to, not equated with, mental imaging: the first lesson we give to students of Romanticism is that, for Wordsworth, Coleridge, Shelley, and Keats, "imagination" is a power of consciousness that transcends mere visualization.[7] We may even go on to note that pictures and vision frequently play a negative role in Romantic poetic theory. Coleridge dismissed allegory for being a mere "picture language," Keats worried about the temptations of description, and Wordsworth called the eye "the most despotic of our senses."[8] It is a commonplace in intellectual history that the relation of the "sister arts" of poetry and painting underwent a basic shift in the early nineteenth century, a shift in which poetry abandoned its alliances with painting and found new analogies in music.[9] M. H. Abrams' story of Romantic poetics as a replacement of the "mirror" (epitomizing passive, empirical models of the mind and of art) by the "lamp" (a type of the active imagination) is simply the most familiar way of schematizing this shift.[10] Coleridge's distinctions between symbol and allegory, imagination and fancy, the "Idea" and the "eidolon," all employ a similar strategy of associating the

[7]I take as exemplary here Coleridge's famous definition of the primary imagination as the "living power and prime agent of all human perception." See *Biographia Literaria*, chapter 13.

[8]Coleridge's comments on allegory as a picture language appear in *The Statesman's Manual* (1816), quoted here from *The Collected Works*, vol. 6: *Lay Sermons*, ed. R. J. White (Princeton, 1972), p. 30. Keats's claim that "descriptions are bad at all times" occurs in his letter to Tom Keats, June 25–27, 1818. Wordsworth's remark on the despotism of the eye comes up in *The Prelude*, both in 1805 (XI.174) and in 1850 (XII.129). For further discussion of Wordsworth's ambivalence about imagery, see my "Diagrammatology," *Critical Inquiry* 7:3 (Spring, 1981), 622–33.

[9]See Roy Park, "Ut Pictura Poesis': The Nineteenth-Century Aftermath," *The Journal of Aesthetics and Art Criticism* 28:2 (Winter, 1969), 155–64.

[10]*The Mirror and the Lamp* (New York, 1953).

49

disparaged terms with pictures and outward, material visibility, the favored term with invisible, intangible "powers" of the mind.

It is tempting to summarize Romantic antipictorialism as a kind of "aesthetic iconoclasm," and to see it as a direct reflection of the political, social, and cultural iconoclasm of the French Revolution. Tempting, but I think misleading, unless we remind ourselves that the "reflection" of political and social patterns in artistic forms is just as likely to include reactionary reversal and inversion as direct imitation. Our suspicion about a direct connection between aesthetic and political iconoclasm during the French Revolution should be especially aroused when we note that the universally acknowledged father of aesthetic iconoclasm in the Romantic era is none other than Edmund Burke, the reactionary politician whose youthful essay on the sublime inaugurated the Romantic critique of pictorialist poetics.[11] Burke started his own minor revolution in poetic theory by attacking the neoclassical "picture theory" of poetic language based in a combination of Classical rhetoric and associationist psychology. Denying that poetry could or should raise clear, distinct images in the mind of the reader, Burke argued that the proper genius of language was to be found in invisible, even insensible matters of feeling and sympathy. Poetry, in Burke's view, is uniquely fitted for presenting the obscure, the mysterious, the incomprehensible— in a word, the sublime. Two things are worth noting here: the first is that Blake alone among the major Romantic poets firmly rejected Burke's doctrine ("Obscurity is Neither the Source of the Sublime nor of any Thing Else").[12] The second is a curious disparity between Burke's aesthetic and political preferences. When Burke confronted a historical event (the French Revolution) that conformed to his concept of sublimity, he could find it only monstrous and disgusting. His notion of the sublime remained safely contained in the realm of aesthetics where it served as a point of departure for writers whose relation to the Revolution was, let us say, uncertain.

The battle lines between the aesthetics of visibility and invisibility become clearer if we take the key terms in their literal sense, and recast the problem in terms of writing. If writing and speech have the same sort of "sisterhood" as painting and poetry—a sisterhood of radical inequality, as Lessing and Burke argued—if writing transforms

---

[11]*A Philosophical Enquiry into the Origin of Our Ideas of the Sublime and Beautiful* (1757). See James T. Boulton's fine introduction to his edition of the *Enquiry* (Notre Dame, 1968) for an account of Burke's influence.

[12]Annotations to Reynolds' *Discourses, The Complete Poetry and Prose of William Blake*, ed. David Erdman (New York, rev. ed., 1982), p. 658. All references to Blake's writings will be to this edition, indicated in parentheses after the quotation by an "E."

invisible sounds into a visible language, then it is bound to be a problem
for writers who want to be imaginative iconoclasts, who want images
that are not pictorial, visions that are not visual, and poetry that need
not be written down.[13] Wordsworth's claim that a poet is a man "speaking" (not writing) to men is no casual expression, but a symptom of
what Derrida would call the "phonocentric" tendency of Romantic
poetics. The projects for recovering or impersonating oral folk traditions
in poetry, the consistent comparison of poetry with music, and the
consistent distaste of the Romantic poets for the vulgar necessity of
submitting their words to material, printed form—all these patterns of
thought reflect a common body of assumptions about the superiority
of word to image, ear to eye, and voice to print. When the printed
word comes to be a highly controversial political instrument in itself,
as it did in the era of the French Revolution, the business of translating
speech into the "visible language" of print can take on an ideological
character in itself.

It is in this sort of context that I would like to situate the question
of visible language and writing in Blake. I have previously discussed
the relation between word and image in his illuminated books in terms
of his commitment to a revolutionary religious and aesthetic sensibility
based in dialectical transformation through conflict. But the specifically
political character of Blake's commitment to making language visible
can best be seen by reflecting on his "graphocentrism," his tendency
to treat writing and printing as media capable of full presence, not as
mere supplements to speech. These reflections will fall into three sections: first, a look at Blake's "ideology of writing" in the context of
Romantic hostility to the printed word; second, a consideration of some
major "scenes of writing" represented in his art; third, some observations on Blake's calligraphy and typography, the "wond'rous art of
writing" which is his "visible language" in what he would call "the
litteral sense."

ROMANTICISM AND THE POLITICS OF WRITING

He who destroys a good booke, kills reason it self, kills the Image of
God, as it were, in the eye.

Milton,
Aereopagitica (1644)

[13]On the "unequal sisterhood" of painting and poetry, see my essay "The Politics of
Genre: Time and Space in Lessing's *Laocoon*," in *Representations* 6 (Spring, 1984).

W. J. T. MITCHELL

The source of the Romantic animus toward "visible language" in general and writing in particular is not far to seek. William Hazlitt put it most succinctly when he suggested that "the French Revolution might be described as a remote but inevitable result of the art of printing."[14] Modern historians like Peter Gay and Elizabeth Eisenstein have echoed Hazlitt in tracing the intellectual roots of the French Revolution to the philosophes' "devotion to the art of writing" rather than to any specific philosophical doctrine.[15] The first French Republic, Eisenstein suggests, grew out of a prior "republic of letters," a polity of unrestrained "speculation" in both the philosophical and financial senses of the term.[16] Nor was the visual sense of "speculation" lost on critics of the Revolution. Burke traced revolutionary fanaticism to an excess of "imagination" (in the visual eighteenth-century sense) and to a deficiency in "feeling," the blind, untutored habits that make for a stable society.[17] And Coleridge identified this tendency to reify and idolize imaginary conceptions as the peculiar defect of the French people: "Hence the *idolism* of the French . . . even the *conceptions* of a Frenchman, whatever he admits to be conceivable, must be imageable, and the imageable must be fancied tangible."[18] The materialism of the French Enlightenment, the pictorialist psychology of empiricism and rationalism, and the emergence of an economy of unfettered philosophical and financial speculation all add up to a coherent pathology called "idolism," the tendency to worship our own created images. Carlyle summarized the iconoclastic English reaction to the French Enlightenment most comprehensively:

> Shall we call it, what all men thought it, the new Age of Gold? Call it at least of Paper; which in many ways, is the succedaneum of Gold. Bank-paper, wherewith you can still buy when there is no gold left; Book-paper, splendent with Theories, Philosophies, Sensibilities, beautiful art, not only of revealing thought, but also of so beautifully hiding from us the want of Thought! Paper is made from the *rags* of things that did

---

[14]*The Life of Napoleon* (1828, 1830).
[15]The phrase is used by Gay in his essay "The Unity of the French Enlightenment," in *The Party of Humanity* (New York, 1964), p. 117.
[16]See *The Printing Press as an Agent of Change* (Cambridge, 1979; one-vol. ed., 1980), pp. 136–38.
[17]See Burke's "Appeal from the New to Old Whigs" (1791): "There is a boundary to men's passions when they act from feeling; none when they are under the influence of imagination." *The Works of Edmund Burke*, 12 vols., ed. George Nichols (Boston, 1865–67), 4:192.
[18]*The Friend, Collected Works*, 4:i 422.

once exist; there are endless excellences in Paper. What wisest Philo-
sophe, in this halcyon uneventful period, could prophesy that there was
approaching, big with darkness and confusion, the event of events?[19]

This is the context that makes Wordsworth's notorious ambivalence
about books intelligible.[20] In the *Lyrical Ballads* Wordsworth associates
printed books with the sterility of "barren leaves," the lifeless knowledge
passed "from dead men to their kind," and with the "dull and endless
strife" of "meddling intellects" who "murder to dissect."[21] These
expressions of bibliophobia have to be taken with some skepticism, of
course, coming as they do in a printed book that Wordsworth hoped
would be widely read. But no appeals to Wordsworthian "irony" can
explain away his anxiety about the printed word. Wordsworth locates
the essence of poetry in speech, song, and silent meditation, and consistently treats writing as a necessary evil, a mere supplement to speech.
A book of poetry is a "poor earthly casket of immortal verse,"[22] and
true moral or political wisdom is not to be found in books of "Science
and of Art," but in the "natural lore" of oral tradition.

Wordsworth and Coleridge seem most sensitive to the visual potential of printed books when their bibliophobia becomes explicitly political. Coleridge describes circulating libraries (which were notorious for
disseminating radical opinions to the populace) as "a sort of mental
camera obscura manufactured at the printing office, which *pro tempore*
fixes, reflects, and transmits the moving phantasms of one man's delirium, so as to people the barrenness of a hundred other brains. . . ."[23]
Wordsworth expresses a similar contempt for the material version of
this popular *camera obscura* in his sonnet "Illustrated Books and News-
papers" (1846): "Avaunt this vile abuse of pictured page! / Must eyes
be all in all, the tongue and ear / Nothing?"[24]

[19]*The French Revolution* (first published 1837; New York, 1859), pp. 28–29.
[20]For an excellent account of Wordsworth and the ideology of writing, see James K.
Chandler, *Wordsworth's Second Nature: A Reading of the Poetry and Politics* (Chicago, 1984),
chapter x.
[21]I quote here from "Expostulation and Reply" and "The Tables Turned," Wordsworth's famous dialogue poems on the merits of "natural lore" versus books. It is worth
noting that Matthew, the defender of books, is commonly identified as William Hazlitt,
whose claim that the French Revolution was caused by the invention of printing was so
widely influential.
[22]See *The Prelude* (1850) V.160–65, where Wordsworth describes the "maniac's fond
anxiety" that entrances him when he holds a volume (i.e., "casket") of Milton or Shakespeare in his hand.
[23]*Biographia Literaria* (1817), ed. John Shawcross (Oxford, 1907), I.34.
[24]*Poetical Works*, ed. Thomas Hutchinson, rev. Ernest de Selincourt (Oxford, 1969),
p. 383.

The battle lines between the conservative oral tradition and the radical faith in the demotic power of printing and "visible language" had been clearly drawn in the famous debate between Thomas Paine and Edmund Burke about the nature of the English constitution. For Burke, the essence of law is to be found in the *unwritten* customs and traditions of a people; writing is only a supplement for "polishing" what has been established by immemorial practice. Thus, "the constitution on paper is one thing, and in fact and experience is another."[25] For Burke, the Enlightenment faith in the unlicensed printing of speculative theories and speculative paper currency was bound to produce a host of speculative constitutions. The National Assembly's Declaration of the Rights of Man was, in Burke's view, nothing more than "paltry blurred shreds of paper" in contrast to the immemorial, invisible sinews of the English constitution.[26] Paine's reply was to insist on the primacy of a written, *visible* constitution: "Can Mr. Burke produce the English Constitution? If he cannot, we may fairly conclude, that although it has been so much talked about, no such thing as a constitution exists. . . . A constitution is not a thing in name only, but in fact. It has not an ideal, but a real existence; and wherever it cannot be produced in visible form, there is none."[27]

Where did Blake stand in this dispute over the political significance of writing and "visible language"? Insofar as Blake was a professed ally of radical intellectuals in the 1790s, we expect him to be on the side of Paine, quite apart from his professional self-interest as a printer, engraver, and painter—a technician of "visible languages" in every sense of the phrase. One way of defining Blake's difference from the other Romantics is to see his lifelong struggle to unite these languages in a "composite art" of poetry and painting as the aesthetic symptom of his die-hard fidelity to the Revolution. Blake would have agreed with Wordsworth's claim that books are an "endless strife," but (like Hazlitt) he thought of this strife as anything but dull. On the contrary, he regarded the battles of books, the "fierce contentions" fostered by a free, independent press, as the very condition of human freedom. While Coleridge and Wordsworth found themselves arguing for censorship of the "rank and unweeded press"[28] that encouraged the excesses of the Revolution, Blake was busy planting new seeds in the fields of

---

[25]"Speech on a Bill for Shortening the Duration of Parliament," in *Works* 7:77.

[26]*Reflections on the Revolution in France* (1790), quoted from Doubleday edition of the Burke-Paine debate (New York, 1961), pp. 98–99.

[27]*Rights of Man* (1791–1792); Doubleday edition, p. 309.

[28]The phrase is Coleridge's. See *A Lay Sermon* (1817), quoted here from *Collected Works*, 6:151.

unlicensed printing.[29] Blake never forsook the "republic of letters" for the tranquillity of the oral tradition. The underground printshop or "Printing House in Hell" that turned out subversive illuminated books in the 1790s expands into the "Wine Press of Los" in the 1800s, becoming the scene of the "Mental Warfare" that Blake hoped would replace the "Corporeal Warfare" ravaging Europe throughout his maturity. Blake continued, in short, to think of writing as a "wond'rous art" when many of his contemporaries were blaming it for all the evils attendant on modernity.

This contrast between radical writers and reactionary speakers is, of course, a vast oversimplification; I present it as a way of foregrounding a subtle tendency in the rhetorical stances taken by intellectuals in the aftermath of the Revolution (my claim is *not*, obviously, that radicals refused oratory, or that conservatives eschewed the written word). There is a kind of writing (call it "natural hieroglyphics") that Wordsworth regularly celebrates, and Blake's encomia on writing are frequently "stained" by irony:

> Piper sit thee down and write
> In a book that all may read.
> So he vanish'd from my sight
> And I plucked a hollow reed.
>
> And I made a rural pen
> And I stain'd the water clear
> And I wrote my happy songs
> Every child may joy to hear.
>
> [E7]

The celebratory emphasis on writing is obvious: Blake's version of the pastoral refuses to keep it in the realm of oral transmission. The hollow reed is not plucked to make the expected flute, but a pen, and the act of writing is immediately identified with the process of publication: "all may read" the books written with this rural pen, and without any loss of the original presence of the speaker: "every child may joy to hear" the voice transmitted in the visible language of writing.

No critical reader of this poem, however, has been able to avoid the ironic undertones. The moment of writing is also the moment when the inspiring child vanishes; the hollow reed and the stained water

---

[29]On Wordsworth's role in the attempt to suppress the anti-Tory *Kendal Chronicle*, see Arthur Aspinall, *Politics and the Press, 1780–1850* (London, 1949; repr. New York, 1974), pp. 354–58.

suggest that a kind of emptiness, darkness, and loss of innocence accompanies the very attempt to spread the message of innocence. What makes this a song of *innocence*, then, is the speaker's unawareness of these sinister connotations. Indeed, we might say that the most literal version of this innocence is the speaker's blithe assumption that the mere act of writing is equivalent to publication and a universally appreciative readership, a bit of wish-fulfillment that every writer will recognize. The piper sees no difference between the creation of a unique, hand-written manuscript and the creation of a text that can be universally disseminated. He is unaware of both the problems and the possibilities of print culture, the culture of mechanical reproduction, what Blake would later call "the Machine of Art."[30]

Blake's struggles with the fearful symmetry of this machine are evident throughout his writings. From his earliest projects for books in illuminated printing we see a man obsessed with the idea of having it both ways—that is, by producing unique, personal texts that would be widely distributed through a new technology combining the arts of poet, printer, and painter. We see his awareness of how easily this dream could become a nightmare in the title page to *The Book of Urizen* (Figure 1), an image that might be labeled "textual man." This image is usually read as a satire on Blake's enemies, as a figure of political, religious, and psychological tyranny—king, priest, and rational censor of the liberating energies of the Revolution. When Urizen is given a more particular historical identity, he is usually equated with English tyrants and reactionaries such as George III, Pitt, or Burke.[31]

But suppose we were to look at this image as a self-portrait of the artist as a solitary reader and writer of texts, a figure of the textual solipsist who insists on doing everything at once—writing his poems with one hand, for instance, while he illustrates them with the other? Or reading the classics and writing commentaries at the same time? Suppose we were to see this, in other words, as a self-parody in which Blake has a bit of fun at his own expense, expressing in a pictorial joke what he cannot quite bring himself to say in print? This reading of the image would also help us, I think, to make a more precise historical identification of the sort of figure Urizen represents in the literary-political battles of the revolutionary era. Instead of representing English reactionaries, Urizen might be seen as a certain kind of French

---

[30]See Morris Eaves, "Blake and the Artistic Machine: An Essay in Decorum and Technology," *PMLA* 92:5 (October, 1977), 907. While Eaves stresses Blake's opposition to mechanical reproduction, my emphasis will be on the evidence for his incorporation of mechanical means into his own expressive project.

[31]David Erdman equates Urizen with Britain and Luvah/Orc with France in *Blake: Prophet against Empire* (Princeton, 1954; 3d ed., New York, 1969), p. 309.

Figure 1. Book of Urizen, title page. By permission of the trustees of the Pierpont Morgan Library.

radical, an elder statesman in the republic of letters, a paragon of the "age of paper."

While I know it is heresy to suggest that Blake could have held any reactionary opinions or agreed with Edmund Burke about anything, it seems to me that certain features of the Urizen figure have to be faced in their historical context.[32] Urizen is no doubt sometimes employed as a figure of English reaction in the late 1790s, but it is also clear that in *The Book of Urizen* (1794) Blake represents him as a revolutionary, utopian reformer who brings new laws, new philosophies, and a new religion of reason. The general prototype for Urizen's "dividing and measuring" is, of course, Edmund Burke's characterization of the "geometrical and arithmetical constitution" of the new French Republic.[33] But Urizen may be identified even more specifically as a composite figure for two French philosophes who were much in the news in the early 1790s. The first is Rousseau, the universally acknowledged intellectual father of the Revolution, whose confessions of self-absorption, onanism, and obsession with "pity" must remind us of the drama of Blake's Urizen.[34] The second is Condorcet, who spent much of his life in attempting to reduce moral and political questions to problems in mathematics, and who was the principal author of the "Principles of the Constitutional Plan" presented to the National Convention in 1793.[35] Condorcet's constitution, like Urizen's "books of brass," attempted to promulgate one rational law to govern France (his scheme to abolish the traditional geographical divisions of France in favor of a geometrical grid became one of Burke's favorite figures of ridicule). Condorcet's Girondin constitution, like Urizen's "iron laws," immediately produced a reaction: Condorcet was ousted by the Jacobins under the leadership of Robespierre and died in prison; Urizen's "laws of peace, love & unity" are spurned by the fiery eternals, and we last see him imprisoned in the web of his own creation. The new leader of the "sons of Urizen" is a fiery rebel named Fuzon who attempts to kill Urizen and is eventually killed by his own "hungry beam" (the guillotine). David Erdman's suggestion that Fuzon represents Robespierre (who deposed the

---

[32]The orthodox view of Blake's political position is that he remained loyal to the ideals and ideology of the French Revolution throughout his life, and criticized France only when it departed from those ideals. Thus, David Erdman: "When Blake reports deteriorative changes in Orc-Luvah he is criticizing not 'the French Revolution' but the Bonapartism that followed and in a sense negated it" (ibid., p. 313).

[33]*Reflections*, p. 67.

[34]Urizen must also remind us of Derrida's Rousseau. See *Of Grammatology* (Baltimore, 1976), pp. 142–52, for Derrida's discussion of Rousseau and writing.

[35]Condorcet's most famous publications in this line were his *Essay on the Application of Mathematics to the Theory of Decision-Making* (1785) and *A General View of Social Mathematics* (1793). See *Condorcet: Selected Writings*, ed. Keith Baker (Indianapolis, 1976).

Girondins and pulled down their statue of Reason in 1794) makes even more sense if Urizen is a figure of Condorcet.[36] We need not see Urizen as a political cartoon, unequivocally linked to Rousseau and Condorcet, to see that he makes considerable sense as a neo-Burkean caricature of revolutionary rationalism and the ethos of letters. But even this interpretation tells us only half the story. It helps us see something of Blake's anxieties about the Revolution and his own role in it as technician of "visible languages"; it shows a world in which the "wond'rous art of writing" has become grotesque and obsessive. But seeing this is not quite the same as understanding the position from which Blake could mount his self-parodic critique of writing. The pure negativity in Blake's attack on rationalist writing is scarcely distinguishable from that of Burke, Coleridge, or Carlyle. We still need to ask, then, how Blake could sustain his faith in the printed word, the visible language that seemed to have brought him and his generation into Urizen's abyss.

The answer, I think, is that Blake never did buy into the rationalist version of the Revolution with the same fervor that Coleridge and Wordsworth did.[37] His understanding of it seems to have been mediated, from very early on, by the typology of seventeenth-century English Puritanism rather than the eighteenth-century French Enlightenment. His faith in writing is grounded not in the brilliance of the modern "republic of letters," but in the tradition of a free English press to be traced back to the English Revolution, Milton's *Aereopagitica*, and beyond that, to the religious reformation fostered by Wyclif's vernacular Bible. More specifically, I suspect that Blake identified himself with the urban guilds of radical printers and engravers whose pamphlets and broadsides helped to bring down Charles I.[38] Blake was, in short, an *English*

---

[36] *Blake: Prophet against Empire*, p. 314. I must add, however, that Erdman has expressed strong reservations about my claim that Urizen has a "French connection."

[37] In the early days of the Revolution Blake sympathized with Voltaire and Rousseau as presiding spirits in the awakening of France to liberty (see *The French Revolution* [1791], E 298–99). But Blake's early suspicion of rationalism is expressed clearly in the *No Natural Religion* tracts (1788) and *The Marriage of Heaven and Hell*, and by the 1800s that suspicion had become explicitly linked with Rousseau and Voltaire's attacks on revealed religion (see the address "To the Deists," which introduces chapter 3 of *Jerusalem*). A good index of Blake's ambivalence about the rationalist ideology of the Revolution is his willingness to find Tom Paine "a better Christian" than Bishop Watson (whose attack on Paine in his *Apology for the Bible* Blake annotated), at the same time that he notes that neither the bishop nor his radical deist opponent quite measures up to Blake's "Everlasting Gospel," the tradition of Puritan radicalism (see "Annotations to an Apology for the Bible," E 619: "The Bishop never saw the Everlasting Gospel any more than Tom Paine").

[38] For the connection between printing and Puritanism in the English Revolution, see Christopher Hill, *The World Turned Upside Down: Radical Ideas during the English Revolution* (Harmondsworth, Middlesex, 1972), pp. 161–62.

W. J. T. Mitchell

revolutionary, a radical throwback to the "Good Old Cause" of Cromwell who was incapable of separating politics from religion, reason from
feeling or imagination.[39] That is why, no matter how mercilessly Blake
satirizes the rationalist corruption of writing, he is still able to maintain
the sort of faith in it that he expresses in the "Introduction" to *Songs
of Innocence,* and in the much later introduction to his long song of
experience, *Jerusalem*:

> Reader! lover of books! lover of heaven,
> And of that God from whom all books are given,
> Who in mysterious Sinais awful cave
> To Man the wond'rous art of writing gave,
> Again he speaks in thunder and in fire!
> Thunder of Thought, & flames of fierce desire:
> Even from the depths of Hell his voice I hear,
> Within the unfathomd caverns of my Ear.
> Therefore I print; nor vain my types shall be:
> Heaven, Earth & Hell, henceforth shall live in harmony
> [E145]

Blake's affirmation that writing is a divine gift must be understood
here in opposition to two contrary ideologies of writing. Blake counters
the conservative hostility to the free press and provides an answer to
poets like Wordsworth who sought an escape from the "dull and endless
strife" of print culture in the traditionalism of oral, rural culture. If
Coleridge could argue that the popular press, especially in the hands
of French writers, was producing a sort of "idolism," Blake's reply is
that there are some kinds of printing (his own, for example) that generate not vain, hollow signifiers or "idols," but efficacious "types" that
are anything but vain.

On the other hand, the die-hard radical would have to read Blake's
account of the divine origin of writing as a direct contradiction of the
rationalist position. When Enlightenment philosophes like Warburton,
Rousseau, Condillac, and Condorcet reflected (as they invariably did)
on the progress of writing as an index to the progress of mankind, they
unanimously debunked the notion of divine origin as an outmoded
superstition. Bishop Warburton even went so far as to deny that writing
had a *human* origin: "it was nature and necessity, not choice and artifice"

---

[39]The basic study of Blake's ties to the Dissenters is still A. L. Morton's classic *The
Everlasting Gospel* (London, 1958).

60

that produced the evolution of writing from pictogram to hieroglyph to phonetic script.[40]

It is easy to see why Blake, an engraver-printer in the tradition of radical English millenarianism, would want to treat the invention of writing as a divine gift. It is also easy to see why this position could be so readily dismissed as superstition, self-interest, and vanity. Benjamin Disraeli suggested that it was a superstition "peculiar" to English calligraphers:

> I suspect that this maniacal vanity is peculiar to the writing masters in England; . . . writing masters or calligraphers, have had their engraved "effigies," with a Fame in flourishes, a pen in one hand, and a trumpet in the other; and fine verses inscribed and their very lives written! They have compared "The nimbly-turning of their silver quill" to the beautiful in art and the sublime in invention; nor is this wonderful since they discover the art of writing, like the invention of language, in a divine original; and from the tablets of stone which the deity himself delivered, they traced their German broad text or their running hand.[41]

Actually, Blake's "maniacal vanity" goes even further, for he is not just claiming a divine origin for writing in the mythic past, but is affirming that his own art of printing, as well as the message it conveys, has been given directly to him as a divine gift in the historical present. Taken literally, Blake's claim is that the writing of *Jerusalem* is on the same level as the writing of the Ten Commandments on Mt. Sinai!

Blake would no doubt answer the charge of vanity by claiming that he, unlike the vain English writing masters, has something important to say. He is not merely playing with empty, ornamental signifiers, but recording a prophecy—that is, speaking his mind on public and private matters. He might answer the charge of superstition by pointing out that the divine origin of writing is synonymous with a *human* origin, since "All deities reside in the human breast" (*MHH* 11; E 38). Blake claims for his writing no more and no less authority than that of Moses—the authority of the human imagination. What he disputes is the rationalist reduction of writing to "nature and necessity" on the one hand, and the phobia about idolatrous writing (and its attendant fetishization of orality and invisibility) on the other.

Blake criticizes both the radical and conservative views of writing from a position which looks irrational and even fetishistic from either

---

[40]*The Divine Legation of Moses Demonstrated* (1740), vol. IV, section 4; quoted from the three-vol. 10th ed. (1848) II:184–85.

[41]Quoted in Donald M. Anderson, *The Art of Written Forms: The Theory and Practice of Calligraphy* (New York, 1969), p. 148.

flank, but which from his own point of view offers a possibility of dialectical struggle and even harmony. He does not single out his own books for unique authority. His writings, like those of Moses (and, presumably, of Warburton, Rousseau, Wordsworth, and even Burke) are gifts of "that God from whom all books are given."[42] And the particular text in question, *Jerusalem*, is presented as a "writing" that unravels all the oppositions that have made books a "dull and endless strife" in Blake's time. "Heaven, Earth & Hell, henceforth shall live in harmony." God speaks in both "thunder" and "fire," a double voice that marries the contraries of thought and desire, reason and energy. This voice is heard both in the "depths of Hell," the underground printshop that produced Blake's radical prophecies of the 1790s, and from the mountaintop, the heaven of Urizenic invention that designs the massive symmetries of *Jerusalem*.

We must notice, finally, that Blake's encomium on writing undoes all the semiotic oppositions that were reified by the political conflicts of his time. Writing and speech, for instance, are not at odds in Blake's scenario of imaginative creation. God speaks to Moses, and in the act of speaking also gives man a new art of alphabetic writing. God (the human imagination) speaks to Blake, and in that speaking gives him symbolic or poetic "types" that will transform the invisible voice and message into a visible language of graphic and typographic signifiers. If Blake's visible language heals the split between speech and writing, it is also designed to undo certain oppositions within the world of textuality, most notably the gap between the pictorial and the linguistic use of graphic figures. Perhaps less obvious is the fact that Blake's composite art is an attempt to fulfill the piper's fantasy of a "writing" that would preserve the uniqueness of the hand-inscribed manuscript and yet be reproducible so that "all may read" and "joy to hear" the poet's message. Blake is perhaps hinting at this marriage of the values of print and manuscript culture when he has God give Moses a "wond'rous art of *writing*" while reserving for himself an art of printed "*types*."

It is one thing to project the goal of an idealized writing that will harmonize all the conflicts an artist may feel; it is quite another actually to achieve such a goal or even to recognize what would count as its realization. In the remainder of this essay I want to examine the way Blake's ideology of writing, his commitment to a divinely given "visible language" that would fulfill the piper's fantasy of full presence, expresses

[42]It has to be noted, however, that the crucial phrase, "all books are given," was etched on plate 3 of *Jerusalem* but never printed. This particular message now comes to us "under erasure," thanks to David Erdman's textual reconstructions.

itself in "scenes of writing" and in his concrete practice as a calligraphic and typographic designer.

THE SCRIBAL SCENE : BOOK AND SCROLL

> And all the host of heaven shall be dissolved, and the heavens shall be rolled together as a scroll.
>
> —Isaiah 34:4

If it is accurate to view Blake the way he regarded himself, as a traditional "History Painter" who depicts (contra Reynolds) "The Hero, & not Man in General" (E 652), then it seems clear that the writer is one of Blake's particular heroes. The moment of writing is, for Blake, a primal scene, a moment of traumatic origin and irrevocable commitment. Inspiration does not come to him from a disembodied spirit into an evanescent voice, later to be recorded in script, but comes directly "into my hand / . . . descending down the Nerves of my right arm / From out the portals of my Brain" (*M* 2:4–6; E 96). And the "Hand" that wields the pen, burin, or paintbrush is as capable of becoming a rebellious demon as a dutiful servant.[43] Writing, consequently, is not just the means of recording epic action: it is itself an activity of world historical significance, worthy of representation in its own right.

The treatment of writing as an epic activity is hardly original with Blake, of course. Ceremonial scenes of writing (the signing of the Declaration of Independence or the Magna Carta) and scenes involving the transmission of sacred texts (the Ten Commandments, the Book of Revelation) were the frequent subjects of history painting, and Blake produced his own versions of these themes. Probably the most important model for his image of the "scribe as hero" was Michelangelo's series of prophets and sibyls in the Sistine Chapel.[44] Blake made pencil copies of engravings after these figures, and employed their postures frequently in his own art—so frequently that the image of writing takes on a heavily elaborated, obsessively repetitious character in his iconography. His illustrations of Milton, Dante, the Book of Job, Young's *Night Thoughts*, and the Bible regularly feature the figure of the reader

[43]See my discussion of Blake's rebellious "Hand" in *Blake's Composite Art* (Princeton, 1978), p. 202.

[44]For a discussion of Blake's use of these figures, see Jenijoy La Belle, "Blake's Visions and Re-visions of Michelangelo," in *Blake in His Time*, ed. Robert Essick and Donald Pearce (Bloomington, Ind., 1978), pp. 13–22.

or scribe. And his choices of unusual subjects (Newton inscribing his mathematical diagrams, the Angel writing the sevenfold "P" on Dante's forehead with his sword, Christ writing on the ground to confound the scribes and pharisees) suggest that the moment of inscription tended to stand out for him as a principal subject for illustration in any narrative. The prominence of these "scribal scenes" is such that it is hard to think of them as metaphors or symbols for something else. We have to say of Blake what Derrida says of Freud: he "is not manipulating metaphors, if to manipulate a metaphor means to make of the known an allusion to the unknown. On the contrary, through the insistence of his metaphoric investment he makes what we believe we know under the name of writing enigmatic."[45]

The clearest indication that writing imposes itself on Blake as enigma rather simply being deployed as an instrument is its inflationary, universal character. For Blake, anything is capable of becoming a text, that is, of bearing significant marks. The earth, the sky, the elements, natural objects, the human body and its garments, the mind itself are all spaces of inscription, sites in which the imagination renders or receives meaning, marking and being marked. This "pantextualism" looks, at first glance, rather like the medieval notion of the universe as God's text and seems quite alien to the modern sense of universal semiosis as an abyss of indefinitely regressive signifiers. But Blake's consistent identification of God with the human imagination makes this abyss an ever-present possibility. "Writing" makes its appearance in Blake's work both as imaginative plenitude and presence and as the void of doubt and nihilism; his pantextualism stands right at the hinge between the ancient and modern view of semiosis. (A similar division was, of course, already latent in the medieval division of the universal text into the Book of Nature and the Book of Scripture.)[46]

This hinge in the textual universe is represented emblematically in Blake's art by a formal differentiation between what I will call, for simplicity's sake, the "book" and the "scroll." In the context of Romantic textual ideology, the book is the symbol of modern rationalist writing and the cultural economy of mechanical reproduction, while the scroll is the emblem of ancient revealed wisdom, imagination, and the cultural economy of hand-crafted, individually expressive artifacts. We might summarize this contrast as the difference between print culture and

[45]"Freud and the Scene of Writing," in *Writing and Difference* (Chicago, 1978), p. 199.

[46]The classic discussion of medieval pantextualism is Ernst Robert Curtius' chapter, "The Book as Symbol," in his *European Literature and the Latin Middle Ages* (1st German ed., Bern, 1948; 1st English ed., New York, 1953).

manuscript culture.[47] Alongside these quasi-historical differentiations, however, Blake treats book and scroll as synchronic emblems of an abiding division within the world of sacred or "revealed" writing. The book represents writing as *law*: it is usually associated with patriarchal figures like Urizen and Jehovah, and Blake regularly uses the rectangular shape of the closed book and the arch shape of the open book to suggest formal rhymes with more primitive textual objects like gravestones, altars, gateways, and tablets. The scroll represents writing as *prophecy*: it is associated with youthful figures of energy, imagination, and rebellion, and its spiraling shape associates it formally with the vortex, the Blakean form of transformation and dialectic.

In the illuminated books Blake's most monolithic presentation of the book motif is, as we would expect, *The Book of Urizen*, which completely excludes the image of the scroll. The only relief from the cave- and grid-like shapes of *Urizen* is the scroll-like posture of the guiding sibyl in "The Preludium" plate. The scroll, by contrast, never seems to dominate any of Blake's illuminated books as an explicit motif the way the book does *Urizen*. It appears in the marginal designs, as a scarcely perceptible extra-textual activity, occasionally to be "blown up" into monumental proportions, as in *Jerusalem* 41 (Figure 2). Here Blake depicts himself as an elfin scribe writing what Erdman calls a "merry proverb" in reversed engraver's writing. The Giant Albion (England/Mankind) is too deeply asleep to notice, much less decipher the prophetic message, but Blake's joke seems to be having its effect nonetheless. The scroll is beginning to "grow" on Albion, becoming one with his garments. The picture cannot tell us whether this is a good or bad thing, but even without Blake's puckish intervention, it is hard to imagine this sleeping giant staying that way indefinitely. His head is buried so deeply in the center of his book that it seems about to break through the spine (as his flowing locks already have) and wake the sleeper with a jolt.

The most systematic use of the book-scroll opposition in Blake's art occurs in his illustrations to the Book of Job, where it serves as a kind of emblematic gauge of Job's spiritual condition. Blake's opening plate (Figure 3) shows Job and his family in a scene of rational, legalistic piety, praying from their books while their musical instruments (several of them shaped like scrolls) hang idle in the tree above their heads. The accompanying text tells us that Job is "perfect & upright"—he

---

[47]For a stimulating discussion of this difference, see Gerald Bruns's essay, "The Originality of Texts in a Manuscript Culture," in *Inventions: Writing, Textuality, and Understanding in Literary History* (New Haven, 1982).

Figure 2. Jersualem, 41. By permission of the Houghton Library, Harvard University.

Figure 3. Book of Job, 1. By permission of Robert Essick.

conforms to the letter of the law—but it also issues a warning (carved on the stone base of a sacrificial altar) about this sort of perfection: "The letter Killeth The Spirit giveth Life." In the final plate of the Job illustrations (Figure 4) all these emblematic signals are reversed: the books have been replaced by scrolls,[48] the musical instruments are being played, reading has been replaced by song, and the inscription on the altar repudiates the altar's function: "In burnt Offerings for Sin thou hast no Pleasure." The stress on oral performance in this final plate is, of course, quite in keeping with Blake's consistent association of the scroll/vortex form with the structure of the ear.[49]

The emblematic opposition of book and scroll settles quite easily, then, into an allegory of good and evil, a code which could be schematized in the following table of binary oppositions:

Book	Scroll
mechanical	hand-crafted
reason	energy, imagination
judgment	forgiveness
law	prophecy
modern	ancient
science	art
death	life
sleep	wakefulness
literal	spiritual
writing	speech/song

The interesting thing about Blake's use of this iconographic code, however, is not just its symmetrical clarity, but the way it disrupts the very certainties it seems to offer. We have to note, for instance, that the final plate of Job has not completely banished the bad sort of text: one of his daughters seems to be holding a book (albeit a rather limp, flexible one).[50] And what are we to make of Blake's depiction of Newton (Figure 5) inscribing mathematical diagrams on a parchment scroll? Everything we know about the "doctrinal" Blake would lead us to expect the great codifier of Natural Law and Reason to be presented as a patriarch with his writings inscribed on books and tablets. Blake

---

[48]In the engraved version one of Job's daughters is holding a book; in the watercolor version, the scroll has completely taken over. See Martin Butlin, *The Paintings and Drawings of William Blake* (New Haven, 1981), cat. 551, 21.

[49]See *Blake's Composite Art*, pp. 62–64, for a discussion of Blake's links between graphic form and sensory structure.

[50]In the engraving, that is. In the watercolor version of this scene, all the texts are scrolls.

Figure 4. Book of Job, 21. By permission of Robert Essick.

Figure 5. Newton. By permission of the Tate Gallery, London.

presents him instead as a youthful, energetic scribe whose writings take the form (perhaps unintentionally) of a prophecy. This is the Newton, not of "single vision" and "sleep," but the "mighty Spirit from the land of Albion, / Nam'd Newton" who "seiz'd the Trump, & blow'd the enormous blast!" (*Europe* 13:4–5; E 65) that awakes the dead to judgment. Or perhaps, more accurately, it is the Newton whose "single vision" is so intensely concentrated that it opens a vortex in his own closed universe, a figure of reason finding its own limit and awakening into imagination.

A similar dialectical reversal occurs in Blake's association of books with sleep, scrolls with wakefulness. We have already remarked on the way the elfin scribe with his prophetic scroll in *Jerusalem* 41 insinuates his message into the garments of the sleeping giant with his Urizenic law book. Blake disrupts the stability of this opposition even further in *Jerusalem* 64 (Figure 6) where the sleeping patriarch has become a scribe pillowing his head on a scroll, and the wakeful figure is poring over a book. The joke is further complicated when we notice that the wakeful reader has been distracted from his text by the lively erotic dream of his sleeping colleague, so much so that he makes a gesture of shielding his book from the tempting vision above him. In that vision, a pair of sylphs soar amid a blast of pollen, unrolling a miniature sexual heaven in the form of a scroll. What is the point of this scene? Are we to take the sleeping writer as a figure of superior imaginative status whose fertile dreams contrast with the barren wakefulness of the inferior reader? (Their position on the page sustains this interpretation, the reader looking up wistfully to the writer, across the gulf of Blake's text.) Or should we take it as a satire on writerly wish-fulfillment, the idle pen of the sleeping writer ironically contrasting with his dream of infinite, pleasurable dissemination of the text, of intellectual radiance (note the aureole around the sleeper's head) combined with sensuous enjoyment (the dream of the unrolling scroll emanates like a giant phallus from the sleeper's loins)? Either way the viewer is confronted with the dilemma of the reader's relation to Blake's authority: Is his work a vision or merely a dream? A prophecy or an idle fantasy? Is his authority, as he claims, on a par with Moses? Or was he a harmless eccentric who had too many ideas and too little talent?

Blake dramatizes the whole issue of scribal authority in plate 10 of *The Marriage of Heaven and Hell* (Figure 7), a scene which brings the emblems of book and scroll into direct contact. The design shows a naked devil kneeling on the ground, dictating from a scroll to two clothed scribes who are copying his words down in books. The devil

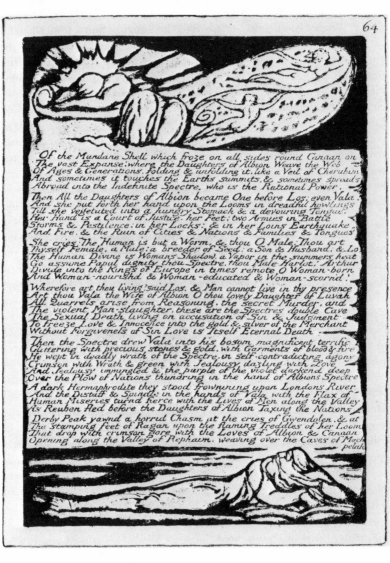

Figure 6. Jerusalem, 64. By permission of the Houghton Library, Harvard University.

Figure 7. The Marriage of Heaven and Hell, 10 (detail). Courtesy of the Library of Congress.

is looking up from his scroll, keeping his place with his finger while he checks on the progress of the scribe at his right. The scribe on his left (who appears slightly feminine in most copies) seems to have finished her secretarial duties, and joins the devil in peering over at the diligent copyist on the other side. When viewed in the context of Michelangelo's prophetic and sibylline scribes in the Sistine Chapel, the image reveals itself as a kind of blasphemous joke. Michelangelo placed naked figures or *ignudi* above his prophets and sibyls to represent the inspiring angels who bring them heavenly wisdom. Blake places his naked devil *below* his angelic scribes, a transformation one can read as a parody of Michelangelo or as an appropriation of angelic authority for Blake's "Infernal Wisdom." The basic point of the design seems to be a conversion of the dialectics of *The Marriage of Heaven and Hell* (Prolific/Devourer; Active/Passive; Energy/Reason; Devil/Angel) into a scene of textual transmission. The devil is the authority figure: he and his scroll represent the primitive original, the "Prolific" source of prophetic sayings like the "Proverbs of Hell" that Blake has been recording in plates 7 through 10. The clothed scribes (whom we are tempted to call "angelic" in their modest, dutiful passivity) are, by contrast, the textual "Devourers," mere middle-men (and women) who copy and perhaps interpret the "original derivations of Poetic Genius." In this reading of the image, all scribal authority is reserved for the prophetic scroll and "the voice of the Devil." The scene may be read, then, as a kind of warning against the transformation of prophetic "sayings" (scroll-writing again associated with oral performance) into the dead, silent form of derivative book-learning.

And yet the image refuses to settle quietly into this "doctrinal" reading of its oppositions. For one thing, the two bookish scribes are themselves divided by an emblematic contrast. Erdman calls them the fast learner and the slow learner, but the sexual differentiation also suggests an allusion to and condensation of Michelangelo's seven (male) prophets and five (female) sibyls, symbols of the distinction between canonical Jewish prophecy and noncanonical "gentile" prophecy.[51] The quick study on the devil's left (a female Daniel, in Michelangelo's idiom) is the figure of un-authorized, noncanonical textual transmission, and she seems to get the prophetic message sooner than her more reputable brother. But a second moment of unsettling occurs when we notice that even the authority of the Devil's voice (and scroll) will not

[51]See Edgar Wind, "Michelangelo's Prophets and Sibyls," in *Proceedings of the British Academy* 51 (1966), 74.

survive extended contemplation. He, after all, is no "author," but merely a reciter, reading off "Proverbs of Hell" which, by definition, can have no author, no individual source. They are impersonal, authorless sayings whose authority comes from their repetition, their efficacy in articulating a collective national "character" ("I collected some of their Proverbs: thinking that as the sayings used in a nation, mark its character, so the Proverbs of Hell, shew the nature of Infernal wisdom better than any description of buildings or garments": *MHH* 6; E 35).

We may say, of course, that this guise of impersonality is a transparent fiction, and we know very well that Blake the historical individual was the author of the Proverbs of Hell. And yet we also have to acknowledge that, for Blake, the claim of individual expressive authority and the disclaimer of authority ("I dare not pretend to be any other than the Secretary the Authors are in Eternity": E730) involves no contradiction, for the universal poetic genius that is God acts only through individuals. That is why Blake can seem to be both the author of original writings and merely a conduit through which innumerable writings (tradition, historical reality, textual and pictorial influence) transmit themselves. All writings, both books and scrolls, are best described by Blake's oxymoron of "original derivation." The attempt to settle the question of origin and authority, to stabilize it in the voice of the Devil, the writing of the Blakean scroll, or the voice of the historical individual William Blake, is precisely what reifies prophecy into law, the bounding lines of the scroll into the closed gates of the book.

Blake's vision of a synthetic text that would reconcile the claims of book and scroll is most directly expressed in the illustrations to the Book of Job. If the first and last plates tell the story of Job as a direct movement from legalistic, bookish religion to the musical, celebratory religion associated with the scroll, the intervening plates treat this movement as a complex struggle between these contrary kinds of writing. The second plate in the Job series (Figure 8) is the opening engagement in this battle of books, every figure in the design except Satan holding some sort of text. As it happens, this textual war is being conducted on two fronts simultaneously, one on earth, the other in "heaven" (generally taken by commentators to be Job's mind). The war on earth seems to follow directly from the scene of plate 1. Job's allegiance to the letter of his law-books is being challenged by two angels who appear on his right offering their scrolls as an alternative to Job's books. Job resists this offer by facing his open book toward the angels, as if projecting the power of its message toward them. It

Figure 8. Book of Job, 2. By permission of the Tate Gallery, London.

appears that his allegiance to the book and resistance to the scroll is supported by all his family except his eldest son, whose offered scroll is rejected by Job's turned back. Meanwhile, in heaven, the same event is being played out as a scene of judgment. God, presented as Job's spiritual double, is besieged by six petitioning angels who cast down scrolls at his feet (S. Foster Damon suggests that these are lists of Job's good deeds).[52] Below these petitioners are two more angels, one holding a book open before Jehovah, the other *withholding* a closed scroll. Presumably these two figures symbolize the balance of mercy and justice one looks for in representations of the Last Judgment; if so, the open book and closed, withdrawn scroll depict the upsetting of this balance, as does the figure of God himself, who ignores the petitioners' scrolls, consults only his book, and issues the condemning judgment on Job. Amid all these textual battles the figure of Satan intrudes as the voice of accusation from beyond the world of writing, disrupting the dialectic between book and scroll, insisting on the unalloyed rule of law. This disruption of the balanced dialectic between book and scroll is reenacted in plate 5, where Blake shows God himself torn between the two alternatives. Instead of a serene, assured judge, we find God writhing on his throne, his left side and upper body (anchored by the book in his left hand) recoiling from the scene of Job's affliction, his right side drawn down in sympathy by the scroll that trails from his right hand.

These scenes of textual warfare are answered in later plates by images of reconciliation. Blake frames his illustration of the Lord blessing Job and his wife (Figure 9) with marginal ornaments that show verses from the Gospel stressing the unity of father and son, the Lord and his people, printed in a display of open books flanking a central scroll. The point here seems to be that the messages of law and prophecy, letter and script, book and scroll have been harmonized in the Gospel, and this reconciliation extends even to the "senses" in which the world and texts are interpreted. Job has previously *heard* a great deal of advice (from his wife and comforters) about God's ways, but what he has *seen* has not been consistent with that advice. Now he says, "I have heard with the hearing of the Ear but now my Eye seeth thee," an experience which, at the level of reading and writing, is something like that of seeing an illuminated book—language made visible—for the first time.

Blake further develops this association between sensory, spiritual, and textual synthesis in his depiction of Job telling his story to his daughters. In the engraved version of this scene (Figure 10), Job instructs

[52]*Blake's Job* (New York, 1966), p. 14.

Figure 9. Book of Job, 17. By permission of the Tate Gallery, London.

Figure 10. Book of Job, 20. By permission of Robert Essick.

his daughters in a room lined with murals showing scenes from his own story. The priority of word and image here is strictly undecidable: Job may be using the pictures to illustrate and embellish his narrative, or he may be using the pictures as the starting point and telling a story by way of interpretation. In his earlier watercolor of the same scene (Figure 11), Blake made these priorities even more complex: here Job gestures, not toward a series of wall-paintings, but toward a cloud-encircled vision that emanates from his head. His daughters do not simply listen passively, but are busy taking down (or taking in) the story in a variety of ways (reading, listening, drawing, or writing) and in a variety of media (book, scroll, and a text or image) which will make the mental images of Job's story into a visible language in the "litteral sense."

Two things should be clear about the motif of book and scroll in Blake's scenes of writing. One is that it forms a fairly consistent iconographic code, expressing in emblematic form the basic contradictions—voice versus print, ancient versus modern textuality, and imaginative versus rational authority—that wracked the Romantic ideology of writing; the second is that Blake consistently uses this code in ways that unsettle its authority and frustrate the straightforward judgments it seems to offer. For Blake, writing does not move in a straight line toward a single version (or vision) of the story. It traces the clash of contraries and subverts the tendency to settle into the fixed oppositions he calls "Negations," whether these are the moral antitheses of law and prophecy, the sensory divide between eye and ear, or the aesthetic gulf between word and image. But we have still seen only his attempt to create this dialectic at the level of ideology (his intellectual "position" on writing) and representation (his treatment of "scenes of writing"). In order to see Blake's visible language directly, in the "litteral sense," we must turn to the material character of the printed word in his illuminated books.

Human Letters

& every Word & Every Character
Was Human according to the Expansion or Contraction,
   the Translucence or
Opakeness of Nervous fibres such was the variation of
   Time & Space Which vary according as the Organs of
Perception vary
                                        —*Jersusalem* 98:35–38; E 258

Figure 11. Job and his daughters. By permission of the trustees of the Pierpont
Morgan Library.

Any attempt to characterize the typography or calligraphy of Blake's illuminated books is frustrated by his subversion of the normal categories into which we sort texts.[53] The distinction between calligraphy and typography, for instance, is impossible to apply to Blake's work, for the art of engraved or etched writing is a composite of the two procedures. It seems odd to think of Blake as a calligrapher, since his texts are not literally autograph manuscripts, written with pen on paper. They are literally books mechanically printed from metal plates on a press. And yet the illuminated books all have the *look* of autograph manuscripts, and the best reconstructions of Blake's reversed writing technique suggest that the letters were traced with a quill or pen on copper, not carved with an engraving tool.[54] It is even more difficult, therefore, to think of Blake as a typographer: although his lettering style sometimes approximates the uniformity of movable type, it never reaches that stage, aiming instead for a various, flexible look that reminds us continually of its manual, nonmechanical origin. Indeed, one hesitates even to invoke a distinction like the "mechanical" versus the "hand-crafted" in describing Blake's books. If Blake's book and scroll symbolize this difference between mechanically reproduced and hand-inscribed texts, his own texts, it seems clear, are both book and scroll— or neither.

A second, even more fundamental distinction that founders on Blake's text is the difference between alphabetic and hieroglyphic or pictographic forms, between writing "proper" and primitive forms or "pre-writing." As we have noted, the history of the evolution from pictorial to alphabetic writing was a central concern of the philosophes in their attempt to trace the growth of human understanding, and it became an especially lively issue in Blake's lifetime with the decipherment of the Rosetta stone. The basic principles that led to decipherment had been laid down in the mid-eighteenth century in Bishop Warburton's famous essay on hieroglyphics.[55] Warburton's theory that the hieroglyphics were to be read not as pictures of objects, but as figures of

[53]I should mention here a recent and excellent book on a closely related topic, Nelson Hilton's *Literal Imagination: Blake's Vision of Words* (Berkeley, 1983). Hilton is mainly interested in Blake's typographic techniques at the level of the *word*, and thus he focuses on aural-visual punning, verbal association, and other modes of polysemic wordplay. My aim here is to characterize the style of Blake's *letters* (in a fairly expansive sense) rather than whole words, but I see this project as integrally related to Hilton's work.

[54]See Robert Essick's chapter "The Illuminated Books and Separate Relief Prints," in his *William Blake, Printmaker* (Princeton, 1980).

[55]For an account of Warburton's role in the decoding of hieroglyphics, see Maurice Pope, *The Story of Archaeological Decipherment* (London, 1975).

speech involving puns, traditional associations and legends, and metaphoric or metonymic abridgments, was repeated by Condillac and Rousseau in their histories of human knowledge and became the basis for Champollion's breakthrough.

There is no question that Blake deliberately violates the boundary between written and pictorial forms; his letters often sprout appendages that are decipherable only in pictorial terms. But the more fundamental problem in viewing Blake's text is deciding just what it means to see something "in pictorial terms." For eighteenth-century aestheticians it usually meant (what it still often means for us) seeing something as a likeness of a previous sense impression, a simulacrum of a "natural" perception. But Blake thought of his pictures in quite different terms, as images of "mental things" or "intellectual vision." They are what is called in the history of writing "ideograms," images which must be construed as representations not just of objects, but of whole conceptions. The problem may be illustrated by asking ourselves whether we see Urizen "in pictorial terms" when we see him as an old man with a white beard, or when we see him as a personification of Reason who belongs in a complex myth. For Blake, this distinction between ideogrammatic seeing and pictorial seeing would be, I suggest, a "cloven fiction," one which separates the mental and physical worlds that his art attempts to marry. In this light, then, we have to say that Blake's text unites poem and picture in a radical sense rather than simply placing them in proximity to one another. Blake treats his pictorial art as if it were a kind of writing and summarizes the entire history of writing from pictogram to hieroglyphic to alphabetic script in the pages of his illuminated books. His images are riddled with ideas, making them a visible language—that is, a kind of writing.[56]

But Blake's art does not just involve pushing painting toward the ideogrammatic realm of writing; he also pushes alphabetic writing toward the realm of pictorial values, asking us to see his alphabetic forms with our senses, not just to read through or past them to the signified speech or "concept" behind them, but to pause at the sensuous surface of calligraphic and typographic forms. What do we see during this pause? Often the symbolic values of Blake's calligraphy seem utterly transparent and straightforward. On the title page of *The Marriage of Heaven and Hell*, for instance, the two contraries of "Heaven" and "Hell"

---

[56]Lessing's strictures against allegorical, ideogrammatic painting are couched in terms of precisely this fear that the practice will lead painting into "abandoning its proper sphere and degenerating into an arbitrary method of writing": *Laocoon* (1766). I quote from Ellen Frothingham's translation (New York, 1969), p. x.

J. T. Mitchell

are printed in austere Roman capitals. The word "Marriage," on the
other hand, is inscribed in flowing engraved calligraphy, and the tails
of the letters merge with the vegetative forms in the pictured scene.
Blake literally embodies in the calligraphic form of "marriage" the
symbolic marriage that his "types" prefigure in the text of *The Marriage
of Heaven and Hell*.

There is a similarly transparent symbolism in the title pages to *Songs
of Innocence and of Experience*, where Blake presents "Experience" in the
stiff mathematical precision of Roman type, and "Innocence" in flowing calligraphy. But there is another pattern in the typography of the
Songs that does not fit this schema so well. Most of the *Songs of Innocence*
is printed in Roman, while the *Songs of Experience* is printed in italic, a
form which is meant to recall the flowing, slanted lines of the calligrapher's running hand. Perhaps Blake is simply resolved to be a "contrary fellow" and wants to keep us off balance (as he does with the
emblems of book and scroll), both to invite and to prevent codification
of his lettering style. Whatever his motives, it is the italic style of *Songs
of Experience* that tends to dominate the typography of the later illuminated books. Roman type appears only in the early philosophical
tracts (*All Religions Are One* and *There Is No Natural Religion*), *Songs of
Innocence*, and the "Proverbs of Hell" section of *The Marriage*. All the
other illuminated books are printed (with variations in size, spacing,
and degree of ornamentation) in italic letters. The general point of this
stylistic choice is not terribly difficult to grasp. Blake wanted a letter
form that would be uniform and readable but would declare its hand-
crafted origins. He also wanted, I suspect, to stress his association with
the great writing masters of the Renaissance, the Italian humanists
who gave "italic" its name and who, along with Italian engraving
masters like Marcantonio Raimondi, provide a model for his graphic
style.[57] This link with the calligraphy of humanism, the "littera humanistica" as it was known, is probably Blake's "litteral sense" when he
claims that "every Word & Every Character / Was Human" in the
visionary discourses that close *Jerusalem*.

The notion of a "Human Character" or "littera humanistica" goes
well beyond the association with humanistic script, however. Readers
of Blake's notebook will recall that he explored the idea of human
letters in drawings which accommodate the human form to the shape
of alphabetic script. These figures illustrate a principle that transcends
the particular conformity of some human posture to the shape of a

---

[57]See Donald Anderson, *The Art of Written Forms*, pp. 112–24, for a discussion of the
Italian calligraphers. Blake's books provided one of the models, of course, for the nineteenth-
century revival of calligraphy led by William Morris.

4

"Y," an "I," an "O," or a "P," and that is the tendency of Blake's graphic art to display "iterated" forms—figures which occur often enough to be recognized as constitutive elements in a code, like the letters of an alphabet. The point is not that a human figure or other graphic form must look like a character in the English or Hebrew alphabet, but that it must be repeated often enough to be differentiated and recognized as a "character" in an ensemble of symbolic forms. And the symbolism of such characters need not be understood as a univocal system of representation: the paired emblems of book and scroll are a perfect example of the use of iterated forms that generate, through patterns of similitude and difference, an infinite range of meanings.

These kinds of repeated iconographic and formal patterns occur in the work of every pictorial artist; they are what Gombrich calls the "schemata" or "grammar" of visual art, and their meaning arises from their resemblance not to natural objects or appearances, but to one another. They are also the constituents of what we call "style" in the graphic arts, a term that suggests, in its connection with the writing tool or *stylus*, the point of convergence between writing and painting. The style is the *signature* of the artist or school, the "characteristic" iterated and reiterated pattern. Blake as a highly self-conscious writer-painter-printer simply foregrounds this general principle of artistic style, making the links between verbal expression, graphic representation, and mechanical reproduction explicit and "litteral."

I have argued elsewhere that Blake's pictorial style is constructed at its deepest level out of four abstract forms or characters (the spiral, circle, S-curve, and inverted U) that correspond to structures Blake associates with sensory openings (ear, eye, tongue, nose).[58] This "alphabet of the senses" would make sense of Blake's claim that the "Human Character" of his art of writing "Was Human according to the Expansion or Contraction, the Translucence or / Opakeness of Nervous fibres such was the variation of Time & Space / Which vary according as the Organs of Perception vary." This is also the point, however, at which Blake's art of writing ceases to be just a *visible* language, and becomes a synaesthetic spectacle that "the eye of man hath not heard, the ear of man hath not seen, man's hand is not able to taste, his tongue to conceive, nor his heart to report." And as Bottom warns us, "Man is but an ass if he go about to expound this dream," this language, or this dream of language.

The good critic, however, like Blake's devil, must always be an ass and rush in to expound where angels fear to read. The dream of a

---

[58]See *Blake's Composite Art*, pp. 58–69.

W. J. T. Mitchell

language that would play upon all the stops of the human senses is more than a proposal for the "improvement of sensual enjoyment" with multimedia devices. It is the use of such devices to create what Marx called "the poetry of the future," a poetry which demands the rethinking of all human discourse and of the social relations inscribed in that discourse. Blake's sensuous alphabet of "human letters" is both a fulfillment of and a tacit critique of the Enlightenment schemes for a "universal character" to unite mankind.[59] Blake wants a writing that will make us see with our ears and hear with our eyes because he wants to transform us into revolutionary readers, to deliver us from the notion that history is a closed book to be taken in one "sense." Northrop Frye made something like this point when he closed *Fearful Symmetry* with the following remark:

> The alphabetic system of writing can be traced back to the Semitic people of "Canaan," and perhaps if we knew more about it we should discover that it was not a moral code but an alphabet that the Hebrews learned at Mount Sinai, from a God with enough imagination to understand how much more important a collection of letters was than a collection of prohibitions.[60]

Blake as a post-Enlightenment poet recognizes that this "collection of letters" was not given by a sky-god with imagination, but that this god *is* the human imagination, the letters a human invention, and that the adequate alphabet for imagination is still being delivered to us—most recently in his own "wond'rous art of writing."

QUESTIONS AND ANSWERS

Question: In discussing Wordsworth and Blake you link their politics to their view of writing. Can you discuss the political implications of Derrida's view of writing?

Answer: In a general sort of way, Derrida's view of writing is insurrectionary and liberationist. He speaks of "The End of the Book and the Beginning of Writing" and presents this displacement as a more or less revolutionary transformation, one that summarizes the epoch

[59]These systems often invoked hieroglyphics and picture-writing as possible models for the "universal character." See James Knowlson, *Universal Language Schemes in England and France, 1600–1800* (Toronto, 1975).
[60]*Fearful Symmetry* (1947; Boston, 1962), p. 416.

of modernity and postmodernity. Like all revolutions, Derrida's presents a double face of fear and hope: fear that the destruction of previous
verities by an unconstrained "writing" will loose mere anarchy on the
world, hope that this anarchy will be less coercive, less destructive to
human life than the order it displaces. The fearful side of Derrida's
view of writing has been perceived by the profession of literary study
in a rather trivial form—the anxiety that we won't be able to "fix" the
meanings of texts (as if there had been a time when we could) and
thus ensure the scientific and professional status of our work. I think
that the fearful, sublime aspects of Derrida's revolutionary writing are
much more threatening than these professional insecurities and that
they have to do with a widespread feeling that our inventions, our sign
systems, media of communication, means of representation and exchange
have gotten out of our control. We live in a world in which both the
environment and the subjective self are enmeshed in mediation and
exchange, in which "presence" and "authenticity" are themselves commodities ("It's the real thing"; "Times like these are made for Taster's
Choice") and thus subject to fetishization. "Writing" is Derrida's name
not just for script in the narrow sense, but for the possibility of semiosis,
grounded in the iteration or repeatability of signs within a system of
differences. It includes all the media, therefore, as well as money, credit,
and cybernetic and biogenetic "programs." "Writing" plays a role much
like the one "media" did in the work of Marshall McLuhan, and
Derrida infuriates traditional humanists because he refuses to make
easy moral judgments on the corruption of modern media and even
seems (sometimes) to be celebrating the textualizing of reality.

I take the hopeful side of Derrida's appraisal of writing to be his
stress on *jouissance* and playfulness as creative strategies for thinking
through this "textual revolution." More seriously, I think Derrida's
message is not so much that this "writing" has a determinate political
content in the traditional sense of aligning itself with conservative,
liberal, or radical causes, but that it is the system within which any
politics is going to find itself inscribed, even a politics (especially a
politics!) that defines itself in reaction against modernity. I think Derrida asks us to consider what kind of politics is possible in a world
where the most advanced economies are producing information rather
than hard commodities.

Question: You suggest that Blake's ideas about writing have a history.
M. H. Abrams suggests—and so have many others—that poststructuralist theory reflects its historical moment, a negative age of skepticism, uncertainty about values, and so on. What historical pressures
do you think Derrida is responding to in his theory of writing?

W. J. T. Mitchell

Answer: I've partially answered this in responding to your first question, and of course I'm a believer in the cliché about theories reflecting historical moments, even though I get very nervous about the metaphor of reflection—especially when we forget what the metaphor entails. Let me evade this question by transposing it to an earlier epoch. I think there really was a fear of "writing" in a much more ordinary, familiar sense (i.e., the printed as opposed to the spoken word) in the early nineteenth century. This fear was based on the widely shared perception that the printing press, in Hazlitt's words, was a "remote but direct" cause of the French Revolution. But it was a fear expressed long before the Revolution in the revulsion of the English Tory satirists against "scribblers," "projectors," and "speculators" of all kinds, and before that, against the pamphlet wars of the English Revolution, and before that, against the Reformation and the printing of vernacular Bibles. "Writing" in this sense has been the threatening "revolutionary medium" for a long time—at least since Plato, in Derrida's view. So it's important not to think of Derrida's notion of an "epoch of writing" as a historical contingency, something that has happened recently, or something to be praised or blamed. I think his claim is that anxiety about writing is built into what Wittgenstein would call our "forms of life," the language games we play with the notion of language itself. It's part of the grammar of our notion of language, and therefore a "necessary" or inevitable development, not a response to or reflection of our modern world of uncertainty. "Our modern world" has always been skeptical and uncertain (in different particular ways, of course) ever since Socrates and the Sophists. Derrida didn't discover skepticism, but he did help us to see how the anxiety it provokes is linked to the fear of writing.

Question: At certain points you seem to want to allow Blake to co-opt Derrida's ideas about writing, with fairly optimistic results. Isn't Derrida's skepticism strong enough to withstand such efforts? You hold up Blake's redemption of writing as a possible "antidote" to deconstruction. How do you think Derrida would respond to your Blakean cure for him?

Answer: I think Derrida would welcome the cure, but not for himself, since he really doesn't need it. The ones who need this cure are those who think that Derrida is a nihilist in some straightforward, programmatic way, who think that he brings a message of despair. Nihilism is always the charge brought against a skeptic who makes the mistake of questioning a fundamental assumption, especially one that underwrites a profession. Blake was a nihilist in this sense as well when he questioned the prevailing notions of artistic excellence and moral propriety

88

in his day and denounced the God of established Christianity as "Nobo-daddy." Blake was (and still is) a rather shocking, antinomian sensi-bility. His skepticism about sexual codes, religious verities, the place of rationality and empirical knowledge strikes me as much more scan-dalous and controversial than the urbane, subtle punning of Monsieur Texte. So I'm far from seeing Blake as a way of saving some sacred object that Derrida wants to destroy. Blake and Derrida are, for me, allies in a culture of artistic and social radicalism that grows out of the Enlightenment and the French Revolution, and that emerges as a strategy for "keeping the Divine Vision in a time of trouble" after the failure or betrayal of revolution—as Milton did after the English Rev-olution, Blake after the French, and Derrida after the experience of the sixties. At any rate, I think this has been the *use* of Derrida in American criticism since the sixties where, it's fair to say, his work has found its most congenial home in feminist and Marxist criticism.

Question: Does Blake's illuminated-book form—which as you say "attempts to marry" the mental and the physical—shed any light on the limitations of Derridean notions of "writing"? Or do Derrida's notions of "writing" make Blake's medium just one more dream of language from which we need to be waked up?

Answer: Blake's composite art of verbal-visual, mental-corporeal "writing" fuses the contraries that Derrida sees as separated in normal, colloquial accounts of writing and in standard "histories of writing." The sensory divide of eye and ear, the historical divisions of pictogram-hieroglyph-alphabetic script, the progression from oral to manuscript to print culture, all these boundaries are transgressed in Blake's text. Most important of all, the traditional distinction (which Derrida dis-cusses at some length) between "divine writing" and "secular" or "human" writing, which is so often figured by the oppositions of inner and outer, presence and absence, nature and convention, is elided in Blake's text. His writing consists in "human forms divine," his text is composed of "characters" that are indecidably sacred and secular. His "books" have the same status as those of the Bible, which means that we either have to look at him as an extraordinary megalomaniac or think of biblical texts in a different way. This "different way," is, I think, already familiar to us in Northrop Frye's work on Blake and biblical tradition as aspects of a universal literary canon, and it is one of the points where Frye's work comes closest to Derrida's—especially in the concluding pages to *Fearful Symmetry* where he discusses the "alphabet of imagination." So Blake's dream of language strikes me as exactly what Derrida is trying to wake us *into* when he criticizes the traditional oppositions that characterize the nature of writing. Blake's technique of contrary or diabolical reading, incidentally, which proceeds by inverting the privileged oppositions in a text (as in his transvaluation of Milton's devils and angels) and then by calling into question the whole system that keeps them opposed, seems to me very close to the method of deconstruction. This isn't to deny that there are important differences between Blake's sensibility and Derrida's. I'm sure Blake would see all the traces of French mocking and doubting in Derrida, the imprint of Voltaire and Rousseau. My point here is that they share a common body of tropes, philosophical problems, images, and intellectual procedures over which they would probably wage fierce contentions—Blake's synonym for friendship.

Question: Can you clarify the connection between Blake's redemption of writing and his invention of illuminated printing? Does Blake's redemption of writing (as a philosophical matter, as an idea) necessitate illuminated printing? Or might Blake's redemption of writing also extend to print?

Answer: I don't think Blake's idea of a redeemed writing necessitates his particular form of illuminated printing. That was just his strategy for confronting the ambivalence about the printed word in his own time with his own talents, but he certainly recognized other strategies. I'm not suggesting that he wanted all books to be illustrated and hand-colored, but that he wanted books to be the products of loving, creative, nonalienated labor. He wanted books, engravings, drawings—representations of all sorts—to bear the imprint of their creators, that is to be expressions of both common human work and unique individuality, the human form divine. To the extent that writing, printing, graphic art, and other media, genres, or styles had become sites of ideological production and reproduction, hieroglyphics of alienation and repression, I think Blake, like the other Romantics, felt that his task was to struggle with and reshape them, not simply to accept them in their received form.

Question: Critical theories seem to have favorite authors (Blake is central to Frye's theory). How do you see Blake's position in the poststructuralist environment—and what does his position reveal about poststructuralist theory?

Answer: This is a very good and very complicated question. The short answer is that Blake has not—apparently—been very important to poststructuralism, and vice versa. The clearest symptom of this fact is that the Yale Romanticists have tended to concentrate on Wordsworth; Harold Bloom's postdiluvian work even expresses regret for his early enthusiasm for Blake. The Blakeans are now catching up, of course, and scholar-critics like Robert Essick and Nelson Hilton are conducting close textual investigations in the spirit of poststructuralist thinking. But there is another way of thinking of Blake's role in contemporary criticism, and that is to see him as the repressed Other who haunts and indirectly dominates the discourse from which he is excluded. I think the Wordsworth of the Yale critics, especially of Bloom and Hartman, is to some extent a Blake *manqué*, a visionary prophet of the imagination for whom Stanley Cavell's "ordinary" is a vehicle and sometimes an obstruction. I'm exaggerating this point, of course, but it comes out of a conversation I had a couple of years ago with the late and much-missed Paul de Man. I asked de Man if he had ever noticed that Blake, unlike the other Romantics, did not consistently privilege voice over writing. De Man replied that of course he had noticed this. Well then, I asked, doesn't this make his work of peculiar interest for deconstruction, particularly its "science of writing" or "grammatology"? De Man's reply: Not at all. Blake's privileging of writing makes him less interesting to deconstruction, because it makes his work less resistant to its strategies. Everything is open to view in Blake. There are no secrets or repressions.

I remember being mystified by this reply at the time, and suspected de Man of teasing. The idea that Blake is "open to view" seemed particularly whimsical to me (though it shouldn't have, given the long tradition of thinking of Blake as "a poet without a mask"). But I think now that I have some glimmer of what he was driving at, and it helps me to see how it makes sense to regard Blake as the secret agenda of poststructuralist Romantic criticism, the marginal figure who infiltrates the center, and who thus cannot be looked at directly but must be mediated through other poets, especially Wordsworth. Of course, there is a simpler explanation for all this, and it is just that the literal sense of Blake's poetry has been so much more difficult to get at than that of the other Romantics. Since deconstruction depends on the existence of a prior construction of secure, stable literal meanings that can be unsettled, and since the reading of Blake's major poems is still relatively unstable, there is no solid surface there to be disrupted. Perhaps this is just a way of simplifying de Man's point about "resistance."

Question: If critical theories privilege authors, perhaps they also privilege literary periods: how does Romanticism fare under poststructuralism?

Answer: Another big question—far too big for me to handle! Am I expected to compare the fortunes of every literary period from the Middle Ages to the modern as it encounters poststructuralism? Of course there is poststructuralist work being done on every one of the traditional "periods" in the academic disciplinization of literary study. My obvious answer to this has to be that the very notion of "periods" comes into question and that poststructuralism is liveliest where it puts pressure on the fundamental ideas of criticism itself—the ideas of genre, representation, style, author, work, reader, text, context, and the "periodic," historical character of all these notions. So poststructuralism thrives, more as a kind of philosophizing itch in the critical community than as a method for getting results. I think it works best (1) where it meets resistance to the programmatic extrapolation of its routines—thus, I like its effects more in the reading of prose than poetry, especially rational, systematic philosophical prose that wants to deny its rhetorical and figurative lapses. Eighteenth-century criticism, aesthetics, and philosophy, with their rational, empirical, secular, and professionalized sense of interpretation are "riper" texts for deconstruction than Shelley's "Ode to the West Wind"; (2) where it offers opportunity for the creation of new disciplines, new topics, new interests and constituents, and (as Stanley Fish would insist) new professional opportunities. Feminist criticism, Marxism, studies in colonial, "third world" literatures, film, media, folklore, popular culture—all these relatively marginal fields (from the standpoint of traditional literary criticism, especially as practiced in American English departments) find aid and comfort in poststructuralism. Which is not to say that everything is fine and we should (as Stanley Fish also insists) "stop worrying and learn to love interpretation." (Is this a deliberate echo of the subtitle of *Dr. Strangelove*?) Poststructuralism is most interesting, in my view, at precisely those moments when it makes us worry about why we do love interpretation so much. Is it really just the Volvos and corduroy jackets and respectful students? Admittedly, a great deal of this "new" stuff is ephemeral fashion. It wouldn't be the first time a marginal social or professional class represented itself as and allied itself with the avant garde, the spirit of the modern, the revolutionary, with somewhat mixed results. No doubt most of this revolutionary energy is co-opted, compromised, or trivialized by its encounter with the stubborn ordinariness of things. All I can say to this is, So what? I still find the problems, questions, and challenges raised by poststructuralist thinking—especially insofar as it confronts the issues of politics, history, and social value in cultural productions—the most exciting area of contemporary intellectual life. But I should perhaps stress that, for me, this sort of thinking does not flow in one-way current from Paris or Europe to the United States, but also has its own fountains in the Anglo-American tradition— in the philosophy of Wittgenstein, Nelson Goodman, John Dewey, and C. S. Peirce; in the work of Stanley Cavell, Richard Rorty, and J. L.

Austin; in the criticism of Kenneth Burke, Edward Said, and Raymond Williams.

Question: You begin your essay with a strong contrast between Wordsworth and Blake, and while Blake is held out as a possible antidote to poststructuralist skepticism, Wordsworth seems to be a victim. One important modern way of thinking about Romanticism—represented, for instance, by Abrams—draws an equally strong contrast between Wordsworth and Blake but puts Wordsworth at the center of Romanticism and Blake at the periphery. Do you think that in recent criticism Wordsworth and Blake are exchanging positions? And what about Coleridge, Keats, Shelley—and perhaps especially Byron, who always seems to be peripheral to recent explanations of Romanticism?

Answer: My essay is in no way meant to be fair to Wordsworth. I've deliberately overstated his anxieties about writing and printing to throw Blake's "graphocentrism" into sharper relief; a study that centered on Wordsworth would show his attitudes to be much more complex than I could represent them here. (I recommend James Chandler's book, *Wordsworth's Second Nature*, on this topic.) But the question of center and periphery, of the "major" canonical writers and the minor, marginal figures, is very complex and interesting. I think it will be one of the major topics in future criticism of the Romantics. On the matter of Blake versus Wordsworth: I think Blake dominated Romantic criticism in the sixties and early seventies, directly in the enormous amount of new work he generated, indirectly in his role as the figure for what Wordsworth "might have been." But there is no denying that, from the standpoint of social history and immediate influence, Wordsworth is the central Romantic poet, and Blake will always be the peripheral Other. That is just a fact, though it is a fact that is felt and imagined in different ways by different generations of interpreters. The other four "major" figures—Coleridge, Keats, Shelley, and Byron—all make clearest historical sense in relation to Wordsworth, whether we construe this sense as one of reaction (Byron), parody, imitation, and continuation (Keats and Shelley), or direct collaboration and competition (Coleridge). Blake just does not figure in this canon in the same direct, historical way that Wordsworth does; but he does figure in an indirect, almost repressed way that is perhaps even more interesting, just because it's harder to talk about.

The other thing that has to be said in answer to this question of the center and periphery is just a reminder that the modern canon of major Romantic poets is largely a Victorian invention. Scott, Moore, Campbell, Southey, Rogers, and Crabbe are the "majors" that the intellectual generation of 1790–1830 would have identified, and we need to recover a more accurate, vivid sense of just how this rather startling shift in evaluation was accomplished.

Question: Abrams, Frye, and Cavell all call themselves *Romantic* critics. Do you consider yourself a Romantic critic?

Answer: Yes, I do consider myself a Romantic critic, in two senses. First, in my concern for the materials of cultural history in the period we call Romantic, and second, in my sense that the values and problems of that period, its very status as a "period" that stands in a number of relationships to modern and contemporary culture, are of the first importance. I think the intellectuals, artists, and poets of the Romantic era, in their struggle with the work of their Enlightenment predecessors, and in their attempts to make sense of the greatest political, social, and cultural revolutions the West has endured, established the basic patterns of thought we have to contend with if we are to fulfill any of the responsibilities of intellectuals. I know that the next question will be, "What are the responsibilities of intellectuals?" and my answer would be, this is the question that must haunt the practice of Romantic criticism. It is the determination, as I said earlier, *not* to "stop worrying and learn to love interpretation," but to make interpretation an anxious, nervous, embattled affair, a radical inquiry into one's own origins, alignments, and affiliations. For me Romantic criticism ought to be a practice of struggle and fierce contention as well as confession and self-criticism. I can't do better than quote Stanley Cavell's "requirements" for an imaginative Wittgensteinian philosophy:

> What I require is a convening of my culture's criteria, in order to confront them with my words and life as I pursue them and as I may imagine them; and at the same time to confront my words and life as I pursue them with the life my culture's words may imagine for me; to confront the culture with itself along the lines in which it meets in me. [*The Claim of Reason*, p. 125]

Question: Where do you think literary theory is headed—and what part do you think Romanticism will play in the future of literary theory?

Answer: I think literary theory is headed for a fall. This intuition is probably nothing more than the usual stock-market sense that what goes up must come down. But it also has to do with certain things that are happening within literary theory, a kind of shifting of emphasis, and some quiet abandoning of questions that seem not so much to be answered as just to dissolve. I suspect that the question of semantic determinacy has just about played itself out. Everyone follows E. D. Hirsch in practice, and everyone suspects that he is wrong in theory. Is this problem likely to be solved by literary theorists or by a theory of meaning imported from philosophy? Are we going to come up with an account of meaning that really settles the question of determinacy and puts our practice on a firm theoretical foundation, giving us secure criteria for separating meaning from significance, intention from accident? It's more likely, in my opinion, that we will, as always, muddle through, and find other points of theoretical pressure to occupy ourselves. I think the grand system-building, speculative phase of theory formation may be over for a while, and that our model building may find itself focusing on more particular problems such as the way histories, classes, cultures, and selves get represented to others and to themselves. Theory seems about to take a plunge back into history, in the form of historical, ideological analyses of theoretical models, as well as in the application of theoretical models to historical problems. Romanticism will play a central role in this plunge, I think, because the pressure of history was so great on Romantic theorizing. Keats's "speculations," Wordsworth's "philosophic mind," Blake's "system," Shelley's "intellectual philosophy" seem to me wonderful sites for the study of literary theorizing as an activity scarred by history. None of these Romantic theories can be taken at face value; none of their self-representations of mastery, comprehension, utopian perfection, or imaginative freedom can be accepted as reliable guides to the understanding of their work, or to our own hopes for theoretical mastery.

The obvious historical scarring of Romantic literary theory has, for me, been an inducement to examine other theoretical texts that are perhaps more cunning in their effacement of playful, uncontrollable literary elements. My interest at this point is not in borrowing "sound" theories from philosophy to apply to literary problems, but in reading philosophical texts against the grain for their figurative, rhetorical features in a historical context. Thus, I'm less interested in refinements in the Marxist theory of ideology at this point than I am in reading Marx's own remarks on ideology, and the critical tradition it inspired, as a body of *writing* imprinted with certain historically potent images or figures. If my interests are at all typical, we should be seeing not new Cartesian or Marxist or Wittgensteinian theories of literature, but new readings of Descartes, Marx, and Wittgenstein that apply to these "foundational" writers the latest techniques of literary history.

J. HILLIS MILLER

On Edge: The Crossways of
Contemporary Criticism

The word "crossways" in my title is meant to suggest borders as well as crossroads. This double image is implicit in the poem by Wordsworth I shall discuss. It is also appropriate to the present state of criticism. Literary study often develops through genetic crossings; it brings together different disciplines or different modes of literary study. I shall attempt now to describe the present moment in literary study. The description will by no means pretend to be a sovereign overview. Any such description is necessarily from within, at the crossroads. This is the case not so much because every view is interested, a biased perspective, as because on principle there is no conceivable metalanguage outside one or another of the languages of criticism.

The institutionalized study of vernacular literature is of course a fairly recent development in the West. Matthew Arnold was in 1857 the first Professor of Poetry at Oxford to give his lectures in English. Although departments of English seem now a necessary part of any college or university—a natural feature of the academic landscape, part of nature, so to speak—until not too many decades ago they did not exist at all. They could of course again easily cease to exist or become marginal, as have, alas, departments of Greek and Latin. Some experts believe that this is in fact happening. A new discipline of rhetoric and the teaching of composition, they say, is developing across the nation.

This essay originally appeared in the *Bulletin of the American Academy of Arts and Sciences* 32 (January 1979) and is reprinted with the Academy's permission.

This new discipline will displace the departments of English or relegate them to the status departments of classics presently hold. This would in fact be a return to the situation in late nineteenth-century America, when all colleges and universities had substantial staffs in composition and in rhetoric. The discipline of the study of vernacular literature was just establishing itself. Thus the presence in American universities of large and strong departments of literary history and literary criticism may be a relatively short-lived phenomenon, lasting less than a century. The alternative would be for them to make changes which would allow them to survive in a new cultural situation.

Changes in literary study, however, as in other disciplines, usually take place with glacial slowness. Such study is strongly institutionalized in secondary school curricula; in college and university departments of English, French, German, comparative literature, and so on; in textbooks and editions; in curricula inscribed in catalogues as though fixed for the ages; and in graduate programs turning out new Ph.D.'s, far too many of them for the available positions. These new Ph.D.'s tend to be trained to teach only literature and to teach it only in certain ways; their training in the teaching of composition is often minimal. The greatest institutionalized resistance to change is in the more or less fixed presuppositions, prejudices, and feelings of those who teach literature and write about it.

This institutional continuity in the study of literature of course has great advantages. It would be impossible for each teacher to make up the whole discipline anew each time he confronted a text or a class. Even the most innovative scholar, teacher, or critic depends on the presence of a relatively stable and conservative academic organization in order to get on with his own work. Much time these days is in fact wasted in the humanities on the endless concoction of new courses and new curricula. There are problems, however, if the institution no longer responds fully to the demands made on it by society, in one direction, nor fits the actual state of the discipline involved, in the other, which, I believe, is to a considerable degree the case at present. Nevertheless, in spite of the inertia of its institutional embodiments, the study of literature in America is at this moment changing with unusual rapidity.

One change is being imposed from outside the discipline, from the direction of society. By society here I mean the context within which literary study in America dwells, which it serves and is served by: parents, school boards, trustees, regents, legislatures, the "media." We teachers of literature have fewer students already and will apparently have still fewer as the years go by, both in individual courses and as majors in the various departments of literature. Those fewer are steadily less well prepared both in literature itself and in what are called "basic language skills." They cannot write well. They cannot read well either. The reading of works of literature appears to be playing every day a less and less important role in our culture generally. The complex social function performed in Elizabethan and Jacobean England by going to the theater and in Victorian England by the reading of novels is performed these days by other activities, mostly, so it seems, by watching television. The reading of a novel, poem, or play, or even the watching of a play, is likely to become an increasingly artificial, marginal, or archaic activity. It is beginning to seem more and more odd, to some people, to be asked to take seriously the literature of a small island on the edge of Europe, a small island, moreover, which has ceased to be a major world power. It might be more important to learn Russian or Chinese or Arabic. At the same time, American society has begun to recognize that we are to a considerable degree a multilingual people, not only because many of us have Spanish or some other tongue as a first language, but because we speak and write many different forms of English besides the idiolect and grapholect of standard English. For better or worse, much "standard English as a second language" must be taught, even to college students.

As College Board scores go down from year to year, our society is demanding in a louder and louder chorus that schools and colleges do something soon about the fact that our young people cannot read and cannot write. This demand, at the college and university level, is being made on professors who have been trained to teach the details of literary history and the intricacies of meaning in works by Shakespeare or Milton, Keats or Woolf. Even before they found themselves asked to teach more and more composition, many departments of English had been demoralized by declining enrollments and had begun to set their Shakespeareans and medievalists to teach classes in modern fiction, in film, or in continental novels in translation, just as the department of classics in one large state university justifies its existence at the undergraduate level by a lecture course on "mythology." A large proportion of the courses offered by the department of English in one good liberal arts college I visited recently included at least one work by J. L. Borges. This department is for all practical purposes a department of foreign literature in translation, and the departments of Spanish, French, and German at the same college are small and ineffective.

In the area of expository writing a large industry is being mobilized to create a new discipline. This mobilization includes distinguished literary theorists and historians like E. D. Hirsch, Wayne Booth, and Stanley Fish, who began as literary critics, not as experts on the teaching of composition. At the same time, more and more bright young people are already making careers in composition, seeking training in rhetoric, in linguistics, and in educational psychology rather than narrowly in traditional literary history and criticism. This is all to the good, but it will obviously weaken further the traditional activities of the study of literature as such.

At the same time, from the other direction, there have been unusually rapid changes within the discipline of literary study proper. Thirty years ago the field of literary study in America was more or less completely dominated by the method of intrinsic reading called the "New Criticism" and by a positivistic literary history committed to gathering facts and establishing texts. The latter mode was associated with the method of scientific research. It descended from such nineteenth-century metaphorical assimilations of literary study to scientific method as that of Hippolyte Taine, as well as from the long European tradition of philology and textual criticism originally coming from the study of Greek and Latin literature and from biblical hermeneutics. The archetypal criticism of Northrop Frye was in 1948 just appearing as the first strong alternative to the New Criticism. There was a somewhat marginal presence of the great German philological tradition in the form of refugee scholars like Erich Auerbach and Leo Spitzer. Some news of continental formalism—Russian, Czech, and Polish—was seeping through in the influential book by René Wellek and Austin Warren called *The Theory of Literature*. In spite of the latter book, however, literary study in America was still insular. It was a more or less self-enclosed Anglo-American tradition confident that it could go on going it alone.

Today the situation is greatly changed. No serious student of literature can fail to think of it as an international enterprise. It is just as important for the student of Chaucer, of Shakespeare, or of Dickens to know about continental criticism and to read such an international journal as *PTL*, which is edited at the Institute for Poetics and Semiotics in Tel Aviv, as it is for him to know the tradition of secondary works on these authors in English or to read *The Publications of the Modern Language Association*.

Moreover, the range of viable alternatives in literary methodology has become bafflingly large. These alternatives can, so it seems, hardly be reconciled in some grand synthesis. *Il faut choisir*. Along with the still powerful New Criticism, archetypal criticism, and positivistic literary history, there is a more or less fully elaborated phenomenological or hermeneutic criticism, a "criticism of consciousness" as it is sometimes called. A new semiotic formalism inspired by linguistics has been developed. There is a structuralist criticism deriving from structural linguistics and structural anthropology. A powerful new form of psychoanalytic criticism, mostly imported from France, has become influential. A revived Marxist and sociological criticism is beginning to take strong hold in America. Another new kind of criticism focuses on reader response and on what is called in Germany *Rezeptiongeschichte*. There is, finally, a form of literary study which concentrates on the rhetoric of literary texts, taking rhetoric in the sense of the investigation of the role of figurative language in literature. This method is sometimes called "deconstruction," which as a name at least has the advantage of distinguishing it firmly from any form of "structuralism." It is associated with the name of Jacques Derrida in France and with certain critics at my own university, Yale, as well as, increasingly, with younger critics at other universities in the United States. It has distinguished native grandsires or at least great-uncles in Kenneth Burke and William Empson. All these new forms are international in scope. The master works in each are as likely to have been written in Russian, German, French, or Italian as in English. This means that the delays and inadequacies of translation have made particular difficulties for literary study recently in America. Few students and young teachers here can read even one foreign language fluently, much less the whole necessary panoply.

This is not the place to attempt a description of each of these modes. It takes a whole semester of an elaborately team-taught course at my university to provide even a relatively superficial introduction to them for undergraduates. My aim here is to suggest that literary study in America now is in an unusually fluid or unstable condition. It is likely to change much more rapidly than usual, as much from forces within itself as from the pressures from without sketched earlier. This makes it somewhat unpredictable; only a remarkably insensitive or secluded person would be complacently at ease. It is in fact an exciting field to work in at the moment, though it is also no wonder so many members of my profession feel on edge, edgy.

In spite of the bewildering array of possibilities in literary methodology, the methods available may, for the purposes to which I want to turn now, be reduced to two distinctly different sorts. One kind includes all those methods whose presuppositions are in one way or another what I would call "metaphysical." The other kind includes those methods which hypothesize that in literature, for reasons which are intrinsic to language itself, metaphysical presuppositions are, necessarily, both affirmed and subverted. By "metaphysical" I mean the system of assumptions coming down from Plato and Aristotle which has unified our culture. This system includes the notions of beginning, continuity, and end, of causality, of dialectical process, of organic unity, and of ground, in short of logos in all its many senses. A metaphysical method of literary study assumes that literature is in one way or another referential, in one way or another grounded in something outside language. This something may be physical objects, or "society," or the economic realities of labor, valuation, and exchange. It may be conscious, the Cogito, or the unconscious, or absolute spirit, or God. An antimetaphysical or "deconstructive" form of literary study attempts to show that in a given work of literature, in a different way in each case, metaphysical assumptions are both present and at the same time undermined by the text itself. They are undermined by some figurative play within the text which forbids it to be read as an "organic unity" organized around some version of the logos. The play of tropes leaves an inassimilable residue or remnant of meaning, an unearned increment, so to speak, making a movement of sense beyond any unifying boundaries. The following out of the implications of the play of tropes leads to a suspension of fully rationalizable meaning in the experience of an aporia or boggling of the mind. This boggling sets up an oscillation in meaning. Dialectical opposites capable of synthesis may break down into contradictory elements which are differences among the same.

This distinction between two kinds of criticism must not be understood, as it sometimes is, to be a historical one; or rather, it challenges a certain historical patterning. What I have been saying must be understood as putting in question the familiar historical scheme which presupposes that there was once an age of faith or of metaphysics which was followed by the skepticism, disintegration, or fragmentation of modern times. The argument, rather, is that the literary and philosophical texts of any period of Western culture contain, in a different way each time, both what I am calling metaphysics and the putting in question of metaphysics. The test of this hypothesis is the interpretation of the texts themselves. It is here that the battle should be fought. What does this given poem or passage *mean?* In principle, and in fact, a Greek tragedy, an episode in Ovid, in Dante, or in *The Faerie Queene* would be as good a testing ground for this as any Romantic or postromantic poem, though I have chosen a well-known text from English Romanticism as my example.

The relation of metaphysics and the deconstruction of metaphysics finds a parable in the strange relation of kinship among apparent opposites in Wordsworth's "A Slumber Did My Spirit Seal." Here is the poem:

A slumber did my spirit seal;
I had no human fears:
She seemed a thing that could not feel
The touch of earthly years.

No motion has she now, no force;
She neither hears nor sees;
Rolled round in earth's diurnal course,
With rocks, and stones, and trees.

This beautiful, moving, and apparently simple poem was written at Goslar in Germany in the late fall or early winter of 1798–1799, during Wordsworth's miserable sojourn there with his sister Dorothy. It seems at first to be organized around a systematically interrelated set of binary oppositions. These seem to be genuinely exclusive oppositions, with a distinct uncrossable boundary line between them. Such a systematic set of oppositions, as always, invites interpretation of the dialectical sort. In such an interpretation, the oppositions are related in some scheme of hierarchical subordination. This makes possible a synthesis grounded in an explanatory third term constituting the logos of the poem. This logos is the poem's source and end, its ground and meaning, its "word" or "message." This particular text, I am arguing, forbids the successful completion of such a procedure. The method does not work. Something is always left over, a plus value beyond the boundaries of each such interpretation.

A surprising number of oppositions are present in the poem. These include slumber as against waking; male as against female; sealed up as against open; seeming as against being; ignorance as against knowledge; past as against present; inside as against outside; light as against darkness in the "diurnal" course of the earth; subject or consciousness, "spirit," as against object, the natural world of stones and trees; feeling as "touch" as against feeling as emotion, "fears"; "human fears" as against—what?—perhaps inhuman fears; "thing" in its meaning of "girl," young virgin, as against "thing" in the sense of physical object; years as against days; hearing as against seeing; motion as against force; self-propulsion as against exterior compulsion; mother as against daughter or sister, or perhaps any female family member as against some woman from outside the family, that is, mother, sister, or daughter as against mistress or wife, in short, incestuous desires against legitimate sexual feelings; life as against death.

The invitation to interpret the poem in terms of oppositions is sustained in part by its syntactical and formal structure. Syntactically it is structured around words or phrases in apposition or opposition. The second line, for instance, repeats the first, and then lines three and four say it over again:

> A slumber did my spirit seal;
> I had no human fears:
> She seemed a thing that could not feel
> The touch of earthly years.

To have no human fears is the same thing as to have a sealed spirit. Both of these are defined by the speaker's false assumption that Lucy will not grow old or die. Formally the poem is organized by the opposition between the first stanza and the second. Each stanza sets one line against the next, the first two against the last two; each also sets line one against line three and line two against line four, by way of the interlaced pattern of rhymes—abab, cdcd. The bar or barrier or blank on the page between the two stanzas constitutes the major formal structuring principle of the poem. In the shift from past to present tense this bar opposes then to now, ignorance to knowledge, life to death. The speaker has moved across the line from innocence to knowledge through the experience of Lucy's death. The poem expresses both eloquently restrained grief for that death and the calm of mature knowledge. Before, he was innocent. His spirit was sealed from knowledge as though he were asleep, closed in on himself. His innocence took the form of an ignorance of the fact of death. Lucy seemed so much alive, such an invulnerable vital young thing, that she could not possibly be touched by time, reach old age, and die. Her seeming immortality reassured the speaker of his own, and so he did not anticipate with fear his own death. He had no human fears. To be human is to be mortal, and the most specifically human fear, it may be, is the fear of death.

Wordsworth, in fact, as we know from other texts both in poetry and in prose, had as a child, and even as a young man, a strong conviction of his immortality. The feeling that it would be impossible for him to die was associated with a strong sense of participation in a nature both enduringly material, therefore immortal, and at the same time enduringly spiritual, therefore also immortal, though in a different way. In this poem, as in so many others by Wordsworth—"The Boy of Winander," the Matthew poems, and "The Ruined Cottage," for example—the speaker confronts the fact of his own death by confronting the death of another. He speaks as a survivor standing by a grave, a corpse, or a headstone, and his poem takes the form of an epitaph.

The second stanza of "A Slumber Did My Spirit Seal" speaks in the perpetual "now" of a universal knowledge of death. The speaker knows his own death through the death of another. Then Lucy seemed an invulnerable young "thing"; now she is truly a thing, closed in on herself like a stone. She is a corpse, without senses or consciousness, unable to feel any touch, unable to move of her own free will, but unwillingly and unwittingly moved by the daily rotation of the earth.

The structure of the poem is temporal. It is also "allegorical" in the technical sense in which that term is used by Walter Benjamin or by Paul de Man. The meaning of the poem arises from the interaction of two emblematic times. These are juxtaposed across an intervening gap. They are related not by similarity but by radical difference. The ironic clash between the two senses of "thing" is a miniature version of the total temporal allegory which constitutes the poem.

The play on the word "thing" exists, it happens, also in German. Two curious passages in Martin Heidegger's work will perhaps help to understand it better in Wordsworth. The first is in a passage in "Der Ursprung des Kunstwerkes" ("The Origin of the Work of Art"), in which Heidegger is giving examples of times when we do or do not call something a "thing":

> A man is not a thing. (*Der Mensch ist kein Ding.*) It is true that we speak of a young girl who is faced with a task too difficult for her (*eine übermäßige Aufgabe*) as being a young thing, still too young for it (*eine noch zu junges Ding*), but only because we feel that being human is in a certain way missing here (*hier das Menschsein in gewisser Weise vermissen*) and think that instead we have to do here with the factor that constitutes the thingly character of things (*das Dinghafte der Dinge*). We hesitate even to call the deer in the forest clearing, the beetle in the grass, the blade of grass a thing. We could sooner think of a hammer as a thing, or a shoe, or an ax, or a clock. But even these are not mere things (*Aber ein bloßes Ding sind auch sie nicht*). Only a stone, a clod of earth, a piece of wood are for us such mere things.

Strangely, though perhaps in response to a deep necessity, Heidegger gives almost exactly the same list of mere things as Wordsworth. His young girl, stone, clod of earth, piece of wood, correspond to Wordsworth's Lucy, rocks, stones, trees, and the earth itself. Moreover, Heidegger, certainly not known for his attention to the sexual aspect of things, finds himself of necessity, in his account of the uses of the word "thing," introducing the fact of sexual difference. A young girl is a thing because something is missing in her which men have. "A man is not a thing." This something missing makes her "too young for it," too young for the burdens of life. She is too innocent, too light.

This lightness of the maiden thing, which makes a young girl both beneath adult male knowledge and lightheartedly above it, appears in another odd passage in Heidegger, in this case in *Die Frage nach dem Ding* (*What Is a Thing?*). Heidegger first recalls the story in Plato's *Thaetetus* about the "goodlooking and whimsical maid from Thrace" who laughed at Thales when he fell down a well while occupied in studying the heavens. In his study of all things in the universe, "the things in front of his very nose and feet were unseen by him." "Therefore," says Heidegger in commentary on Plato's story, "the question 'What is a thing?' must always be rated as one which causes housemaids to laugh. And genuine housemaids must have something to laugh about (*Und was eine rechte Dienstmagd ist, muss doch auch etwas zum Lachen haben*)." The question, "What is a thing?", which is the question implicit in "A Slumber Did My Spirit Seal," would be a laughable nonquestion to Lucy. She would not understand it because she *is* a thing. Being a thing makes her both immeasurably below and immeasurably above laughable man with his eternal questions. By dying Lucy moves from the below to the above, leaving the male poet in either case in between, excluded, unable to break the seal.

As the reader works his or her way into the poem, attempting to break its seal, however, it comes to seem odder than the account of it I have so far given. My account has been a little too logical, a little too much like Thales' account of the universe, an analogical oversimplification. For one thing, the speaker has in fact not died. Lucy, it may be, has achieved immortality by joining herself to the perpetual substance of earth, which cannot die, as Wordsworth very forcefully says at the beginning of Book V of *The Prelude*. The speaker by not dying remains excluded from that perpetual vitality. His immortality is the bad one of a permanent empty knowledge of death and a permanent impossibility of dying. The "I" of the first stanza ("I had no human fears") has disappeared entirely in the impersonal assertions of the second stanza. It is as though the speaker has lost his selfhood by waking to knowledge. He has become an anonymous impersonal wakefulness, perpetually aware that Lucy is dead and that he is not yet dead. This is the position of the survivor in all Wordsworth's work.

Moreover, an obscure sexual drama is enacted in this poem. This drama is a major carrier of its allegorical significance. The identification of this drama will take the reader further inside. As we know from *The Prelude* as well as from the Lucy poems, nature for Wordsworth was strongly personified. It was, oddly, personified as both male and female, as both father and mother. The earth was the maternal face and body he celebrates in the famous "Infant Babe" passage in the earliest version of *The Prelude*, written also in Goslar in 1798:

> No outcast he, bewilder'd and depress'd;
> Along his infant veins are interfus'd
> The gravitation and the filial bond
> Of nature, that connect him with the world.

Nature was also, however, in certain other episodes of the earliest *Prelude*, a frightening male spirit threatening to punish the poet for wrongdoing. The poem "Nutting," also written at Goslar and later incorporated into *The Prelude*, brings the two sexes of nature together in the astonishing scene of a rape of female nature which brings the terror of a reprisal from another aspect of nature, a fearsome male guardian capable of revenge.

Wordsworth's mother died when he was eight, his father when he was thirteen. His father's death and Wordsworth's irrational sense of guilt for it are the subject of another episode of the two-book *Prelude*, another of the "spots of time." His mother's death, however, is curiously elided, so that the reader might not even be sure what the poet is talking about:

> For now a trouble came into my mind
> From obscure causes. I was left alone. . . .

The death of Wordsworth's mother hardly seems an "obscure cause" for sorrow, and yet the poet wants to efface that death. He wants to push the source of the sorrow of solitude further back, into deeper obscurity. In the Lucy poems the possession of Lucy alive and seemingly immortal is a replacement for the lost mother. It gives him again that direct filial bond to nature he had lost with the mother's death. It perhaps does not matter greatly whether the reader thinks of Lucy as a daughter or as a mistress or as an embodiment of his feelings for his sister Dorothy. What matters is the way in which her imagined death is a reenactment of the death of the mother as described in *The Prelude*.

The reenactment of the death of the mother takes a peculiar form in "A Slumber Did My Spirit Seal," however. This poem, and the Lucy poems as a group, can be defined as an attempt to have it both ways, an attempt which, necessarily, fails. Within his writing, which is what is meant here by "Wordsworth," the poet's abandonment has always already occurred. It is the condition of life and poetry once Wordsworth has been left alone, once he has become an outcast, bewildered and depressed. His only hope for reestablishing the bond that connected him to the world is to die without dying, to be dead, in his grave, and yet still alive, bound to maternal nature by way of a surrogate mother, a girl who remains herself both alive and dead, still available in life and yet already taken by Nature. Of course this is impossible, but it is out of such impossibilities that great poems are made.

Wordsworth's acting out of this fantasy is described in an extraordinary passage by Dorothy Wordsworth. This is her entry in the "Grasmere Journals" for April 29, 1802, three and a half years after the composition of "A Slumber Did My Spirit Seal":

> We then went to John's Grove, sate a while at first. Afterwards William lay, and I lay in the trench under the fence—he with his eyes shut and listening to the waterfalls and the Birds. There was no one waterfall— it was the sound of waters in the air—the voice of the air. William heard me breathing and rustling now and then but we both lay still, and unseen by one another. He thought that it would be as sweet thus to lie so in the grave, to hear the *peaceful* sounds of the earth and just to know that our dear friends were near.

"A Slumber Did My Spirit Seal" dramatizes the impossibility of fulfilling this fantasy, or rather it demonstrates that it can only be fulfilled in fantasy, that is, in a structure of words in which "thing" can mean both "person" and "object," in which one can have both stanzas at once, and can, like Lucy, be both alive and dead, or in which the poet can be both the dead-alive girl and at the same time the perpetually wakeful survivor. To have it as wordplay, however, is to have it as the impossibility of having it, to have it as permanent loss and separation, to have it as the unbridgeable gap between one meaning of the word "thing" and the other.

In "A Slumber Did My Spirit Seal" this simultaneous winning and losing, winning by losing, losing by winning, is expressed in a constant slipping of entities across borders into their opposites. As a result the mind cannot carry on that orderly thinking which depends on keeping "things" firmly fixed in their conceptual pigeon-holes. Lucy was a virgin "thing." She seemed untouchable by earthly years, that is, untouchable by nature as time, as the bringer of death, as death. The touch of earthly years is both a form of sexual appropriation which leaves the one who is possessed still virgin if she dies young, and at the same time it is the ultimate dispossession which is death. To be touched by earthly years is a way to be sexually penetrated while still remaining virgin.

The speaker of the poem rather than being the opposite of Lucy, male to her female, adult knowledge to her prepubertal innocence, is the displaced representative of both the penetrated and the penetrator, of both Lucy herself and of her unravishing ravisher, nature or death. The speaker was "sealed," as she was. Now he knows. He is unsealed, as she is. To know, however, as the second stanza indicates, is to speak from the impersonal position of death. It is to speak as death. Death is the penetrator who leaves his victim intact, unpierced, but at the same time wholly open, as an unburied corpse is exposed, open to the sky, like rocks and stones and trees. The speaker's movement to knowledge, as his consciousness becomes dispersed, loses its "I," is "the same thing" as Lucy's death. It finds its parable in that death.

Whatever track the reader follows through the poem he arrives at blank contradictions. These contradictions are not ironic. They are the copresence of difference within the same, as, for example, time in the poem is not different from space but is collapsed into the rolling motion of the earth, or as Lucy in her relation to the speaker blurs the difference of the sexes. Lucy is both the virgin child and the missing mother, that mother earth who gave birth to the speaker and has abandoned him. Male and female, however, come together in the earth, and so Lucy and the speaker are "the same," though the poet is also the perpetually excluded difference from Lucy, an unneeded increment, like an abandoned child. The two women, mother and girl child, have jumped over the male generation in the middle. They have erased its power of mastery, its power of logical understanding, which is the male power *par excellence*. In expressing this, the poem leaves its reader with no possibility of moving through or beyond or standing outside in sovereign control. The reader is caught in an unstillable oscillation unsatisfying to the mind and incapable of being grounded in anything outside the activity of the poem itself.

"A Slumber Did My Spirit Seal" shimmers between affirming male mastery as the consciousness which survives the death of the two generations, mother and daughter or sister, and *knows*, and lamenting the failure of consciousness to join itself to the dead mother, and therefore to the ground of consciousness, by way of its possession of the sister or daughter. On the one hand, he does survive; if he does not have possession or power, he has knowledge. On the other hand, thought or knowledge is not guiltless. The poet has himself somehow caused Lucy's death by thinking about it. Thinking recapitulates in reverse mirror image the action of the earthly years in touching, penetrating, possessing, killing, encompassing, turning the other into oneself and therefore being left only with a corpse, an empty sign.

Lest it be supposed that I am grounding my reading of the poem on the "psychobiographical" details of the poet's reaction to the death of his parents, let me say that it is the other way around. Wordsworth interpreted the death of his mother according to the traditional trope identifying the earth with a maternal presence. By the time we encounter her in his writing she exists as an element in that figure. His life, like his poetry, was the working out of the consequences of this fictitious trope, or rather of the whole figurative system into which it is incorporated. This incorporation exists both in Wordsworth's language and in the Western tradition generally, both before and after him. To put this as economically as possible, "A Slumber Did My Spirit Seal," in the context of the other Lucy poems and of all Wordsworth's work, enacts one version of a constantly repeated occidental drama of the lost sun. Lucy's name of course means light. To possess her would be a means of rejoining the lost source of light, the father sun as logos, as head power and fount of meaning. As light she is the vacant evidence that that capital source seems once to have existed. Light is dispersed everywhere but yet may not be captured or held. It is like those heavens Thales studied. To seek to catch or understand it is to be in danger of falling into a well. The fear of the death of Lucy is the fear that the light will fail, that all links with the sun will be lost, as, in "Strange Fits of Passion," another of the Lucy poems, the setting of the moon, mediated female image of the sun, makes the poet-lover fear Lucy's death:

> "Oh mercy!" to myself I cried,
> "If Lucy should be dead."

The fulfillment of that fear in her actual death is the loss both of light and of the source of light. It is the loss of the logos, leaving the poet and his words groundless. The loss of Lucy is the loss of the poet's female reflex or narcissistic mirror image. In the absence of the filial bond to nature, this has been the only source of his solid sense of selfhood. In one version of the Narcissus story, Narcissus' self-love is generated by the hopeless search for a beloved twin sister, who has died. For Wordsworth, "The furiously burning father fire" (Wallace Stevens' phrase) has sunk beneath the horizon, apparently never to return. In spite of the diurnal rotation of the earth that earth seems to have absorbed all the light. Even the moon, reflected and mediated source of sunlight at night, and so the emblem of Lucy, has set. The consciousness of the poet has survived all these deaths of the light to subsist as a kind of black light. His awareness is the light-no-light which remains when the sun has sunk and Lucy has died, when both have gone into the earth.

This loss of the radiance of the logos, along with the experience of the consequences of that loss, is the drama of all Wordsworth's poetry, in particular of "A Slumber Did My Spirit Seal." In the absence of any firm grounding the poem necessarily takes on a structure of chiasmus. This is the perpetual reversal of properties in crisscross substitutions I have tried to identify. The senses of the poem continually cross over the borders set up by the words if they are taken to refer to fixed "things," whether material or subjective. The words waver in their meaning. Each word in itself becomes the dwelling place of contradictory senses, as though host and parasite were together in the same house. This wavering exceeds the bounds of the distinction between literal and figurative language, since literal ground and figurative derivative change places too within the word, just as do the other opposites. This wavering within the word is matched by an analogous wavering in the syntax. That in turn is matched by the large-scale relation of going and coming between the two stanzas. Each of these waverings is another example of the disparate in the matching pair which forbids any dialectical synthesis. The tracing out of these differences within the same moves the attention away from the attempt to ground the poem in anything outside itself. It catches the reader within a movement in the text without any solid foundation in consciousness, in nature, or in spirit. As groundless, the movement is, precisely, alogical.

This explanation of Wordsworth's little poem has led me seemingly far away from a sober description of the state of contemporary literary study. It is meant, however, to "exemplify" one mode of such interpretation. In a passage in *The Will to Power* Nietzsche says: "To be able to read off a text as a text without interposing an interpretation is the last-developed form of 'inner experience'—perhaps one that is hardly possible." If it is hardly possible, it may not even be desirable, since interpretation, as Nietzsche also elsewhere says, is an active, affirmative process, a taking possession of something for some purpose or use. In the multitudinous forms of this which make up the scene of literary study, perhaps the true fork in the road is between two modes of this taking possession, two modes of teaching literature and writing about it. One mode already knows what it is going to find. Such a mode is controlled by the presupposition of some center. The other alternative mode of reading is more open to the inexhaustible strangeness of literary texts. This enigmatic strangeness much literary study busily covers over. The strangeness of literature remains, however. It survives all attempts to hide it. It is one of the major correlatives of the human predicament, since our predicament is to remain, always, within language. The strangeness lies in the fact that language, our Western languages at least, both affirm logic and at the same time turn it on edge, as happens in "A Slumber Did My Spirit Seal." If this is the case, the alternative mode of literary study I have tried to exemplify both can and should be incorporated into college and university curricula. This is already happening to some extent, but, as I see it, the development of programs for this, from basic courses in reading and writing up to the most advanced graduate seminars, is one task in humanistic studies today.

POSTSCRIPT 1984

Reading Meyer Abrams' "Construing and Deconstructing" and trying to remember what was going on in my mind when I was writing "On Edge," now five years ago, I do not quite want to say what Thomas Hardy said of *Tess of the d'Urbervilles: "Melius fuerat non scribere.* But there it stands." Though I would not write "On Edge" in the same way today, I am glad I wrote it, and in any case, there it stands. As with any piece of writing, the passage of time has detached it more and more from its author, who is no longer quite the same person. Perhaps he was made a somewhat different person by the act of writing it. "On Edge" must now in any case make its own way in the world, as a fatherless orphan who can only go on saying the same thing, over and over, in answer to any questions, such as those Meyer Abrams puts to it.

The situation of literary studies in the United States today, moreover, is markedly different from what it was in 1979. It is my impression that Meyer Abrams is now trying to come to terms with a *fait* largely *accompli.* A good bit at least of what I hoped for then has now occurred, namely the widespread assimilation of new rhetorical methodologies into normal practice in the study and teaching of literature in America. The frontier or edge of literary study has moved on to a different location, a new asking of questions about the relation of literature to history and to society *in the light of* recent rhetorical and linguistic insights. For better or for worse, the study of literature in the United States has been permanently altered by structuralist and poststructuralist methods. Not that there is not still opposition, but that opposition has gone into a new phase, I suppose predictable, but nonetheless deplorable; I mean a phase of irrational polemic, sometimes by distinguished older scholars who apparently feel so threatened by these new directions of literary study that they are willing to abandon all traditions of scholarly accuracy and responsibility in order blindly to attack what they appear to have made no attempt to understand. Meyer Abrams by no means belongs in that category. He has read Derrida and me with great care. His essay has considerable importance as one of the most serious and detailed attempts by a scholar-critic of a different set of commitments to come to terms with so-called deconstruction. With Meyer Abrams one can differ and still talk, and all honor to him and to his essay for that.

My reply, though I am sure my claim that he has not entirely understood deconstruction will not fill him with delight, is meant nevertheless to keep the door open for further dialogue between us, and between people like him and people like me. I have attempted especially to try to answer the question of why Abrams and I, two literary scholars brought up in somewhat the same tradition and both with presumably some competence as readers, nevertheless read Derrida so differently and why we read "A Slumber Did My Spirit Seal" so differently. I find that a puzzling question. I think I have found the answer to it, an answer that lies not in the highfalutin altitudes of pure literary theory but in the lowlands of basic and instinctive orientation toward language, literary or otherwise.

Controversy and polemics in literary study rarely accomplish much. Neither side is likely to cover itself with glory, and much foolishness may be spoken. Nevertheless, the stakes are high enough in this case perhaps to justify a brief response to Abrams' essay. Though I am of course grateful to him for the careful attention he has given to an essay of mine and to a selection of the work of Derrida, he nevertheless seems to me a striking example of the way a man can be learned, distinguished, generous and open minded, at least to a degree, and yet, in this case at least, miss major points in the texts on which he is commenting. Something could be said about more or less every line or sentence of Abrams' essay, something, it seems to me, identified as slightly askew in his formulations and conclusions. In the interests of brevity I shall first identify several less than pervasive though by no means insignificant points of misunderstanding or errancy and then move quickly on to the fundamental misunderstanding which underlies Abrams' whole essay.

First smaller point: I am much troubled by the remarks toward the end of Abrams' essay about the way young people today use so-called deconstructive methods because they produce new and publishable readings and are a way of getting ahead in the academic world, getting promotion and tenure, etc. Abrams here seems to me, if I may say so, shockingly cynical. He shows an amazing lack of confidence in the intellectual integrity of the young people in our profession. Surely he knows that good work was never yet done with that kind of motivation. The only hope in literary study and teaching is to say it like it is as one sees it. Of those sentences in Abrams' essay one can certainly say: *melius fuerat non scribere.*

Second point: Abrams' discussion of Derrida, though it makes a somewhat wider sweep through his writings than many more reductive accounts of it do, is nevertheless primarily based on quite early work, especially *De la grammatologie* and other early essays. Though Derrida would not, I think, by any means repudiate what he wrote then, he has of course published many books and essays since. His new work should surely now form the essential context for any reading of what he wrote earlier, and the early work itself can hardly be understood in isolation from the context of the relation of Derrida's first books to Husserl, to Heidegger, and even to Sartre or to French existentialism of that time generally. If Abrams wanted to make a more solidly based assessment of the implications of Derrida's work for literary study, it might have been better to discuss *Glas*, or *La carte postale*, or *Signéponge*. The same thing might be said in a somewhat different way of his treatment of my essay. Though, as I have said, I am grateful for the careful attention he has given my discussion of "A Slumber Did My Spirit Seal," it seems to me a shaky use of synecdoche to make it stand for my work in general or for American deconstructive criticism in general, in its presumed deviation from Derrida. Abrams' generalizations here are built on an excessively fragile foundation.

Final preliminary point: Abrams often talks as if he thinks it is being claimed that so-called deconstruction is a wholly new and unheard of mode of interpretation, based on new insights into language, something that has never been done before. Nothing could be further from the truth. What is being claimed, rather, is that deconstruction is only the current version of a long tradition of rhetorical study going back especially to the Greeks, though to some degree to an aspect of Greek thought that has tended to be obscured or effaced—even by the Greeks themselves, as by Plato. Good writers and good readers have always known what deconstruction knows, for example about figurative language. What Abrams calls his own "oldreading" is in fact the Johnny-come-lately. It is based on a quite recent set of assumptions about literary interpretation, assumptions narrowly circumscribed within a certain historical situation, that of nineteenth- and twentieth-century humanism in literary study. Like so-called aestheticism, of which it is the mirror image or twin, this humanism tends to sequester literary texts from fundamental ontological, metaphysical, or religious questions.

Now the most important point: The major misunderstanding in Abrams' essay might be approached by way of his title, "Construing and Deconstructing." If these two terms are translated into their more traditional equivalents, Abrams' title would be "Grammar and Rhetoric," that is, the names of two of the three branch-roads of the medieval trivium, the third being logic. Abrams' error is the aboriginal one of assuming that the grammar of a language, for example the language of Wordsworth's little poem, is a first and fundamental level of easily identifiable meaning to which figurative language, the deviant realm of tropes, is added as a nonessential second layer open to what Abrams, in a nice little play of double meaning of his own, calls "over-reading." First there is under-reading, or the construing of plain grammar, and then, if you happen to want it (though why should you?) there is over-reading, the interpretation of figures, what is sometimes called deconstruction. The latter is a kind of supererogatory fiddling with the text. It is altogether dependent, to boot, on the fact that the deconstructor has first performed, like every other reader, the under-reading of the text, that construing of its plain sense which all competent readers spontaneously and successfully accomplish.

The claim of the tradition to which Derrida and I belong is that this is a false picture both of language and of the process of good reading. The major presupposition of deconstruction and of the long tradition to which it belongs is that figurative language goes all the way down, so to speak. It is not something added on top of an easily construable grammar. The language of poems, novels, philosophical texts, or of any other genre, for example literary criticism, is not like that honey pot with which Pooh in A. A. Milne's story fears he may have baited the trap for heffalumps, honey on top, product of the sweet flowers of rhetoric, and cheese at the bottom, the plain food of literal language. Language is honey all the way to the bottom, and the bottom is a long way down. All language is irreducibly and fundamentally figurative, as in my play on words for bottom or ground here. All good reading is therefore the reading of tropes at the same time as it is the construing of syntactical and grammatical patterns. Any act of reading must practice the two forms of interpretation together. This means that there is no such thing as that plain under-reading which Abrams hypothesizes. With the collapse of this hypothesis Abrams' whole argument against deconstruction, his aberrant reading of it, as well as his proposal of an alternative pedagogy, falls to the ground. There is only and always, from the beginning, one form or another of over-reading, the reading of grammar and tropes together, more or less adequately.

One evidence of the nonexistence of the grammatical under-reading Abrams imagines is the wild diversity of "first readings" of any given text one gets from so-called competent readers. Abrams presents, almost in spite of himself, one example of this in his brief discussion of previous commentary on "A Slumber Did My Spirit Seal." Anyone who has followed the history of the interpretation of any major works in the canon of Western literature, even the most apparently "simple" ones, will have encountered other versions of this diversity. What Abrams really means by "we under-readers who start and stop with the plain sense everyone can agree on" is "I, Meyer Abrams, and those I can persuade to accept my reading." The evidence against the notion of a broad agreement on the plain construed sense of literary works is overwhelming.

Any good reader confronted with the words of "A Slumber Did My Spirit Seal," as Abrams cites it at the end of his essay, will be assailed by a swarm of questions, not by any means faced with a clear, spontaneously generated, construed meaning on the basis of which he can execute arabesques of irresponsible or ungrounded "over-readings." Some of these questions are "grammatical": e.g., why does the poem say "did . . . seal" rather than use the simple past tense, "sealed"? Some are "rhetorical" or have to do with tropes: e.g., what does it mean to say someone's "spirit" "slumbers"? what does it mean to say that someone's "spirit" (whatever *that* means in this case) is "sealed"? does it mean as an envelope, or as a bit of wax, or as a tomb, or as someone's lips are "sealed," or what? All these enigmas are on the same level, so to speak. Each enters into the others, is intertwined with them, so that one cannot be "solved" without the others. Their failure to form a hierarchy forbids the certain establishment of that plain sense or under-reading which Abrams wants to make the basis of literary study.

All the other conclusions of Abrams' essay are vitiated by the insubstantiality of his initial premise, in particular his way of reading deconstructive texts by Derrida and by me, his questioning of my placing of "A Slumber Did My Spirit Seal" in a wide context of passages by Wordsworth and by others, and his picture of a proper pedagogy as beginning with construing or grammar and then going on, for very advanced students, to deconstruction, that is to rhetoric as the understanding of tropes.

The whole effort of deconstructive criticism has been to demonstrate, patiently, over and over again, with many different texts of different sorts—poems, novels, philosophy, criticism, prefaces, and so on—the exact opposite of what Abrams wants to say, namely to demonstrate that the plainest grammatical sense is already turned aside from itself by tropes of one sort or another. Far from building his reading of Rousseau on an under-reading which everyone accepts, Derrida wants to show both that a specific reading, namely the "logocentric" one, is inevitable for any reader at any time in our culture and at the same time that such a reading always contains the traces, vestiges, or latent indications of another reading undoing the first. Deconstruction displaces or reorients that metaphysical reading by following those traces and thereby placing the logocentric reading in a different context. This new context turns the logocentric reading into something other than itself. This procedure shows that the logocentric reading is something far different from the solidly based under-reading Abrams presumes it to be, namely that it is but one strand in a complex fabric.

As for what Abrams says about my initial paraphrase of "A Slumber Did My Spirit Seal," I am sorry to say that he has missed the point of what I was trying to do, and for a reason which may have a profound significance for the differences between us. My initial paraphrase was meant to be ironic, that is, to display its manifest inadequacy, as a way of preparing for the attempt later on to account for this inadequacy and to try to repair it. The reader was meant to recognize that there is something strangely incomplete or lacking in such an account of the poem and to expect something more as an attempt to repair that incompleteness. As someone has said, there should be a mark of punctuation for irony.

On the question of context: Abrams assumes that there is a solid context for the reading of detached texts, such as a short lyric poem like "A Slumber Did My Spirit Seal," in the grammatical competence of any reader or speaker of the language in which it is written. Derrida knows French, therefore he can read Rousseau, just as any other Frenchman can. I know English, so what's my problem with "A Slumber Did My Spirit Seal"? If Derrida and I are right, and we are, about the enigmas introduced into even the most apparently simple passage by its permeation or pervasion by figurative language, one of the effects of this is to make each piece of language idiosyncratic, idiomatic, the generator of an idolect of its own. It follows from this that the presumed sufficient context in standard French or English is an illusion.

We need in such an emergency all the help we can get. One such help is other "similar" passages in the same writer or in other writers, in a widening field which, as Derrida puts it, can never be "saturated," and which of course creates as many problems as it solves, especially by way of what is problematic about that "similarity." In what way, exactly, do the so-called Lucy poems form a group? I agree with Abrams that this is a problem, but I do not think the problem can be solved by pretending there is no relation among them. The other "similar" passages will not "solve" the enigmas, which are in any case insoluble in the sense of being incapable of being untied, made clear once and for all, but the analogues will perhaps assist the reader in catching a glimpse of what is heterogeneous, incommensurate, idiolectal, idiomatic, or even "idiotic" (in the sense of being unconstruable) in the text at hand. All this depends, of course, on the capacity to see it as, on the first and most immediate level, strange, puzzling, lacking in transparency of meaning.

Finally, on the question of pedagogy: As I have already hinted, it would follow from the pervasion of grammar by rhetoric which deconstruction patiently demonstrates, that Abrams' model for teaching is an impossibility. He imagines that it is possible to teach novices first "to write texts that will say, precisely and accurately, what they mean, and to construe, precisely and accurately, the texts that they read." Then possibly, at some much later stage, in advanced seminars, as an unnecessary frill, the "equilibristic art" of deconstruction might be taught. Alas, this will not work. There is no grammar without rhetoric, as teachers of composition have always known, and as they are finding out again in different ways today. Students will learn neither to write well nor to read well unless they are taught both grammar and rhetoric together from the beginning. That this makes difficulties for the devising of curricula in composition and in literature (and for the training of teachers of both) I would be the last to deny, but so have recent advances in physical and biological knowledge made great problems for the teaching of those disciplines. The difference is that the inherence of tropes, including the trope of irony, in ordinary as well as in literary language has been known since Plato and the Greek rhetoricians. To say that rhetoric or the knowledge of tropes should not be taught from the beginning, along with grammatical competence, in courses in composition and reading is like saying schools should first teach that the sun moves around the earth or that lice are bred from human sweat, and then let a few advanced students know it is not so simple.

There is no help for it. If language is "perfidious," to use Abrams' somewhat invidious word, then students even at the most preliminary level should be told this truth, just as beginning courses in biology or physics must try to explain the latest knowledge of genetics or of particle physics. That there are special difficulties in using language to explain language, as a teacher of composition or rhetoric must do, there can be no doubt, but there is no alternative but to try. Once more I think Abrams is surprisingly condescending both to teachers of composition and reading and to their students in suggesting that they will necessarily fail in this attempt.

I conclude by asking again why it might be that there is such a great gulf between Abrams and me in what happens when we first encounter something like those eight lines of "A Slumber Did My Spirit Seal" he cites at the end of his essay as the final challenge to deconstruction. What I have said already about his failure to identify the trope of irony in my essay may give the clue. I am reminded of the passage in George Eliot's *Daniel Deronda* describing Gwendolen's blindness to religious experience and to economic or political knowledge:

> She had no permanent consciousness of other fetters, or of more spiritual restraints, having always disliked whatever was presented to her under the name of religion, in the same way that some people dislike arithmetic and accounts: it has raised no other emotion in her, no alarm, no longing; so that the question whether she believed it had not occurred to her, any more than it had occurred to her to inquire into the conditions of colonial property and banking, on which, as she had had many opportunities of knowing, the family fortune was dependent. [Chap. 6]

Just as, so I have gradually come to believe, there are people learned, sensitive, and intelligent for whom metaphysical or religious questions are nonquestions, or people, also learned, sensitive, and intelligent, for whom social or political questions are nonquestions, so it may be that there are people who have a blind spot in the area of recognizing the strange things tropes do to a given piece of language. This may especially appear in an insensitivity to irony, which is like failing to see the point of a joke. Nothing is more annoying than to be told one has not seen that a joke is a joke, an irony an irony. Disagreements about the way to take a possibly ironic passage are likely to give rise to the bitterest and most acrimonious controversies, such as those I began this post-script by deploring. Something of this sort, nevertheless, may be the cause of the fissure or cleft between Meyer Abrams and me, though I continue to hope that he will come over to my side of the chasm. Perhaps it is the fissure between all under-readers and all over-readers, though I should prefer to make it a distinction between worse and better reading as such, for example of "A Slumber Did My Spirit Seal."

QUESTIONS AND ANSWERS

Question: You seem to make two different claims for deconstruction, one soft and the other hard. The soft claim seems to be that deconstruction is simply an attempt to test or question the weight-bearing capacity of the ground assumed by a text. The hard claim seems to be the conclusion that the ground in each case can't bear the weight imposed on it. I think that a critic of deconstruction like Walter Jackson Bate wouldn't oppose the first notion; he's not against testing or questioning texts. But it's the second notion that alarms him.

Answer: I agree. The second part is the specifically skeptical aspect of deconstruction that does annoy and alarm people like Professor Bate. My answer to that would be to say to him or to anyone else, let's look at the works together. Let's read them together and do that testing and we'll see whether you can persuade me that the ground of a text does bear the weight. That's what I mean by the claim that deconstruction is simply good reading and that the best places for discussing deconstruction are to be found in shared acts of reading, not in pure theory. In the latter, untested preconceptions about what goes on in Kant or Wallace Stevens, for example, move very easily into polemical statements.

Question: If Bate read further into deconstruction, don't you think that he would find comfort in the obvious conservatism that has developed there? It seems to me that the conclusion to your questioning is predetermined; that is, you already know that literature won't sustain the meanings imposed on it. But faced with that fact you finally develop the conservative argument that since there's no way in which you can justify *any* map of literary history, for example, you're justified in holding on to the map you've got. Do you think that deconstruction consequently shelters academic and intellectual conservatives who in a previous era would have been New Critics?

Answer: I don't agree that my conclusions are predetermined. I'm still looking and would be glad to find solid ground to stand on. As for the map of literary history, I believe a new one on the basis of new developments is possible. Drawing that map is a major task today. Insofar as deconstruction is simply good reading or careful reading, then it is a form of reading in general of which the New Criticism was another form. Unlike the New Critics, deconstructionists argue that you can't take it for granted that a good work of literature is going to be organically unified. Deconstruction sees irony as not necessarily (or perhaps ever) a trope of determinable meanings (saying one thing and meaning another identifiable thing) and puts more emphasis than Brooks did on such problematic tropes, however much interest he took in them. Deconstruction is more Empsonian or Burkean than Brooksian. I would say that it's all there in Kenneth Burke and Empson: you don't need Derrida if you have read Burke. Derrida has, however, applied notions about language like Burke's to a larger variety of works. He is interesting to me not only as a theorist but also as a reader.

J. HILLIS MILLER

Question: Sometimes you seem to be suggesting that a poem is a speech act, in which case it would follow that we need to consider the situation of the poem as we read it. If the poem is a speech act, then how do you justify your analysis of "parasite" and "host," for example, where you take these words back to their origins and thus ignore the context of the texts in which they appear?

Answer: In my view, words retain some of their historical force in whatever situation they're used. Therefore the poem is not for me a vacant place given meaning by one or another community of readers, as it is for Stanley Fish. The poem has power, even dangerous power, over me when I read it. One of its powers is the inhabitation in words of some aspect of historical meaning. I stand by my history of "parasite" and "host," though it was meant to some degree to be playful. I was trying to show that these words tend to liberate, in a canny user of them like Shelley, not their whole history but a significant part of it. Arguing from etymologies, as Heidegger, for example, does, is dangerous because there may have been a break in the history of a word's meaning. That history is not all necessarily preprogrammed in the word's root. On the other hand, I don't think a word is entirely defined by its situations; it is not a blank sound or mark to which I give meaning freely or because I belong to some interpretative community. Literature is always full of surprises for even the halfway good reader.

Question: In "The Function of Rhetorical Study at the Present Time," you say that you think it's more important to read Shakespeare, Spenser, and Milton than Borges or Virginia Woolf, and in another place you state that it's important to read "the best" literature. What criteria or resources does deconstruction offer to help us determine the "best" literature?

Answer: I originally made that remark at a meeting at Texas A & M before a gathering of chairmen of departments of English. I was trying to affirm the conservative side of my position. I meant there's too much attention paid to modern literature. I picked Virginia Woolf as a writer whom you can spend too much time studying, however important she is. One needs to know what she knew, including all those male writers she has such an uneasy relation to in *A Room of One's Own*. Although I think that Virginia Woolf is important, I also think that one shouldn't only read twentieth-century literature. Deconstruction is conservative as far as the canon goes. There's been relatively little fiddling with the canon on the part of the deconstructionists, though even slight rearrangements, for example putting Hegel side by side with Genet, as Derrida does in *Glas*, may have more than trivial consequences. There's a rereading of the canon by the deconstructionists, but the people that

120

we read are essentially the ones that everybody else reads. Because the canon is pretty well taken for granted in deconstruction, this particular form of criticism hasn't discovered all that many great writers whom nobody else had noticed. Derrida, for example, teaches philosophy. He teaches mostly the central canon of major philosophers, Plato, Leibnitz, Descartes, Kant, Hegel, Heidegger, just as any other historian of philosophy would do.

Question: Suppose you were a student whose education stopped about 1965. You knew about the New Criticism, rhetorical criticism, and reader-response criticism, but nothing about deconstruction. If you were such a student, how would you read a poem differently from the way you do now? What would you fail to see in it that you think you can now see?

Answer: Nothing, if I had been a good reader. That's what I mean when I say that you don't need Derrida or deconstruction if you have not so much Brooks and Warren as Empson and Burke, that side of the New Criticism that's slightly more radical in its view of figures of speech and so on. I would also say, however, that by putting in question the assumption that a good literary work is going to be organically unified, deconstruction has freed me to deal with aspects of works which are not easily assimilated on the assumption of unity. The deconstructionist critics have called attention to the special power of catachresis, a figure of speech, if you can call it that, to which the New Critics did not pay much attention. (Derrida's "White Mythology" is of course a key text here.) Catachresis and prosopopoeia have been important in my recent work. They are limits where rhetorical analysis of literary texts based on the opposition between literal and figurative languages breaks down and where there may be a glimpse, as in the wink of an eye, of something beyond language. That "something," it may be, forbids language, the language of poems for example, to "come clear." Catachresis and prosopopoeia converge, as in "face of a mountain," but have different temporal orientations, catachresis toward the present and toward the "making present" by naming of what would otherwise slip away, prosopopoeia toward the past, the invocation of the absent, inanimate, or dead by giving it the mask of personification, speaking to it or of it as though it were a living person: "Ye knew him well, ye cliffs and islands of Winander." As my example shows, apostrophe and prosopopoeia are of course closely connected. I have tried to work some of this out in *The Linguistic Moment*.

Question: But I would say that in *The Linguistic Moment* you give an organic reading of Yeats's "Nineteen Hundred and Nineteen." By showing that there's disorder in each of the individual parts of the poem, you suggest that the poem consistently creates an image of disorder. I am consequently still not sure what is new about your reading.

Answer: What you say is based on a misunderstanding of the opposition between an "organically unified" reading and a deconstructionist one. A deconstructionist reading can be quite specific about the particular ways a given poem, say Yeats's "Nineteen Hundred and Nineteen," does not hang together or cohere, is heterogeneous, defies the unifying power of logical reason, the logos, without thereby making for an organically unified reading. Nor does such a reading mean that it's a free-for-all, that one is free to make any reading whatsoever of the poem. I would say that I think my reading of Yeats's poem is right, that all right-thinking people will come, given enough time, to my reading. When one speaks of undecidability as a feature of deconstructive criticism, one doesn't mean a free-for-all but a very precise identifiable movement back and forth among possibilities, each of which can be articulated phrase by phrase. My notion is that a poem has a coercive effect on any reader and on any reading, even an inadequate one. Even the most evasive paraphrase contains latently the meanings it tries to suppress, for example Abrams' reading of "A Slumber Did My Spirit Seal." The exemplary statement of this is in Paul de Man's foreword to Carol Jacobs' *The Dissimulating Harmony*. To de Man's statement I give my entire allegiance. Here are his words, if I may be allowed, belatedly and in his memory, to read them into the record:

> Understanding is not a version of one single and universal Truth that would exist as an essence, a hypostasis. The truth of a text is a much more empirical and literal event. What makes a reading more or less true is simply the predictability, the necessity of its occurrence, regardless of the reader or of the author's wishes. "Es ereignet sich aber das Wahre" (not *die Wahrheit*) says Hölderlin, which can be freely translated, "What is true is what is bound to take place." And, in the case of the reading of a text, what takes place is a necessary understanding. What marks the truth of such an understanding is not some abstract universal but the fact that it has to occur regardless of other considerations . . . it is not a matter of choice to omit or to accentuate by paraphrase certain elements in a text at the expense of others. We don't have this choice, since the text imposes its own understanding and shapes the reader's evasions. The more one censors, the more one reveals what is being effaced. A paraphrase is always what we called an analytical reading, that is, it is always susceptible of being made to point out consistently what it was trying to conceal.

Question: I'm always surprised when you talk about the coerciveness or independent status of the poem. How can you exempt the poem from the skepticism in deconstruction that seems to undermine every other presence?

Answer: I need something to hang on to or to stand on. It's those words on the page. They are not so much "presence" as what Mallarmé calls "une apparence fausse de présence." In giving that nonpresent presence irresistible power I'm testifying to my experience with literature, which is that I can't make George Eliot's *Middlemarch* or Stevens' "The Rock" mean anything that I want it to mean. Such a text that has coercion over me may be complicated, heterogeneous, enigmatic, but that doesn't make it disappear or free me to make it mean anything I want. This fact preserves the possibility of saying to somebody, "You're wrong in this case." Luckily, since a teacher needs to feel able to say that. This power of the text over its readers also opens up the possibility of dialogue among readers in which you could actually work out whether somebody was right or wrong. It follows that the real way to get at Derrida—it would be hard to do—would be to try to demonstrate that he is wrong about Plato or Ponge or Hegel, that his readings are wrong. This would be far more to the point than arguing in a vacuum about his "theories."

Question: How does Frye's theory of archetypes fit in with your view of deconstruction?

Answer: For Frye, archetypes tend to be thought of as preceding or exceeding any of their embodiments. Therefore, though Frye's theory is not openly Jungian, he nevertheless suggests that there is a reservoir of archetypes somewhere, and that they have to reappear out of some place. For me or for Derrida, the patterns exist only in their bodies; there is no *ur* example. There is no origin other than a movement of differentiation. Frye has not been much talked about or criticized by deconstructionists as far as I know, but in "Structure, Sign, and Play" Derrida explicitly criticizes a nostalgia for an original happy savage state in Lévi-Strauss. In the Lévi-Straussian or structuralist anthropological view of myth, you have two, three, five, a dozen, a hundred different examples of the myth you have gathered, and it looks as if they bend back toward some original myth of which they are all representative, though Lévi-Strauss correctly sees that as an anaclastic illusion. Frye sometimes seems to yield to that illusion.

Question: M. H. Abrams has used your essay "On Edge" to make a sharp distinction between Derrida's linguistic philosophy and the use made of it in American deconstructive criticism. Do you see any grounds for distinguishing between your literary criticism and Derrida's philosophy?

Answer: I should hope there would be a difference! On the other hand it would be a mistake to assume too easily that American deconstruction is necessarily all that tame or conservative. Profound changes in curriculum and departmental organization are already beginning in American colleges and universities as a result of deconstruction. Your question has been raised by people quite different from Abrams in orientation. For example, Rodolphe Gasché in an essay in *Glyph* makes the point rather aggressively that Derrida belongs to a certain European context, that he is genuinely revolutionary in that context, that he is a philosopher, not a literary critic, and that when he is appropriated in the United States primarily by literary critics and for the purposes of reading, he is tamed and made more conservative. The people who do this kind of criticism in America, moreover, tend to be in elitist institutions, say some of our critics, and therefore uphold the status quo, vote conservatively, and so on. Deconstructionists find themselves in the strange situation of being attacked by both sides: by conservatives like Bate and Wellek and Gerald Graff for being nihilistic and by Marxists for not changing the institution one iota. On the one hand we do nothing, on the other are violent anarchists. I don't see how our opponents can have it both ways. In fact both are grievously in error. I would agree that there is a change when you move from one institutional context to another. Derrida, it is true, is supposed to be a philosopher, and most of the people in America who do this kind of criticism are literary critics, though Derrida's influence on philosophy proper in America is beginning to be strongly felt. This fact is resisted and deplored by philosophers like Searle. On the other hand, I do think that Gasché is wrong in ignoring the fact that Derrida is primarily a reader of pieces of language and that among the things that he has read are works of literature. It's not necessarily the case, then, that a critic of literature must be less radical than Derrida. It's not intrinsic in the transfer that deconstruction must be weakened over here. Changed, yes, but after all Derrida teaches at Yale a few weeks each year and lectures widely in the States. At least to that degree his activity is transferred to the United States.

Question: You no longer feel that there is any sort of interaction between the self and language?

Answer: I'm skeptical about whether you can think of the self as something inside me like a grain of sand, as Yeats put it, something like a definite hard object. It seems to me that the self is a function primarily of language rather than a preexistent given which uses language. Language is prior to selfhood rather than the other way around, though the latter is what Georges Poulet, along with so many other distinguished critics, appears to think. Once you see the self as generated by language, then selfhood becomes much more varied, precarious, and complicated. I agree with Nietzsche here. He defines the self as a congeries of warring selves. The issue of selfhood is of great importance in the criticism of fiction. It is traditional to assume that a good work of fiction is going to present characters each of whom has a total unity. It seems to me, on the contrary, that one of the major things the tradition of realistic fiction does is to put that notion of selfhood in question. A marvelous example of this is Meredith's *The Egoist*. Clara Middleton discovers that though her act of promising to marry Willoughby presupposes a fixed and unified self on the basis of which promises can be made, she does not in fact have such a self. She is rather "a multitude of flitting wishes." It's not, then, that there's necessarily no such thing as selfhood but that it cannot be taken for granted. The nature of selfhood is one of the things that literature makes problematic or about which literature raises questions.

Question: But in "The Function of Rhetorical Study at the Present Time" you suggest that calling into question the notion of the self eventually affirms the self.

Answer: Well, the self is a hard thing to do without—almost impossible, in fact, even in the most practical sense. Suppose I could say that yesterday I signed that promissory note or took out that mortgage but I'm not the same person today that I was yesterday, so you can't hold me to the mortgage payment. Obviously that would cause great problems. It seems like a trivial example, but our whole social life depends on the possibility of holding somebody to promises and commitments that presuppose you're somehow the same person from day to day and from year to year. It's a serious business, this question of self, not just a theoretical speculation. This is why I think it's better that questions about it should be raised in a relatively safe area like novels rather than in other areas. That is one of the things we need novels for, to assuage our anxiety about a subject by allowing questions to be raised about it and perhaps to lead us, as *The Egoist* does, to a happy ending, thereby calming our fears. In *The Egoist* the idea of selfhood as a fixed, preexisting thing is replaced by a much more precarious notion of selfhood, a notion which would be a little harder to live with if it were widely accepted.

Question: But doesn't deconstruction, in practice, affirm the self that it wants to question?

Answer: Yes, though perhaps in a form which is slightly shaken or transformed. Nietzsche is a good example of this. Book III of *The Will to Power* is one of the most powerful puttings into question of the notion of selfhood I know. Nietzsche argues subtly and overtly that there is no such thing as the self, that it is just a changing set of functions, linguistic conventions, etc. But notice the way Nietzsche says this: "*I hold* [*Ich halte*] that there's no such thing as the self." He cannot perform the activity of deconstructing the self without at the same time affirming it. It is a splendid example of your point.

Question: Where do you see literary study going in the immediate future? Are significant further changes likely to take place?

Answer: I think the frontier or border on which we stand now is very different from our situation five years ago when I wrote "On Edge: The Crossways of Contemporary Criticism." We stand at a different crossroads and have different choices to make. The assimilation of poststructuralist modes of criticism into college and university curricula for which I called then has to a considerable extent occurred or is occurring. The danger now is that deconstruction might petrify, harden into a dogma, or into a rigid set of prescriptions for reading, become some kind of fixed method rather than a set of examples, very different from one another, of good reading. I see the frontier of literary study at the present time as involving the genuine assimilation of the lessons of deconstruction (no easy matter, involving as it does the careful reading of the work of de Man, Derrida, et al.) and then requiring us to move on as they are (or rather as Derrida is and as de Man was in work done shortly before his death) toward the difficult questions of what these new developments mean for ethics, for the institutionalizing of literary study, and for the broadest and most fundamental questions of literary history, of history as such, of social policy and social organization, of the role of literature in society. The stakes here are enormous. The most prudent and careful as well as the most courageous work of thought will be necessary, but if literature, as a mode of the aesthetic, is to have the role allotted to it by Kant, and ever since Kant, as the bridge between epistemology and ethics, the new developments in literary study have important implications not only for the bridge but for those realms the bridge is supposed to join. So we may be not so much at a frontier or at a crossroads as standing on a bridge—a bridge, moreover, that has received in recent years a new testing, shaking, or solicitation.

M. H. ABRAMS

Construing and
Deconstructing

This age of critical discourse is the best of times or it is the worst of times, depending on one's point of view; but there is no denying that it is a very diverse and lively time. Never have the presuppositions and procedures of literary criticism been put so drastically into question, and never have we been presented with such radical alternatives for conceiving and making sense of literary texts. Among the competing theories of the last several decades we find reader-response criticism (itself divisible into a variety of subspecies), reception criticism, anxiety-of-influence criticism, structuralist criticism, semiotic criticism, and—most ominous to many traditional ears—deconstructive criticism. It was not many years ago that announcements of jobs for professors of literature began to be supplemented by requests for professors of literary criticism. Now we find increasing requests for professors of the theory of criticism—professors, that is, whose profession is metacriticism.

The new theories are diverse in principles and procedures, but in their radical forms they converge in claims that have evoked indignation from many traditional critics. One claim is that it is impossible even to identify anything called "literature" by establishing boundaries, or specifying features, which set it off from other forms of writing. Another and related claim is that criticism is in no way attendant upon or subordinate in function to the literature which, over the centuries since Aristotle, critics have set themselves to classify, analyze, and elucidate; criticism, it is now often said, is a mode of writing which does not discover, but "produces" the meanings of the texts that it engages, hence is equally entitled to be "creative." Most dismaying to traditionalists is the claim, diversely argued, that no text, either in its component passages or as an entity, has a determinable meaning and therefore that there is no right way to interpret it; all attempts to read a text are doomed to be misreadings.

Among these innovations in literary theory and practice, the signs are that deconstruction, based primarily on writings of Jacques Derrida since the late 1960s, will be predominant. Within the last ten years deconstructive criticism has generated a flood of books and articles which exemplify it, describe it, attack it, or defend it; the articles appear not only in several journals devoted primarily to deconstruction, but increasingly in the most staid of publications, including the alleged stronghold of the critical establishment, *PMLA*. Its focal center in America has been Yale University, whose faculty includes those exponents whom their colleague, Geoffrey Hartman, has genially labeled "boa deconstructors"—especially Derrida himself, Paul de Man, and J. Hillis Miller. Radiating from that center, the movement has captivated, in varying degree, a number of younger teachers of literature and many among the brightest of graduate students, including some who have written their theses under my direction. By J. S. Mill's maxim that the opinions of bright people between twenty and thirty years of age is the best index to the intellectual tendencies of the next era, it seems probable that the heritage of deconstruction will be prominent in literary criticism for some time to come.

I shall try to locate the deconstructive enterprise on the map of literary theory by sketching its overlap with, as well as its radical departures from, traditional treatments of literature. It is impossible to do so except from some point of view. I shall try to make allowances for mine, which is that of a traditionalist who has staked whatever he has taught or written about literature, and about literary and intellectual history, on the confidence that he has been able to interpret the textual passages he cited with a determinacy and an accuracy sufficient to the purpose at hand.

I

One must approach deconstructive literary criticism by way of the writings of Jacques Derrida, the founder, namer, and prime exemplar of deconstruction-in-general. To be brief about so protean, oblique, and tactically agile a writer cannot escape being selective and reductive.

It seems fair to say, however, that in terms of the traditional demarcations among disciplines, Derrida (though he has commented on some literary texts) is to be accounted a philosopher, not a literary critic, and that his writings undertake to reveal the foundations presupposed by all precedent Western philosophies and ways of thinking, to "undermine" or "subvert" these foundations by showing that they are illusions engendered by desire for an impossible certainty and security, and to show the consequences for writing and thinking when their supposed foundations are thus undermined.

Some commentators on Derrida have remarked in passing that Derrida's conclusions resemble the skeptical conclusions of David Hume. I want to pursue this comparison; not, however, in order to show that, despite his antimetaphysical stance, Derrida ends in the classical metaphysical position called radical skepticism, but in order to bring out some interesting analogues between the procedures of these two very diverse thinkers. These analogues will highlight aspects of Derrida's dealings with language, emulated by his followers in literary criticism, which are inadequately stressed, both by proponents who assert that Derrida has totally revolutionized the way we must from now on read texts and by opponents who assert that Derrida cancels all criteria of valid interpretation, in an anarchical surrender to textual "freeplay."

We can parallel three moments in the overall procedures of Hume and Derrida:

(1) The point of departure in Hume's *Treatise of Human Nature* is that "nothing is ever really present with the mind but its perceptions," which consist of "impressions" that are "immediately present to our consciousness" and the "ideas" that are the fainter replica of these impressions.[1] Beginning with these as the sole givens which can be known with certainty, Hume proceeds to show that, in all reasoning and knowledge concerning "matters of fact," we can never get outside the sense-impressions which were his starting point, nor establish the certainty of any connections between the single sense-impressions which constitute immediate awareness. He thus disintegrates all grounds for certain knowledge about the identity of any two impressions separated in time, about the existence of material objects in an external world, about the relation of cause and effect between any two occurrences, and about the reality even of "personal identity" or a conscious "self." All these entities and relations, Hume contends, since they cannot be established by demonstrative reasoning from his premised single

---

[1] David Hume, *A Treatise of Human Nature*, ed. L. A. Selby-Bigge (Oxford, 1928), pp. 67, 73, 197, 265.

impressions, are the products of the "imagination" and of "custom," and have the status not of knowledge but merely of "fallacies," "fictions," or "illusions."

To Derrida's way of thinking, Hume's starting point in the *hic et nunc* of a nonmediated, hence certainly known perception would be a classic example of the way Western philosophy, in all its forms, is based on a "presence," or indubitable founding element independent of language; so that Hume's skeptical conclusions from this given, to Derrida, would be merely a negative counterpart of the cognitive dogmatism that it challenges. As Derrida has put it: "Perception is precisely a concept, a concept of an intuition or of a given originating from the thing itself, present itself in its meaning, independently from language, from the system of reference."[2] Hence, he declares, "I don't believe that anything like perception exists." Instead of positing a foundational given, Derrida establishes a point of view. "The axial proposition of this essay," he declares in *Of Grammatology*, is "that there is nothing outside the text" ["*il n'y a rien hors du texte*," or alternatively, "*il n'y a pas de hors-texte*"[3]]. This assertion is not offered either as the point of departure or as the result of a philosophical demonstration. It functions as an announcement of where Derrida takes his stand, and that is within the workings of language itself, in order to show us what standard philosophical problems, premises, and intellection look like when viewed from this stance and point of vantage. In many of its consequences, nonetheless, Derrida's counterphilosophical linguistic ploy converges with those of Hume's skeptical philosophy. Hume, premising only single impressions, showed that there is no way to establish identity or causal connections among impressions, nor to match impressions to material objects, a world, or a self to which we have access independently of impressions. Derrida, taking his stand within language, disperses the seemingly determinate meanings of terms such as "identity," "cause," "material objects," "the external world," "the self," and shows that there is no way to match such terms to a reality to which we have access independently of the language we use to represent it.

Derrida's way of carrying out his project is to offer "readings" of passages in Western thinkers, from Plato to the ordinary-language philosopher John Austin, in order to reveal their common "logocentrism." This term denominates his claim that Western philosophical

<hr/>

[2]Jacques Derrida, "Structure, Sign, and Play in the Discourse of the Human Sciences" in *The Language of Criticism and the Sciences of Man*, ed. Richard Macksey and Eugenio Donato (Baltimore, 1970), "Discussion," p. 272.

[3]Jacques Derrida, *Of Grammatology*, trans. Gayatri Spivak (Baltimore, 1976), p. 163; see also p. 158.

discourse—and indeed all modes of discourse, since none can escape the use of terms whose significance is "sedimented" by their role in the history of philosophy—is predicated on the existence of a logos. The logos is Derrida's overall term for an absolute, or foundation, or ground, whose full, self-certifying "presence" is assumed to be given in a direct cognitive encounter which is itself unconditioned by the linguistic system that incorporates it, yet relies on it as a foundation. Such a presence, for example, is sometimes posited as an immediately known intention or state of consciousness in a speaker while speaking, or as an essence, or as a Platonic Form accessible to mental vision, or as a referent known in its own being; in any case, it constitutes a "transcendental signified" which, though inevitably represented by a signifier, is regarded as an unmediated something that is unaffected by the signifying system which represents it.

Derrida's readings are oriented toward showing that any philosophical text can be shown to rely on a ground which is indispensable to its argument, its references, and its conclusions, but turns out to be itself groundless, hence suspended over an "abyss." Derrida's view, furthermore, is that a logos-centered philosophy is a voice-centered philosophy. In consequence, one of his characteristic procedures, often misunderstood, is to overcome Western "phonocentrism" (the reliance on the speaking voice as the linguistic model) by positing an admittedly nonexisting "arche-écriture," "writing-in-general." By asserting the "priority" of writing (in the sense of writing-in-general) both to speech and to writing (in the ordinary sense of putting words on paper), Derrida is not claiming that the invention of writing preceded speech in history; he is deploying a device designed to get us to substitute for the philosophical idiom of speaking the alternative idiom of writing, in which we are less prone to the illusion, as he conceives it, that a speaker in the presence of a listener knows what he means independently of the words in which he expresses it, or that he establishes the meaning of what he says to the listener by communicating his unmediated intention in uttering it.

From his elected stance within language, Derrida replaces the view that language developed by a matching of words to the given world by positing an internal linguistic principle of "*différance.*" This term, like "writing-in-general," is offered as a heuristic fiction, in which the "a" in the written form, Derrida tells us, indicates the conflation of the incompatible senses of the French word *différer* as "to differ" and "to defer." In accordance with the insight of the linguist Saussure that both a signifier and what it signifies are constituted not by their inherent features, but by a network of "differences" from other signifiers and

131

signifieds, Derrida posits *différance* as generating internally the differential verbal signs, while deferring the presence of what they signify through endless substitutions of signifiers whose ultimate arrest in a determinate and stable meaning or reference never is, but is always about to be. For according to Derrida, in the lack of any possible "transcendental," or extralinguistic referent unconditioned by the differential economy of language, there is no stopping the play of meanings. In one of Derrida's formulations: "The absence of the transcendental signified extends the domain and the interplay of signification *ad infinitum*."[4] Or, in another of his punning, deliberately contrarious terms, which in this case exploits a double etymology, any text, under radical inquisition, "disseminates": it sows its seed, and in that process loses its seeming semantic determinacy, by scattering into a regress which inevitably involves an "aporia"—that is, a deadlock between incompatible meanings which are "undecidable," in that we lack any certain ground for choosing between them.

(2) Having reached his skeptical conclusions, Hume finds himself, he tells us, in a condition of "melancholy" and "despair," "affrighted and confounded with that forelorn solitude, in which I am plac'd in my philosophy."[5] Hume's solitude is beyond solipsism, for the solipsist is certain at least of the reality of his conscious self, while Hume is reduced to knowing only present perceptions which yield no implication of a conscious self that knows. From this dire condition he finds himself rescued not by further reasoning, but by the peremptory intrusion of a life-force—"an absolute and uncontrollable necessity" that he calls "nature." "Nature herself . . . cures me of this philosophical melancholy and delirium. . . . I dine, I play a game of back-gammon, I converse, and am merry with friends; and when after three or four hours' amusement, I wou'd return to these speculations, they appear so cold, and strain'd, and ridiculous, that I cannot find in my heart to enter into them any farther." Hume finds that he cannot live in accordance with his skeptical philosophy; yet his impulse to philosophical reasoning is no less compelling than his instinct to participate in human society in accordance with its shared beliefs. As a consequence, Hume finds himself living (and recommends that others should also live) a double life: the life of human society, and the life of the reason that disintegrates all the beliefs on which social life is based into fictions and illusions: "Here then I find myself absolutely and necessarily determin'd to live, and talk, and act like other people in the common affairs of life." Yet

[4]"Structure, Sign, and Play," p. 249. See also Derrida, *Dissemination*, trans. Barbara Johnson (Chicago, 1981), p. 5.
[5]Hume, *Treatise*, p. 264.

"in all the incidents of life we ought still to preserve our skepticism. If we believe, that fire warms, or water refreshes, 'tis only because it costs us too much pains to think otherwise."[6]

Derrida's conduct of language is analogous to Hume's double mode of necessarily continuing to live in accordance with shared beliefs that he is rationally compelled to subvert. Derrida in fact describes the deconstructive enterprise as a deliberate and sustained duplexity—"a double gesture, a double science, a double writing."[7] And in reading texts there is a double procedure, "two interpretations of interpretation," which play a simultaneous role in life, and which, though irreconcilable, permit no option between them:

> There are more than enough indications today to suggest we might perceive that these two interpretations of interpretation—which are absolutely irreconcilable even if we live them simultaneously [*même si nous les vivons simultanément*] and reconcile them in an obscure economy—together share the field which we call, in such a problematic fashion, the human sciences.
>
> For my part, although these two interpretations must acknowledge and accentuate their difference and define their irreducibility, I do not believe that today there is any question of *choosing.* . . . [8]

We mistake Derrida's own procedure if we overlook the fact that his deconstructive readings of philosophical passages involve both these interpretive modes and consist of a deliberate double-reading—we may denominate them as reading$_1$ and reading$_2$—which are distinguishable, even if they are irreconcilable, sometimes concurrent, and always interdependent. Reading$_1$ finds a passage "lisible" and understandable, and makes out, according to a procedure that he shares with common readers, the determinate meanings of the sentences he cites. (For convenience let us say that in reading$_1$ he *construes* the passage.) Reading$_2$, which he calls a "critical reading," or an "active interpretation," goes on to disseminate the meanings it has already construed.

Derrida accounts for the possibility of reading$_1$ by attributing to differance the production of the "effect" in language of a fundamental presence—not a real presence, or free-standing existent, but one which is simply a "function" of the differential play—as well as the production of all the other "effects" on which the common practice of reading depends, including the "effects" of a conscious intention, of a specific

---

[6]Ibid., pp. 265, 183, 269–70.
[7]Derrida, "Signature Event Context," *Glyph*, 1 (1977), 195.
[8]Derrida, "Structure, Sign, and Play," pp. 264–65.

speech act, and of a determinate meaning or reference.[9] In this way, he explains, "the metaphysical text is *understood*; it is still readable, and remains to be read."[10] And this standard reading and understanding, though only an initial "stage," is indispensable to the process of deconstruction.

For example: most of Derrida's *Of Grammatology* presents readings of selected passages from Rousseau's *Essay on the Origin of Language*. In great part Derrida, with no lack of assurance, construes these passages as conveying determinate meanings, with tacit confidence that his own readers will assent to his construal—a confidence I find well founded, because Derrida is an uncommonly proficient and scrupulous reader of texts in the standard fashion. In this process, he attributes the writing of the *Essay* to an individual named "Rousseau," and has no hesitation in specifying what "Rousseau affirms . . . unambiguously," or what "Rousseau says . . . clearly in the *Essay*" and "also invariably says . . . elsewhere" (pp. 173, 184), nor in attributing what the text says to Rousseau's "intention" to say it, or to what it is that "Rousseau wishes to say." In the course of this reading₁, Derrida paraphrases Rousseau's assertions and identifies recurrent "themes" in variant phrasings of the same assertion (p. 195; see also p. 133); undertakes to establish the time of his life in which Rousseau wrote the *Essay* on the basis of two kinds of evidence, which he describes as either "internal" or "external" to the *Essay* itself (pp. 171, 192); and, though he detects "massive borrowings" in the *Essay* from earlier writers, affirms the essential "originality" of Rousseau as a theorist of language (pp. 98, 272, 281). Derrida also accepts as accurate some interpretations of Rousseau's text by earlier commentators, but corrects others which he describes, politely, as the result of "hasty reading" (pp. 189, 243). And he is able to find Rousseau's text "readable" in this fashion because the language that Derrida has inherited, despite some historical changes, is one that he possesses in common with Rousseau; as Derrida puts it: "Rousseau drew upon a language that was already there—and which is found to be somewhat our own, thus assuring us a certain minimum readability of French literature" (p. 160).

Thus far, Derrida's reading proceeds in a way that is congruent with the theories of many current philosophers that communication depends on our inheritance of a shared language and shared linguistic practices or conventions, and that when, by applying the practice we share with

[9]See, for example, "Structure, Sign, and Play," "Discussion," pp. 270–71; "Signature Event Context," pp. 174, 193; *Dissemination*, pp. 43–44.

[10]"Differance," in Derrida, *Speech and Phenomena*, trans. David B. Allison (Evanston, Ill., 1973), p. 156.

a writer, we have recognized what he intended to say, then we have understood him correctly. Many of these philosophers also agree with Derrida that there is no extralinguistic, nonconventional foundation for our linguistic practice which certifies its rules and their application and guarantees the correctness of a reader's interpretation; in justifying an interpretation, when we have exhausted appeals to shared, though contingent, linguistic and social conventions, in Wittgenstein's phrase, "the spade turns." Derrida's radical innovation does not, therefore, consist in his claim that no such foundation exists, but in his further claim that such a foundation, though nonexistent, is nevertheless indispensable, and that in its absence there is no stopping the continuing dissemination of construed meanings into undecidability.

In accordance with this view, Derrida designates his reading$_1$—the determinate construal of the "legibility" of passages in Rousseau—as no more than a "strategic" phase which, though indispensable, remains "provisional" to a further "critical," or deconstructive reading (pp. 99, 149). One of Derrida's moves in this critical reading is to identify strata, or "strands" in Rousseau's text which, when read determinately, turn out to be mutually contradictory (pp. 200, 237, 240, 245). A number of earlier commentators, of course, have found Rousseau's linguistic and social theories to be incoherent or contradictory, but have regarded this feature as a logical fault or else as assimilable to an overall direction of his thinking. Derrida, however, regards such self-contradictions not as logical mistakes which Rousseau could have avoided, but as inescapable features not only in Rousseau's text but in all Western texts, since all rely on a fixed logocentric ground yet are purely conventional and differential in their economy. In his critical "sub-reading" of Rousseau's texts, Derrida asserts that their determinate reading always leaves an inescapable and ungovernable "excess" or "surplus" of signification, which is both the index and the result of the fact that "the writer writes *in* a language and *in* a logic whose proper system, laws, and life his discourse by definition cannot dominate absolutely"; a critical reading must aim at detecting the "relationship, unperceived by the writer, between what he commands and what he does not command . . . " (p. 158). Derrida's reading$_2$ of Rousseau thus repeatedly uncovers opposed meanings between what Rousseau "wishes to say" and what "he says without wishing to say it," or between what Rousseau "declares" and what the text "describes" without Rousseau's wishing to say it (pp. 200, 229, 238). What Rousseau declares and wishes to say is what is construed by a standard reading; what the text ungovernably goes on, unbeknownst to the writer, to say is what gets disclosed by a deeper deconstructive reading.

Derrida's commentary on John Austin, an ordinary-language philosopher who disclaims any extralinguistic foundation for the func-
tioning of language, couches Derrida's views in terms which bring them
closer to the idiom familiar to Anglo-American philosophers. In discussing Austin's theory of a performative speech-act, Derrida points
out that all words and verbal sequences are "iterable," or repeatable
in diverse linguistic and social circumstances, with a consequent diversity both in the nature of the speech-act and the signification of its
words. Derrida construes Austin to make the claim that the total verbal
and social context, in a clear case, establishes for certain the nature
and communicative success of a speech-act. Derrida's counterclaim is
that we never find an absolutely clear case, in that we can never know
for certain that all the necessary and sufficient conditions for determining a specific and successful performative have in fact been satisfied.
(In Derrida's parlance, no context is ever "saturated," so as to make
it "entirely certain," or "exhaustively determinable," which is "the
sense required by Austin."[11]) He stresses especially Austin's reiterated
references to the intention of the speaker—necessary, for example, in
order to determine a speaker's sincerity and seriousness—as a condition
for the success of a speech-act. The speaker's intention, Derrida asserts,
is a condition whose fulfillment neither the speaker nor his auditor can
know with certainty and one which cannot control or "master" the
play of meaning. Derrida's conclusion is that there can be no "communication," as he puts it, "that is unique, univocal, rigorously con-
trollable, and transmittable," and no way of achieving certainty about
the "purity," in the sense of "the absolutely singular uniqueness of a
speech act."[12] To this conclusion Austin himself would surely agree.
Language, as a shared conventional practice, cannot provide grounds
for absolute certainty in communication; even in the clearest case, it
always remains possible that we have got an interpretation wrong.
Language nonetheless is adequate for communicating determinate
meanings, in that the shared regularities of that practice can provide,
in particular circumstances, a warranted assurance about what someone has undertaken to say. For Derrida, however, it is a matter of all-
or-nothing; there is no intermediate position on which a determinate
interpretation can rest, for if no meanings are absolutely certain and
stable, then all meanings are unstable and undecidable. "Semantic

---

[11]"Signature, Event, Context," pp. 174, 192. See also Derrida, "Living On: Border
Lines," in *Deconstruction and Criticism*, ed. Geoffrey Hartman (New York, 1979), p. 78:
"Hence no context is saturable any more. . . . No meaning can be fixed or decided upon."
And p. 81: "No meaning can be determined out of context, but no context permits
saturation."

[12]"Signature, Event, Context," pp. 172, 186, 191.

communication," or the successful achievement of a performative or other speech-act, is indeed an "effect"; but it is, he says, "only an effect," and as such incapable of arresting the dispersal of signification in "a *dissemination* irreducible to *polysemy*."[13]

In the process of his critical reading, Derrida identifies various features of a philosophical text which inescapably "exceed" the limits of what its writer set out to assert. One of these features is the use in the argument of key equivocations that cannot be used to specify one meaning without involving the opposed meaning. In Rousseau's theory of language, for example, the argument turns on the duplicitous word "supplement" (meaning both something added to what is itself complete and something required to complete what is insufficient); in reading other authors, Derrida identifies other Janus-faced terms such as *pharmakon* and *hymen*. Another feature is the presumed reliance of a text on a logical argument which turns out to involve nonlogical "rhetorical" moves. Prominent in Derrida's analysis of the inherent rhetoricity of philosophical reasoning is the disclosure of the role of indispensable metaphors that are assumed to be merely convenient substitutes for literal or "proper" meanings, yet are irreducible to literal meanings except by applying an opposition, metaphoric/literal, which is itself a consequence of the philosophy which presupposes it. A third feature is the unavoidable use in a text of what are presumed to be exclusive oppositions; Derrida undertakes to undermine such oppositions by showing that their boundaries are constantly transgressed, in that each of the terms crosses over into the domain of its opponent term. Prominent among the many unsustainable oppositions to which Derrida draws our attention is that of inside/outside, or internal/external, as applied to what is within or outside the mind, or within or outside the system of linguistic signs, or within or outside a text (a book, a poem, or an essay) which is ostensibly complete in itself.

Derrida's view of the untenability of the distinction between what is inside or outside a text has had, as we shall see, an especially important impact on the procedures of deconstructive literary criticism. "What used to be called a text," Derrida says, has "boundaries," which were thought to demarcate "the supposed end and beginning of a work, the unity of a corpus"; such a designation, however, applies only on the condition that "we accept the entire conventional system of legalities that organizes, in literature, the framed unity of the corpus," including the "unity of the author's name . . . registration of the copyright, etc."[14] Derrida's double-reading, reading$_1$ and reading$_2$, in fact produces two

[13]Ibid., pp. 174, 193, 195.
[14]"Living On: Border Lines," pp. 83, 142.

texts. One is the text, such as Rousseau's *Essay*, which he reads by accepting, in a provisional way, the standard conventions and legalities that establish as its boundaries the opening and closing lines of its printed form. Text$_2$ is produced "by a sort of overrun [*débordement*] that spoils all these boundaries and divisions and forces us to extend the accredited concept, the dominant notion of a 'text,' of what I still call a 'text,' for strategic reasons." This second text is "no longer a finished corpus of writing" by a particular author, but a text as an aspect of textuality in general—of "a differential network, a fabric of traces referring endlessly to something other than itself, to other differential traces." Text$_2$, however, does not simply annul the constraints and borders that function in the reading of text$_1$ for, though it "overruns all the limits assigned to it so far," it does so not by "submerging or drowning them in an undifferentiated homogeneity, but rather making them more complex. . . . "[15]

This last quotation brings out what commentators overlook who claim that Derrida's emphasis on "freeplay" in language is equivalent to "anything goes in interpretation," and that is his repeated emphasis that a deconstructive reading$_2$ does not cancel the role of intention and of the other conventions and legalities that operate in a determinate reading of a limited text, but merely "reinscribes" them, as he puts it, so as to reveal their status as no more than "effects" of the differential play.[16] Derrida insists that the standard mode of "doubling commentary"—a commentary, that is, which simply undertakes to say in other words what it is that the author undertook to say—"should no doubt have its place in a critical reading." "To recognize and respect all its classical exigencies [*i.e.*, of reading$_1$] is not easy and requires all the instruments of traditional criticism. Without this recognition and this respect, critical production [*i.e.*, reading$_2$] would risk developing in any direction at all and authorize itself to say almost anything. . . . "[17]

The deliberate anomaly of Derrida's double interpretive procedure, however, is patent. He cannot demonstrate the impossibility of a standard reading except by going through the stage of manifesting its

[15] Ibid., pp. 83–84.
[16] E.g., *Of Grammatology*, p. 243: Rousseau's "declared intention is not annulled . . . but rather *inscribed* within a system it no longer dominates." "Signature, Event, Context," p. 192: In "a differential typology of forms of iteration . . . the category of intention will not disappear; it will have its place, but from that place it will no longer be able to govern the entire scene and system of utterance."
[17] *Of Grammatology*, p. 158. Derrida adds (pp. 158–59) that the exigencies of standard interpretive commentary, though it is an "indispensable guardrail," "has always only *protected*, it has never *opened* a reading." A critical reading, however, which recognizes that, in the inescapable lack of a "natural presence," a text "has never been anything but writing"—that is, "substitutive significations which could only come forth in a chain of differential references"—"opens" meaning and language, as he puts it, "to infinity."

possibility; a text must be read determinately in order to be disseminated into an undecidability that never strikes completely free of its initial determination; deconstruction can only subvert the meanings of a text that has always already been construed. And even if a reader has been persuaded that Derrida has truly discovered a force in language (seemingly unsuspected, or at least unexploited, before Nietzsche) which forces him to overrun all the constraints and borders of standard construal, he has no option except to begin by construing a text, including Derrida's own text; or more precisely, his only option is whether or not to read French, or English, or any other natural language.

(3) In addition to subverting all the convictions of our common life and common thought, then to asserting the inescapable need for a double life and double thinking, Hume's epistemology contains a third moment that has an analogue in Derrida's theory of language. This is the moment when Hume turns his skepticism back upon itself, by what he calls "a reflex act of the mind" upon "the nature of our understanding, and our reasoning." In doing so he finds himself involved in "manifest absurdities" and "manifold contradictions," including the absurdity that his skeptical argument has no recourse except to use reason itself in order "to prove the fallaciousness and imbecility of reason." Hence "the understanding . . . entirely subverts itself, and leaves not the lowest degree of evidence in any proposition, either in [skeptical] philosophy or common life."[18] As the only reasonable way to cope with the diverse illogicalities of his philosophical and his social life, Hume recommends that we replace "the force of reason and conviction" by an attitude of insouciance—"a serious good-humor'd disposition" and a "careless" [i.e., carefree] conduct of philosophy, and a diffidence about the conclusions reached by that philosophy. "A true skeptic will be diffident of his philosophical doubts, as well as of his philosophical conviction."[19]

In a parallel way, Derrida turns deconstruction back upon itself. Since, he says, it has no option except to take all "the resources of subversion" from the logocentric system that it subverts, "deconstruction always in a certain way falls prey to its own work." Even the assertion that the play of writing is incomprehensible by the categories of "the classical logos" and "the law of identity" cannot escape reference

---

[18]Hume, *Treatise*, pp. 182, 186–87, 267. Hume's idiom for describing his dilemmas at times converges with that favored by Derrida. For example, he declares in the *Treatise* that in reconsidering his section on the self, or personal identity, he finds himself "involv'd in such a labyrinth, that . . . I neither know how to correct my former opinions, nor how to render them consistent," and ends in the undecidability of what Derrida calls the "double bind" of an "aporia": "In short there are two principles, which I cannot render consistent; nor is it in my power to renounce either of them" ("Appendix," pp. 633, 636).

[19]Ibid., pp. 270, 273.

to the logocentric logic that it flouts; and "for the rest," he allows, "deconstruction must borrow its resources from the logic it deconstructs." In addition, as Derrida says, his own deconstructive "production is necessarily a text."[20] Hence in his writing about writing, Derrida has no option except to "communicate" his views in language intended to be understood determinately by his readers, knowing that, to the extent that his own text is understood, it becomes a victim of the dissemination it asserts. The "work of deconstruction," then—since it is forced to use linguistic tools which are themselves deconstructed by the work they perform, in a play of illogicalities which cannot be named except by the logic it undermines—cannot escape the "closure" of logocentrism; it can only provide the "crevice through which the yet unnamable glimmer beyond the crevice can be glimpsed." And to this glimpse of what Derrida can designate only by terms borrowed from the logocentric system—"the freeplay of the world," "*genetic* indetermination," "the *seminal* adventure of the trace"—he too recommends that we assume an attitude. This is not, in his case, Hume's attitude of urbane "carelessness," but a Nietzschean attitude of gaiety: a "joyous affirmation" which is "without *nostalgia*," "with a certain laughter and with a certain dance."[21]

Where, according to Derrida, does deconstruction leave both our ordinary use of language and the philosophical and other specialized uses of language? Apparently, pretty much where they are now. He disclaims any possibility of a superior truth which would allow us to replace, or even radically to reform, our current linguistic procedures. "Deconstruction," he insists, "has nothing to do with destruction." "I believe in the necessity of scientific work in the classical sense, I believe in the necessity of everything which is being done."[22] He does not, he says, "destroy" or set out to "discard" concepts; he merely "situates" or "reinscribes" them in an alternative system of differance, in order to reveal that they indeed function, but only as "effects" which lack absolute foundation in an ontological given. What he can be said to reveal, in a change of vocabulary, is that the communicative efficacy of language rests on no other or better ground than that both writers and readers tacitly accept and apply the regularities and limits of an inherited social and linguistic contract.

[20] *Of Grammatology*, pp. 24, 314, 164; also "Structure, Sign, and Play," pp. 250–51: "We have no language—no syntax and no lexicon—which is alien to this history [of metaphysics]; we cannot utter a single deconstructive proposition which has not already slipped into the form, the logic, and the implicit postulations of precisely what it seeks to contest. . . . Every particular borrowing drags along with it the whole of metaphysics."
[21] *Of Grammatology*, p. 14; "Structure, Sign, and Play," p. 264; "Differance," p. 159.
[22] "Structure, Sign, and Play," "Discussion," p. 271.

II

Derrida has attracted little sustained comment from English and American philosophers, and that comment has been, with few exceptions, dismissive. One reason is that his writings, in addition to being abstruse, variable in procedure, and inveterately paradoxical in the give-yet-take of their "double gestures," are also outlandish. I do not mean only in the sense that they employ what, to the mainstream Anglo-American philosopher, is the foreign idiom of continental philosophy from Hegel through Heidegger. They are outlandish also because there is an antic as well as a sober side to Derrida's philosophical writings. He likes to give rein to his inventive playfulness in order to tease, or outrage, philosophers who regard the status and role of philosophy with what he takes to be excessive seriousness. He is fond—increasingly in recent publications—of exploiting Janus-faced neologisms, deliberately far-fetched analogues, bizarre puns, invented etymologies, straight-faced and often sexual jokes, and dexterous play with his own signature, and also of intercalating incongruous texts by diverse authors, in order to shake, shock, or beguile us out of our ordinary assurance about the enabling conditions that establish the limits of a textual entity or yield a determinate and stable interpretation.

It is not on Anglo-American philosophy, but on Anglo-American literary criticism that Derrida has had a strong and increasing effect. Some reasons for this specialized direction of influence are obvious. Derrida's examples of textual readings became widely available to English readers in the 1970s, when what was called the "New Criticism" was some forty years old. The New Criticism was only the most prominent mode of a procedure that had dominated literary criticism for almost a half-century, namely the elaborate explication, or "close reading," of individual literary texts, each regarded as an integral and self-sufficient whole. A representative New Critic defined a literary work as a text which, in contradistinction to "utilitarian" discourse, uses a language which is metaphorical and "ambiguous" (that is, polysemous, multiply meaningful) rather than literal and univocal, to form a structure which is a free-standing organization of ironies and paradoxes, instead of a logically ordered sequence of referential assertions. By the mid-1970s this once-innovative critical procedure had come to seem confining, predictable, stale. The very features of what Derrida calls his "style" of philosophical reading which made him seem alien to Anglo-American philosophers—his reliance on the elaborate analysis of particular texts, his stress on the covert role of metaphor and other rhetorical figures, his dissemination of ostensibly univocal meanings into paradoxes and aporias—made his writings seem to Anglo-American critics to be familiar, yet generative of radically novel discoveries. Far from offering his style of reading philosophical texts as a model for literary criticism, however, Derrida has emphasized its subversion of the metaphysical concepts and presuppositions that occur in all modes of discourse without exception: there are no features, metaphorical or other, which distinguish a specifically literary use of language; and dissemination, he insists, is "irreducible" to polysemy (a set of determinate meanings), for dissemination is an "overloading" of meanings in an uncontrollable "spread" that cannot be specified as a finite set of determinate signifieds.[23] Critical followers of Derrida have nonetheless assimilated deconstruction to their preexisting critical assumptions and procedures. The result has been in various degrees to domesticate, naturalize, and nationalize Derrida's subversiveness-without-limit, by accommodating it to a closer reading of individual works which serves to show, as Paul de Man has put it, that new-critical close readings "were not nearly close enough."[24] The process is well under way of providing a rival deconstructive reading for each work in the literary canon which had earlier been explicated by one or another New Critic.

What we tend to blanket as deconstructive criticism is in fact highly diverse, ranging from an echoing of distinctive Derridean terms—"presence," "absence," "difference," "effacement," "aporia"—in the process of largely traditional explication, through foregrounding the explicit or implied occurrence in a work of a Derridean theme (especially the theme of writing, or inscription, or decoding), to a radical use of Derridean strategies to explode into dissemination both the integrity and the significance of the literary text that it undertakes to explicate. Instead of generalizing, I shall analyze a single example of the radical type—the reading of Wordsworth's "A Slumber Did My Spirit Seal" by one of the "boa deconstructors," J. Hillis Miller, in an essay of 1979 entitled "On Edge: The Crossways of Contemporary Criticism." I choose this instance because Miller presents his reading explicitly "to 'exemplify,' " as he says, the deconstructive mode of literary interpretation;[25] because Wordsworth's poem is only eight lines long, so that we can have the entire text before us as we go along; because Miller specifies some of the theoretical underpinning of his enterprise and is

---

[23]"White Mythology: Metaphor in the Text of Philosophy," *New Literary History* 6 (1974), 48–49; "Living On," p. 91; *Dissemination*, pp. 25–26. See also "Signature, Event, Context," pp. 173, 181, 188, 195.

[24]Paul de Man, "Introduction" to the special issue entitled "The Rhetoric of Romanticism," *Studies in Romanticism*, 28 (1979), 498.

[25]P. 110, above. All the succeeding page references in the text are those of the essay in this volume.

a lucid and lively expositor of its results—and also, I admit, because some of these results will be so startling to oldreaders as to inject drama into my presentation. My intention is not polemical, but expository, to bring into view some of the unexpressed, as well as explicit, procedures in this instance of radical literary deconstruction; if my tone is now and then quizzical, that is because it would be both disingenuous and futile to try to conceal my own convictions about the limits of a sound interpretation.

III

> A slumber did my spirit seal;
> I had no human fears:
> She seemed a thing that could not feel
> The touch of earthly years.
>
> No motion has she now, no force;
> She neither hears nor sees;
> Rolled round in earth's diurnal course,
> With rocks, and stones, and trees.

The "battle" between the earlier, metaphysic-bound reading and the deconstructive reading, Miller says, is joined in the alternative answers they offer to the question "What does this given poem or passage *mean?*" (p. 101). Early on in answering this question, he shows that the poem means to him very much what I and other oldreaders have hitherto taken it to mean. I quote from Miller's deft and lucid exposition of this moment in his deconstructive double-reading:

> This beautiful, moving, and apparently simple poem was written [by Wordsworth] at Goslar in Germany in the late fall or early winter of 1798–1799. . . .

> To have no human fears is the same thing as to have a sealed spirit. Both of these are defined by the speaker's false assumption that Lucy will not grow old or die.[26]

[26]Miller identifies the "she" referred to in the poem as "Lucy" on the standard ground that we have convincing reasons to believe that Wordsworth intended "A Slumber" to be one of a group of five short lyrics—what Miller calls "the Lucy poems as a group" (p. 106). In the other four poems, the girl is named as "Lucy," and Lucy, as one of the poems puts it, "is in her grave, and, oh, / The difference to me!"

. . . the shift from past to present tense [between stanza 1 and stanza 2] . . . opposes then to now, ignorance to knowledge, life to death. The speaker has moved across the line from innocence to knowledge through the experience of Lucy's death.

The poem expresses both eloquently restrained grief for that death and the calm of mature knowledge. Before, he was innocent. His spirit was sealed from knowledge as though he were asleep, closed in on himself. . . . Lucy seemed so much alive . . . that she could not possibly be touched by time, reach old age, and die. . . . Then Lucy seemed an invulnerable young "thing"; now she is truly a thing, closed in on herself, like a stone. . . . unable to move of her own free will, but unwillingly and unwittingly moved by the daily rotation of the earth. (Pp. 102–3)

Thus far Miller, with no want of assurance, has read the text, in its parts and as a whole, as having determinate meanings. He has, to use my term, construed the text and gone on to explicate the implied purport of these meanings in ways closely tied to the construal. Here are some features of Miller's reading₁:

(1) He accepts the historical evidence that the poem was written by an individual, William Wordsworth, during a particular span of time, 1798–1799. And in the assurance with which he construes the poem, it seems that Miller assumes, as standard readers do, that Wordsworth deployed an acquired expertise in the practice of the English language and of short lyric poems, and that he wrote his text so as to be understandable to readers who in turn inherit, hence share, his competence in the practice of the language and the conventions of the lyric.

(2) By implicit reference to this common practice, Miller takes it that, whatever the intended thematic relation to other Lucy poems, Wordsworth undertook to write a poem, beginning with the words "A slumber" and ending with the words "and trees," which can be understood as an entity complete in itself.

(3) Miller takes the two sentences which constitute the poem to be the utterance of a particular lyric speaker, the "I" of the text, and to be about a girl, who is referred to by the pronoun "she." And he takes the tense of the verbs in the first sentence-stanza ("did . . . seal," "had," "seemed"), as signifying an event in the past, and the tense of the verbs in the second sentence-stanza ("has . . . now," "hears," "sees") as signifying a state of affairs in the present—the sustained "now," that is, of the speaker's utterance.

(4) He takes the three clauses in the first sentence, although they lack explicit connectives, to be related in such a way that the assertions

in the second and third clause make more specific, and give reasons for, the assertion in the first clause, "A slumber did my spirit seal." As Miller puts it, perhaps a bit flatly, "the second line . . . repeats the first, and then lines three and four say it over again" (p. 103). Miller also takes the assertions in the first sentence plainly to imply that the girl was then alive, and the assertions in the second sentence (augmented by the stanza-break) to imply that the girl is now dead.

(5) So far, I think, most standard readers of the poem will concur. Miller also goes on to specify the lyric speaker's state of feeling, now that the girl is dead. Since the second stanza does not advert to the speaker's own feelings, but leaves them to be inferred from the terms with which he asserts a state of affairs, the text allows standard readers considerable room for variance in this aspect of interpretation.[27] Miller's statement on this issue seems to me sensitive and apt: "The poem expresses both eloquently restrained grief for that death and the calm of mature knowledge" (p. 103).

(6) Note also that Miller reads the poem as a verbal presentation of a human experience which, as he says, is both "beautiful" and "moving"; that is, its presentation is ordered—especially in the sharp division of the stanzas between the situation then and the situation now—so as to effect an emotional response in the reader. That experience might be specified as the shocking discovery, by a particular

---

[27]The disagreement about "A Slumber" between Cleanth Brooks and F. W. Bateson (which E. D. Hirsch has publicized and made a notable interpretive crux) has to do solely with this issue. (See E. D. Hirsch, Jr., *Validity in Interpretation* [New Haven and London, 1967], pp. 227–30.) Both readers construe the text as signifying that a girl who was alive in stanza one is dead in stanza two; their disagreement is about what we are to infer about the speaker's state of mind from the terms in which he represents the circumstances of her death. Brooks says that the closing lines "suggest . . . [his] agonized shock at the loved one's present lack of motion . . . her utter and horrible inertness"; Bateson claims that his "mood" mounts to "the pantheistic magnificence of the last two lines. . . . Lucy is actually more alive now that she is dead, because she is now a part of the life of Nature, and not just a human 'thing.' " Miller's description of the lyric speaker's state of mind seems to me much more attuned to what the speaker says than either of these extreme versions.

Almost all of the many critics who have written about "A Slumber" agree with Miller's construal of the basic situation—a lyric speaker confronting the fact that a girl who seemed invulnerable to aging and death is now dead; they differ mainly in their explication of the overtones and significance of the presented facts. The one drastic divergence I know of is that proposed by Hugh Sykes Davies, in "Another New Poem by Wordsworth," *Essays in Criticism*, 15 (1965), 135–61. Davies argues against the evidence that Wordsworth intended "A Slumber" to be one of the Lucy group and suggests that Wordsworth intended the "she" in the third line to refer back to "spirit" in the first line; hence that the text is to be construed as a poem about a trance-state of the speaker's own spirit. Such a reading seems to me to be not impossible, but extremely unlikely. What Davies' essay does serve to indicate is that no construal of a poem can, by reference to an infallible criterion, be absolutely certain; it is a matter of adequate assurance, as confirmed by the consensus of other competent readers.

person in a particularized instance, of the awful suddenness, unexpectedness, and finality of death.

These are features of Miller's reading of Wordsworth's lyric, phase one: the determination of specific meanings in the poem read as an entity. Phase two, the deconstructive reading, follows from Miller's claim that, since literature is not "grounded in something outside language," the determinate bounds of its meanings are "undermined by the text itself," in a "play of tropes" that "leaves an inassimilable residue or remnant of meaning . . . making a movement of sense beyond any unifying boundaries" (p. 101). The intrinsic anomaly of the deconstructive procedure is apparent: in claiming that a determinate interpretation is made impossible by the text, Miller has already shown that it is possible, for he deconstructs a text that he has already determinately construed.

We find the same double-reading—the first performed, but declared to be in some sense impossible, the second held to be made necessary by the text itself—in Paul de Man, whose deconstructive criticism is often said to be closest in its "rigor" to the model of reading established by Derrida himself. As it happens, in an essay of 1969 entitled "The Rhetoric of Temporality," de Man dealt with this very poem by Wordsworth; and he there construes the text in a way that, for all its difference in idiom, emphasis, and nuance, approximates the way that Miller, and I, and almost all traditional readers, construe it. In the two stanzas,

> we can point to the successive description of two stages of consciousness, one belonging to the past and mystified, the other to the *now* of the poem, the stage that has recovered from the mystification of a past now presented as being in error; the "slumber" is a condition of non-awareness. . . .

> The curious shock of the poem . . . is that this innocuous statement ["She seemed a thing . . . "] becomes literally true in the retrospective perspective of the eternal "now" of the second part. She now has become a *thing* in the full sense of its word. . . .

De Man also reads the poem as the utterance of its first-person speaker whose responses we can infer from the way he describes the situation then and the situation now:

> The stance of the speaker, who exists in the "now," is that of a subject whose insight is no longer in doubt. . . . First there was error, then the death occurred, and now an insight into the rocky barrenness of the human predicament prevails.[28]

[28]Paul de Man, "The Rhetoric of Temporality," *Interpretation: Theory and Practice*, ed. Charles S. Singleton (Baltimore, 1969), pp. 205–6.

In this early essay de Man goes on to describe the poem he has so read as, in a special sense, an "allegory." He thus opens the way to the intricate deconstructive strategy exemplified in his later *Allegories of Reading* (1979). "The paradigm for all texts consists of a figure (or a system of figures) and its deconstruction." But such a reading engenders a second-order "narrative" which he calls an "allegory"—of which the tenor, by the inherent nature of discourse, is invariably the undecidability of the text itself: "Allegories are always allegories of metaphor and, as such, they are always allegories of the impossibility of reading."[29]

To return to Miller's engagement with Wordsworth's text: I shall first list some of the significations into which (forced, he asserts, by an "inassimilable residue" in the text itself) he disperses the meaning that he has already construed as "apparently simple"; I shall then go on to inquire into the operations which enable him to arrive at these multiplex and self-conflicting significations.

(1) "An obscure sexual drama is enacted in this poem. This drama is a major carrier of its allegorical significance" (p. 105). Miller explains that he applies " 'allegorical' in the technical sense in which that term is used by Walter Benjamin or by Paul de Man," with temporal reference to "the interaction of two emblematic times," that of stanza one and that of stanza two (p. 104).

(2) "The possession of Lucy alive and seemingly immortal is a replacement for [Wordsworth's] lost mother," who had died when he was eight years old. It follows that Lucy's "imagined death is a reenactment of the death of the mother," hence a reenactment of the loss of "that direct filial bond to nature" which his mother, while alive, had established for him (p. 106).

(3) "Lucy was [line 3] a virgin 'thing.' " In fact she was, by Miller's account, a very young virgin thing, in that she was viewed by the adult and knowledgeable male "speaker of the poem" as possessing a "prepubertal innocence." Consonantly Miller interprets "the touch of earthly years," line 4, to be "a form of sexual appropriation"; but since time is the death-bringing aspect of nature ("earthly years"), that touch is also "the ultimate dispossession which is death." Yet, since Lucy had died so young as to remain intact, "to be touched by earthly years is a way to be sexually penetrated while still remaining virgin" (p. 107).

(4) "The speaker of the poem" (signified by "I,") is not, as it initially seemed, "the opposite of Lucy, male to her female, adult knowledge to her prepubertal innocence." In Miller's disseminative reading of the speaker's temporal transition to knowledge in the second stanza, he becomes "the displaced representative of both the penetrated and the

[29]Paul de Man, *Allegories of Reading* (New Haven, 1979), p. 205; see also p. 131.

147

penetrator, of both Lucy herself [thus also of the mother whom Lucy has replaced] and of her unravishing ravisher, nature or death." "The speaker's movement to knowledge," Miller remarks, "as his consciousness becomes dispersed, loses its 'I' " (p. 108). The I-as-construed, we can add, is dispersed not only into a "he" (the knowledgeable male), but also into a "she," a "they" (Lucy and his mother), and, as the representative of nature, an "it."

(5) "Lucy is both the virgin child and the missing mother. . . . Male and female, however, come together in the earth, and so Lucy and the speaker are 'the same'. . . . The two women, mother and girl child, have jumped over the male generation in the middle. They have erased its power of mastery, its power of logical understanding, which is the male power *par excellence*" (p. 108).

(6) Climactically, in his deconstructive second-reading, Miller discovers that the poem "enacts one version of a constantly repeated occidental drama of the lost sun. Lucy's name of course means light. To possess her would be a means of rejoining the lost source of light, the father sun as logos, as head power and fount of meaning. . . . Her actual death is the loss both of light and of the source of light. It is the loss of the logos, leaving the poet and his words groundless. . . . As groundless, the movement is, precisely, alogical" (pp. 109–10). The poem thus allegorically reenacts the inescapable dilemma of our logocentric language, and that is the reliance on a logos, or ground outside the system of language which is always needed, always relied on, but never available.[30] From this ultimate alogicality stem the diverse aporias that Miller has traced. As he puts it: "Whatever track the reader follows through the poem he arrives at blank contradictions. . . . The reader is caught in an unstillable oscillation unsatisfying to the mind and incapable of being grounded in anything outside the activity of the poem itself" (p. 108).

IV

Now, what are the interpretive moves by which Miller deconstructs his initial construal of the poem into this bewildering medley of clashing significations? In a preliminary way, we can describe these moves as designed to convert the text-as-construed into a pre-text for a supervenient over-reading that Miller calls "allegorical." There are of course

---

[30]As Miller puts it, the poem instances the way in which, in any "given work of literature . . . metaphysical assumptions are both present and at the same time undermined by the text itself" ("On Edge," p. 101).

precedents for this tactic in pre-deconstructive explications of literary texts. The old-fashioned close reader, however, undertook to over-read a text in a way that would enlarge and complicate the significance of the text-as-construed into a richer integrity; the novelty of Miller's deconstruction is that in his over-reading he "undermines," as he says, the text, then detonates the mine so as to explode the construed meaning into what he calls, in one of his essays, "an undecidability among contradictory alternatives of meaning."

Miller's first move is to identify in Wordsworth's poem an "inter-related set of binary oppositions. These seem to be genuinely exclusive oppositions, with a distinct uncrossable boundary line between them" (p. 102). He lists almost a score of such oppositions; among the more obvious ones are "slumber as against waking; male as against female; sealed up as against open; . . . past as against present; . . . self-propulsion as against exterior compulsion; . . . life as against death." About such linguistic oppositions Miller, following the example of Derrida, makes a radical claim. This is not the assertion, valid for standard readers, that the boundary between such opposed terms is not a sharp line, but a zone, and that the locus of this boundary is not fixed, but may shift between one utterance and another. Miller's claim is that the seeming boundary between each pair of these terms dissolves into what he calls an inevitable "structure of chiasmus"; that as a result there is "a constant slipping of entities across borders into their opposites" so as to effect a "perpetual reversal of properties"; and that this "cross over" is forced on the reader by a "residue" of meaning within the text of Wordsworth's poem itself (pp. 110, 107, 101).

When we examine Miller's demonstrations of these crossovers and reversals, however, we find, I think, that they are enforced not by a residue of meaning in the two sentences of Wordsworth's "A Slumber," but only by these sentences after they have been supplemented by meanings that he has culled from diverse other texts. Miller acquires these supplementary meanings by his next move; that is, he dissolves the "unifying boundaries" of the poem as a linguistic entity so as to merge the eight-line text into the textuality constituted by all of Wordsworth's writings, taken together. ("His writing," Miller explains, " . . . is what is meant here by 'Wordsworth' " [p. 106].) This maneuver frees "A Slumber" from the limitations involved in the linguistic practice by which Miller himself had already read the text as a specific *parole* by a specified lyric speaker. Miller is now licensed, for example, to attribute to the "I" in line 1, initially construed as a particular speaker, and the "she" in line 3 and elsewhere, initially construed as a particular girl, any further significances he discovers by construing, explicating, and over-reading passages that occur elsewhere in Wordsworth's total *oeuvre*.

149

M. H. Abrams

By way of brief example: Miller reads "other texts both in poetry and prose" as providing evidence that Wordsworth (whom he now identifies with the unspecified "I" of the poem) "had as a child, and even as a young man, a strong conviction of his immortality," and that this conviction "was associated with a strong sense of participation in a nature both enduringly material, therefore immortal, and at the same time enduringly spiritual, therefore also immortal" (p. 103). Miller reads other passages in Wordsworth as evidence that "nature for Wordsworth was strongly personified," though "oddly, personified as both male and female, as both father and mother." He cites as one instance of the latter type of personification the passage of *The Prelude* in which the "Infant Babe," learning to perceive the world in the security of his mother's arms, and in the assurance of her nurturing love, comes to feel in his veins "The gravitation and the filial bond / Of nature, that connect him with the world." Miller interprets this statement to signify that the "earth was [to Wordsworth] the maternal face and body." In other episodes in *The Prelude* and elsewhere, on the other hand, nature is "a frightening male spirit threatening to punish the poet for wrongdoing," hence representative of his father. Miller points out that "Wordsworth's mother died when he was eight, his father when he was thirteen," leaving Wordsworth feeling abandoned by the death of the former and irrationally guilty for the death of the latter. He then cites another passage, this time not directly from Words- worth but from his sister Dorothy's journal, in which she describes how she and her brother lay down in a trench, and Wordsworth "thought that it would be as sweet thus to lie so in the grave, to hear the *peaceful* sounds of the earth and just to know that our dear friends were near"; this remark Miller identifies with Wordsworth's "fantasy" of Lucy lying in the earth in stanza two of "A Slumber" (p. 107).

It is only by conflating the reference and relations of the "I" and "she" in "A Slumber" with these and other passages that Miller is able to attribute to Wordsworth's text the oscillating, contrarious meanings that Lucy alive was a replacement for the lost mother, while her death reenacts the death of the mother, hence the loss of the "filial bond to nature" which his mother had established for him; and the further meaning that Wordsworth's "only hope for reestablishing the bond that connected him to the world is to die without dying, to be dead, in his grave, and yet still alive, bound to maternal nature by way of a sur- rogate mother, a girl who remains herself both alive and dead, still available in life and yet already taken by Nature" (p. 107). And it is only by merging the reference of the "I" with other passages, interpreted as expressing Wordsworth's sense of participation in an enduring, immortal nature, or as signifying Wordsworth's experience of a nature which is male and his father as well as female and his mother, that Miller achieves the further range of simultaneous but incompatible meanings that "the speaker of the poem rather than being the opposite of Lucy, male to her female . . . is the displaced representative . . . of both Lucy herself and of her unravishing ravisher, nature or death" (p. 108).

It might seem that Miller acts on the interpretive principle that whenever Wordsworth uses a narrative "I" or "she" in a poem, the pronouns inescapably carry with them reference to everything the author has said, in any of his texts, about himself and any female persons and about their relations to each other and to nature. In fact, however, Miller's procedure is constrained in various ways. It is constrained by Miller's tacit requirement of some connection to partial aspects of the text as initially construed, as well as by his tacit reliance on plausible bridges for the crossovers between the "I" and "she" and the various personages and relationships that he finds, or infers, elsewhere in Wordsworth's writings. These are primarily doctrinal bridges, whose validity Miller takes for granted, which serve to warrant his "allegorical" reading—in other words, to underwrite his over-readings of the text of "A Slumber." Some underwriters remain implicit in Miller's essay. He relies throughout, of course, on the views, terms, and strategies of Derrida. He patently accepts Freud's doctrines about the unconscious attitudes of a male to his mother, father, and lover, and the disguised manifestations of these attitudes in the mode of symbolic displacements, condensations, and inversions. And in his discussion of Wordsworth's lyric as simultaneously affirming and erasing "male mastery" and the male "power of logical understanding," Miller manifests a heightened consciousness of the relations of men to women in a patriarchal society, as delineated in recent feminist criticism.

Some of his connective bridges, however, Miller explicitly identifies; and one of these is Martin Heidegger's assertions about the use of the word "thing" in German. I want to dwell on this reference for a moment, as representative of the way Miller both discovers and corroborates some startling aspects of the allegorical significance of "A Slumber" as "an obscure sexual drama."

Miller cites (and construes determinately) a passage in which Heidegger points out that in German, we do not call a man a thing (*Der Mensch ist kein Ding*); and that "only a stone, a clod of earth, a piece of wood are for us such mere things." We do, however, "speak of a young girl who is faced with a task too difficult for her as being a young thing, still too young for it (*eine noch zu junges Ding*)" (p. 104). This is a striking quotation, with its parallel (of the sort Miller is often and impressively able to introduce) between Heidegger's "a stone, a clod of earth, a piece of wood" and Wordsworth's triad, "with rocks, and stones, and trees." As Miller implies, this sexual a-symmetry in the application of the term "young thing" applies to English as well as German. Among speakers of English, women as well as men are apt to refer to inexperienced or innocent girls, but not to inexperienced or innocent boys, as "young things." On this feature of the language Miller largely relies for important elements in his sexual drama. By referring to her as "a thing," the speaker invests the girl with a virginal innocence— a "prepubertal innocence," in fact—which nature tries, only half in vain, to violate; by the same epithet, he implicitly stresses his own male difference, and claims superiority over the young virgin in knowledge, experience, physical attributes, and logical power; only to have the oppositions dissolved and the claims controverted by implications derived from crisscrossing "A Slumber" with other texts in Wordsworth.

There comes to mind a familiar folk song in English, not cited by Miller, whose parallel to Miller's disseminative second-reading of "A Slumber" seems a good deal closer than the German passage in Heidegger. In this song the term "young thing" is again and again applied to a girl who resists (or seems to resist) the advances of an importunate and experienced male. Her age—or rather ages—are compatible with her being prepubertal, nubile, and maternal too:

> Did she tell you her age, Billy boy, Billy boy,
> Did she tell you her age, charming Billy?
> She's three times six, four times seven,
> Twenty-eight and near eleven,
> She's a young thing, and cannot leave her mother.

In the concluding stanza the young thing is represented as vulnerable, acquiescent, yet unpenetrated by her lover:

> Did she light you up to bed, Billy boy, Billy boy,
> Did she light you up to bed, charming Billy?
> Yes, she lit me up to bed,
> But she shook her dainty head,
> She's a young thing, and cannot leave her mother.[31]

---

[31] From *The Abelard Folk Song Book*, ed. Abner Graboff (New York and London, 1958).

Now, what is the relevance of the gender-specific uses of "young thing," whether in German or English, to the third line of Wordsworth's poem—which does not call the girl a "young thing" at all, nor even simply "a thing," but that term as qualified by a clause Miller had initially construed to signify that she was a thing so vital "that she could not possibly be touched by time, reach old age, and die"? To oldreaders like myself, they have no relevance whatever. But to a second-order reading which has deliberately cut itself free from the limitations in construing the poem as a specific lyric *parole*, such uses help to endow the text with a diversity of contradictory sexual significations.

There remains the last feature that I have listed in Miller's deconstructive reading of "A Slumber," the discovery of a general aporia that underlies and necessitates all the local aporias; and to track down this discovery requires us to identify a final interpretive operation. This move (already suggested by Miller's reference to the use of *junges Ding* in German, and by his comment [p. 109] that Wordsworth's "identifying the earth with a maternal presence" repeats a trope that exists "in the Western tradition generally") is to dissolve linguistic boundaries so as to merge "A Slumber" not only with Wordsworth's other writings, but into the textuality constituted by all occidental languages taken together. In this all-embracing linguistic context, by way of the etymological link between "Lucy" (a name not mentioned in the poem) and the Latin *lux*, or light, the death of the girl is read as enacting "a constantly repeated occidental drama of the lost sun . . . the father sun as logos, as head power and fount of meaning" (p. 109).

The implicit warrant for this over-reading of the "she" in "A Slumber" is a remarkable essay by Derrida, "White Mythology: Metaphor in the Text of Philosophy." There Derrida undertakes to show that metaphysics is inescapably metaphorics, and that the founding metaphors of philosophy are irreducible. All attempts to specify the literal meaning, in implicit opposition to which a metaphor is identified as metaphoric, and all attempts to translate a metaphor into the literal meaning for which it is held to be a substitute, are incoherent and self-defeating, especially since the very distinction between metaphoric and literal meaning is a product of the philosophical system it purports to found, or "subsume." Derrida stresses particularly the reliance of traditional philosophical systems on metaphors, or "tropes," in which terms for visual sense-perception in the presence or absence of light are applied in what purports to be the mental or intellectual realm. Philosophers claim, for example, that they see the meaning or truth of a proposition, or they distinguish clear and distinct from obscure ideas, or they appeal to contemplative vision and to the natural light of reason;

all are instances of standing at gaze before something which compels belief, in the way that we are supposedly compelled to believe in the presence of a thing perceived by our sense of sight. Such mental tropes, like their visual correlates, must assume a source of light, which is ultimately the sun; and with his customary wit, Derrida names this key trope (that is, "turn") of Western thought—which as metaphor is also an instance of what are traditionally called "flowers of rhetoric"— the "heliotrope"; that is, a kind of sunflower of rhetoric. But the visible sun, itself ever turning, rises only to set again; similarly, the philo- sophical tropes turn to follow their analogous sun, which appears only to disappear, even though, as the source of light, it constitutes the necessary condition for the very opposition between seeing and not- seeing, hence between presence and absence. The sun thus serves Der- rida himself as a prime trope for the founding presence, or logos, which by our logocentric language is ever-needed and always-lost.

Miller, it is evident, has plucked Derrida's heliotrope and carried it over, via the unnamed Lucy, into the text of Wordsworth's poem. (Derrida himself remarked, possibly by way of warning, that "the heliotrope may always become a dried flower in a book";[32] it may become, that is, a straw-flower.) As a radically deconstructive critic of literature, Miller always knows in advance that any literary text, no less than any metaphysical text, must be an allegorical or "tropological" vehicle whose ultimate tenor is its constitutional lack of a required ground. And by ingeniously transplanting the heliotrope, he is indeed enabled to read the death of the "she" in Wordsworth's short lyric as an allegory for "the loss of the logos, leaving the poet and his words groundless" (p. 109).

V

Miller introduces his exemplary analysis of Wordsworth's poem in the middle of an essay which begins and ends with a discussion of literary study in the university, and in the course of this discussion he raises a pressing issue for the teaching of literature. He divides the "modes of teaching literature and writing about it" into two kinds. One kind is the deconstructive "mode of literary study I have tried to exemplify"; the other comprehends all the more traditional modes. And, he declares, "both can and should be incorporated into college and university curricula" (p. 111).

[32]Derrida, "White Mythology," p. 74.

I am not at all opposed to incorporating deconstructive theory and deconstructive critical practice as subjects for study in university curricula. They have become the focus of the kind of vigorous controversy which keeps a discipline from becoming routine and moribund, and have had the salutary result of compelling traditionalists to reexamine the presuppositions of their procedures and the grounds of their convictions. The question is: when, and in what way, to introduce this subject?

Miller's answer is to incorporate it at all stages, "from basic courses in reading and writing up to the most advanced graduate seminars." The basic courses are presumably freshman and sophomore courses. Such early and reiterative presentation of the subject would seem to rest on the conviction that Derrida's theory, which deconstructs the possibility of philosophical truth, is itself the truth about philosophy, and furthermore, a theory capable of being taught before students have read the philosophy on which it admittedly depends even as it puts that philosophy to radical question. And how are we to introduce Derrida's theory and practice of deconstructing texts to novices at the same time that we are trying to teach them to write texts that will say, precisely and accurately, what they mean, and to construe, precisely and accurately, the texts that they read? In his sustained "double gestures" Derrida is an equilibrist who maintains a precarious poise on a tightrope between subverting and denying, between deconstructing and destroying, between understanding communicative "effects" and dissolving the foundations on which the effects rely, between deploying interpretive norms and disclaiming their power to "master" a text, between decisively rejecting wrong readings and declaring the impossibility of a right reading, between meticulously construing a text as determinate and disseminating the text into a scatter of undecidabilities. In this process Derrida is also a logical prestidigitator who acknowledges and uses, as a logocentric "effect", the logic of noncontradiction, yet converts its either/or into a simultaneous neither/nor and both/and, in a double gesture of now-you-see-it, now-you-don't, of giving and taking back and regiving with a differance. I find it difficult to imagine a population of teachers of composition and reading who are so philosophically adept and pedagogically deft that they will be able to keep novices from converting this delicate equilibristic art into a set of crude dogmas; or from replacing an esteem for the positive powers of language by an inveterate suspicion of the perfidy of language; or from falling either into the extreme of a paralysis of interpretive indecision or into the opposite extreme of interpretive abandon, on the principle that, since both of us lack a foundation in presence, my misreading is as good as your misreading.

Miller's recommendation to teach deconstruction as a subject to advanced students—after, it is to be hoped, a student has become competent at construing a variety of texts, and knowledgeable about traditional modes of literary criticism, and has also achieved the philosophical sophistication to understand the historical position and the duplexities of Derridean deconstruction—seems to me unobjectionable. No student of literature, in fact, can afford simply to ignore deconstruction; for the time being, it is the focus of the most basic and interesting literary debate. And it is only fair to add that, if a graduate student elects to adopt, in whole or part, this strategy for liberating reading from traditional constraints, it offers, in our institutional arrangements for hiring and advancing faculty, certain practical advantages. It guarantees the discovery of new significations in old and much-criticized works of literature, hence is eminently publishable; and while, because of the built-in conservatism of many literary departments, it still incurs institutional risks, it increasingly holds out the promise of institutional rewards.

As a long-time observer of evolving critical movements and countermovements, I am not disposed to cavil with this latest innovation; I do want, however, to express a few caveats. In appraising the old against the new mode of teaching and writing about literature, Hillis Miller declares that the old mode, since it is "controlled by the presupposition of some center," "already knows what it is going to find," while the deconstructive mode "is more open to the inexhaustible strangeness of literary texts" (p. 110). I recognize the justness of the second clause in this claim, but not of the first. As Miller's reading of "A Slumber" demonstrates, deconstruction has indeed proved its ability to find strange meanings that make the most ingenious explorations of new-critical oldreaders seem unadventurous—although it should be noted that deconstructive readings are adjudged to be strange only by tacit reference to the meanings of the text as already construed. But surely it is deconstructive criticism, much more than traditional criticism, which is vulnerable to Miller's charge, in his first clause, that it "already knows what it is going to find." Whatever their presuppositions, traditional modes of reading have amply demonstrated the ability to find highly diverse structures of meaning in a range of works from Wordsworth's "A Slumber" through Shakespeare's *King Lear*, George Eliot's *Middlemarch*, and the rhymes of Ogden Nash. But as Miller himself describes deconstruction, it "attempts to show that in a given work of literature, in a different way in each case," following out "the play of tropes leads to . . . the experience of an aporia or boggling of the mind" (p. 101). This presupposition makes a deconstructive reading not merely goal-oriented, but single-goal-oriented. The critic knows before he begins to read what, by deep linguistic necessity, he is going to find—that is, an aporia—and sure enough, given the freedom of interpretive maneuver that deconstruction is designed to grant him, he finds one. The readers of radically deconstructive critics soon learn to expect that invariable discovery. So one of my caveats is this: for all the surprising new readings achieved en route, I do not see how Derrida's counterphilosophical strategy, when transposed to the criticism of literature, can avoid reducing the variousness of literary works to allegorical narratives with an invariable plot.

Another caveat: to be successful in his chosen métier, the apprentice needs to approximate the proven strengths of the masters of deconstruction: their wide-ranging and quite traditional learning, for example; their quick eye for unexpected similarities in what is taken to be different and of differences in what seems to be the same; their ingenuity at finding openings into the linguistic substructure of a work and resourcefulness at inventing diverse tactics in the undeviating deconstructive quest; and not least, the deftness, wit, and wordplay which often endow their critical writings with their own kind of literary value.

My third warning is this: Derrida is careful to point out, as I have said, that deconstruction does not destroy, and cannot replace, traditional humanistic pursuits, including presumably literary criticism; nor can it, as his own theory and practice demonstrate, dispense with a determinate construal of a text, as a necessary stage toward disseminating what has been so construed. Above all, then, the young practitioner needs to be sure that he establishes his credentials (as Derrida, Miller, de Man, and other adepts have impressively established theirs) as a proficient, acute, and sensitive construer and explicator of texts in the primary mode of literary understanding. Otherwise, as traditional literary readings may degenerate into exercises in pedantry, so deconstructive readings may become a display of modish terminology which never engages with anything recognizable as a work of literature.

My final point has to do with the difference between traditional and deconstructive motives for reading literature, and the distinctive values that each reading provides. To read a text in the traditional way, as a work of literature, is to read it as a human document—a fictional presentation of thinking, acting, and feeling characters who are enough like ourselves to engage us in their experiences, in language which is expressed and ordered by a human author in a way that moves and delights the human reader. Deconstructive critics, if they acknowledge such features at all, treat them as unauthored, linguistically generated illusions, or "effects." Literature has survived over the millennia by

M. H. Abrams

being read as a presentation of human characters and matters of human interest, delight, and concern. It is far from obvious that the values in such a reading can for long be replaced by the value, however appealing in its initial novelty, of reading literature as the tropological vehicle for a set of conundrums without solutions.

I am reassured, however, by the stubborn capacity of construed texts to survive their second-order deconstruction. When, for example, I turn back from Miller's essay to Wordsworth's "A Slumber," I find that it still offers itself, not as a regress of deadlocked "double-binds," but as what Wordsworth's friend Coleridge found it to be when he called it a "sublime elegy," and what Miller himself at first found it to be, when he described it as a "beautiful" and "moving" poem—beautiful in the terse economy, justness, and ordering of its verbal expression, and moving in that it presents a human being at the moment in which he communicates the discovery, in a shocking instance, of the suddenness, unexpectedness, and finality of death. Let's put the text to trial:

> A slumber did my spirit seal;
> I had no human fears:
> She seemed a thing that could not feel
> The touch of earthly years.
>
> No motion has she now, no force;
> She neither hears nor sees;
> Rolled round in earth's diurnal course,
> With rocks, and stones, and trees.

Questions and Answers

Question: In "Behaviorism and Deconstruction" (1977) you wrote that you expected deconstruction to pass on soon. Do you see that prophecy coming true?

Answer: It probably hasn't reached its climacteric, although things turn faster and faster in the carrousel of literary theory these days. Look at the New Criticism, which came into dominance in the thirties. It reigned—though not unchallenged—a good quarter century before there appeared a serious rival in Frye's archetypal criticism. If I were forced to guess, I would say that deconstruction will be crescent for another five or ten years, after which it will pass on; but it won't pass away. In the Hegelian term, it will be *aufgehoben*; that is, it will be canceled, yet survive at another level. That higher level is the traditional way of reading works of literature, which has shown over the centuries a powerful survival value. Because it has enormous inertia (based, I believe, on its grounding in enduring human concerns and needs), traditional criticism assimilates innovations and continues on, although sometimes with important and positive differences.

It's now the fashion to derogate the New Criticism. We forget that the sustained close reading of literary texts had almost no precedent before the New Critics showed us how to do it. I was in mild opposition to some manifest deficiencies of the New Criticism during the earlier part of my critical career. I must say now, however, that there isn't anyone I know who teaches literature or writes about it who hasn't learned a lot from the New Criticism. Because I manifest a skeptical stance toward the radical claims or procedures of deconstruction, don't assume that I think that everything the deconstructionists say is wasted. Deconstruction raises important questions and has some important things to tell us, too.

Question: Wouldn't the deconstructionists concede your point about the staying power—or inertia, or durability—of traditional criticism? They often say that there's no escaping the metaphysics that underlies traditional criticism. Why do they try to escape a tradition that they themselves acknowledge cannot finally be escaped?

Answer: If you return to the fountainhead, Derrida himself, he would indeed claim that there is no escaping Western metaphysics, because it is involved in our very language: the minute you use language you accede to its fallacy of presence, the ground for which there is no ground, always needed but never in fact available. But I don't think he means that we can never get rid of a particular philosophical position within that overall frame.

In any case, I think that many of Derrida's followers are less consistently aware than he is of the implications of their position, which makes everything that they themselves say vulnerable to deconstruction. For Derrida, the writing in which you undermine any other piece of writing is equally subject to being undermined. That's a persistent admission on his part, and he means it; but some of his followers seem to make truth-claims without awareness of the rebound, or ricochet, of their operations upon themselves. Perhaps because it's a rather unpleasant thing to contemplate: what's the use of deconstructing others if you're deconstructing yourself in the process?

Question: I've heard it suggested that certain kinds of literature bring about certain kinds of theories about literature. People have proposed that modern literature helped bring about the New Criticism, which was promoted by critics who were also modern poets. If the same thing can be said of deconstruction—that it was the natural product of certain kinds of postmodern literature, criti-fiction and so on—is its usefulness limited to helping us understand that particular kind of literature, or can it be useful in dealing with other kinds?

Answer: I agree that deconstruction feeds upon certain phenomena in literature of the last couple of decades or more. Whether that's a sufficient explanation of its emergence or vogue is another question. You can easily move to a higher explanatory level and claim that certain kinds of postmodern literature and deconstruction are both manifestations of a skepticism about the bases of Western culture that is part of the intellectual ambience of our time: the literature undertakes to subvert the basic assumptions and conventions on which earlier literary documents were built, and the criticism undertakes to subvert the bases of all earlier modes of reading and of Western thinking in general.

But at any rate they do feed on each other. Derrida learned from Barthes, while Barthes, who before his death became more deconstructive in his mode, picked up ideas from Derrida. Barthes's early criticism was based in large part on experimental fiction like the *nouveau roman*, which undertakes to subvert prominent features of the implicit social contract involved in storytelling which had been the grounds of almost all earlier fiction. But both deconstructive literature and deconstructive criticism flourish because they appeal to the temper of the times—a dangerous temper, one that worries me—in which we tend to be much more hospitable to negative modes of thinking and writing than to positive modes. A vigorous culture can never do without the negatives; traditionalists need to be driven to reexamine and reconstitute their premises and to refresh their procedures. But the negative seems to be what at present absorbs the interest and enthusiasm of many of the younger intellectuals—graduate students, teachers, writers. Sometimes the ready hospitality to negative ideas appears to me to be ominous; but it's reassuring to remember the attested power of traditional criticism to adapt itself to—even, selectively, to absorb—ideas which seem to threaten its own survival.

I think that deconstruction leaves radically out of account features of works of literature which have been essential to their survival as presentations of human matters and concerns which themselves embody human values. That doesn't mean, however, that deconstruction, *en passant*, may not reveal other features of these works which have been neglected. My own position is that of a critical perspectivist; it seems to me that a new mode of criticism, insofar as it has validity, throws a strong shaft of light on features in literature we're apt to have overlooked or insufficiently stressed, but throws into shadow, even into darkness, things which have hitherto been central in our view of literature. In the process of achieving its own aims, deconstruction has in fact been constructive; for example, in drawing attention to the subtle play in a literary work of figurative language, concealed rhetorical devices and modes, and so on. The claim of a radically deconstructive critic, following Derrida's lead, is that these figures uncontrollably get out of hand and subvert the very grounds of the literary document within which they were meant to be constructive. I don't agree to the force of this claim; it can be maintained only by setting up a rationale for waiving the rules for the practice of writing and understanding language on which the deconstructor himself tacitly relies, in presenting his own claims in language that he intends his readers to understand. But I believe nonetheless that one can profit from a deconstructive critic's sensitivity to certain aspects of the play of language, which goes beyond the range of perception of the New Critics, however much they did to open our eyes to the play of figuration in a literary text.

Question: Speaking of the relatively hospitable climate that Derrida has found among literary critics, can you explain the neglect of Derrida by Anglo-American philosophers?

Answer: Neglect, or sometimes contempt. The standard procedure in philosophy is to read other philosophers to get at the content of their thought by looking through their language to the doctrines, and the arguments for those doctrines, that the language is taken more or less transparently to convey. Derrida's procedure is quite different. Derrida insists that language, even at its most abstract and logical, is never transparent to meaning; he reads selected passages of a philosophical text minutely, with close attention to the play of language and figuration as indiscriminable from the doctrines and arguments—and indeed, as ultimately subversive of the doctrines and arguments. Such close reading, which foregrounds the linguistic medium itself, seems strange, or aberrant, to most American philosophers, but much more familiar to literary critics nurtured on the close reading of the New Criticism. So, once we got habituated to the repertory of special terms, neologisms, and analytic maneuvers that Derrida deploys, what he was doing did not seem all that strange to us.

The relatively few Anglo-American philosophers who take Derrida seriously enough to read him with some care interpret his central assertion about the lack of "presence," hence of a "ground," in metaphysics to be coincident with the assertion by American pragmatists, and one especially familiar in Anglo-American philosophy since Wittgenstein, that there is no ultimate "foundation" on which metaphysical truth-claims can rest. This seems to me to be on the right track. The distinctive and radical aspect of Derrida's thinking, however, as I put it in 1979 (in "How to Do Things with Texts"), is that he "is an absolutist without absolutes"; that is, though he denies the possibility of the traditional metaphysical claim that there is an absolute foundation for valid knowledge, he tacitly accepts the metaphysical assumption that such an absolute foundation is indispensable to valid truth-claims and indeed indispensable to all determinate communication that is more than an illusory "effect" of the internal, differential play of language; Derrida's "dissemination" of seemingly determinate meanings, like his subversion of metaphysical claims to an absolute truth, rests on this presumption of the indispensability, yet radical absence, of an absolute foundation for language. To this, I think, the proper response is that a language is a highly complex conventional practice that requires no ontological or epistemological absolute or foundation in order to do its work; furthermore, that we have convincing evidence that as speakers or auditors, writers or readers, we share the regularities of this practice in a way that makes possible determinacy of communication and also makes it possible to utter assertions that can not only be understood determinately, but adjudged validly to be true or false. Such understanding can never be absolutely certain, nor can the asserted truths be absolute truths; understanding can at best be an adequate or practical assurance, and the truths practically certain within the limits of a given frame of reference. That is simply our human condition. But we should not let what Derrida calls our human "nostalgia" for absolute certainties blind us to the fact that, as an inherited and shared practice, and despite the attested failures in some attempts at communication, language in fact can work, can work determinately, and can work wonderfully well—in literature as in other modes of discourse.

Question: Do you think there's any truth to the charge that deconstruction, despite its distressed, radical rhetoric, actually shelters conservative ideas about literature and literary criticism, especially by isolating the literary work from life in a way that's comfortable for at least some old New Critics? Does the "autonomous" literary work that we heard so much about from the New Criticism reappear as the self-reflexive, self-subversive work—a work that talks mainly about itself—that we're hearing about now?

Answer: Yes, in a way. One of the standard claims in poststructuralism generally is that literature and criticism can't be distinguished, that they're both equally creative, equally interesting, equally figurative, equally fictive, and so on. But then, as you suggest, many critics—such as Hillis Miller—are writing deconstructive close readings of the same literary texts that the New Critics wrote new-critical close readings of. Such deconstructors, like the New Critics, are thereby—in a way—maintaining the autonomy of the work they're dealing with, both by separating it from specific relevance to human life and human concerns and by treating it as a self-sufficient, self-reflexive linguistic entity.

In a way, and up to a point: there is always, in other words, a point at which Miller, for example, crosses over. He first deals with Wordsworth's "A Slumber Did My Spirit Seal" as a separate poem—an independent textual entity. But then he goes on to dissolve its boundaries and to merge it first into all of Wordsworth's other writings, then into the differential play of language throughout the Western world. It's only in the initial moment, or aspect, of his criticism that Miller resembles a new-critical close reader of an autonomous text, before he proceeds to dissolve that text into what Edward Said has called the sea of textuality. But of course he continues to sustain the view that a literary text, as a self-enclosed play of linguistic differance, makes none but illusory references to the experienced world, human life, and human concerns.

Question: At the end of your essay "Behaviorism and Deconstruction: A Comment on Morse Peckham's 'The Infinitude of Pluralism,' " you write of a "central Romantic hope" for the reintegration of the self, of the self with a community, and of the self with a humanized nature. Deconstruction, you say there, is a "subversive" kind of criticism leading to "cultural vacuum"—refuting Peckham's notion that deconstruction, despite its problems, may at least manage to destroy the sometimes violent and authoritarian side of the Romantic ideology of "secular redemptionism" (pp. 184–85, 193). In some respects J. Hillis Miller's criticism seems to fit this Romantic pattern. His use of violent analysis to move the reader to the abyss of underlying nothingness perpetuates a revolution of the spirit in the affirmation of a personal code, thus allowing him to say "I believe in the traditional canon of English literature and the validity of the determinate text" ("The Function of Rhetorical Study at the Present Time," p. 12). The ultimate outcome of the secular ritual of repeatedly affirming the unit of the self over the abyss sounds much like the Romantic affirmation you have described: "life, love, liberty, hope, and joy." Can't one see Miller within the Romantic tradition?

Answer: I haven't seen the essay you allude to, but it doesn't surprise me to find Hillis Miller reaffirming the traditional literary canon and the determinacy of a text. As you suggest, he can be viewed as recapitulating the process of many Romantic writers in England and America, who moved from a literal belief in violent revolution as carrying out the millenarian prophecies of the Bible to a translation of central elements of biblical and exegetical ethics into a secular, humanistic

163

ethos. I think I'm right in saying that Hillis Miller is the son of a preacher, and he is certainly imbued with the humanistic ethos derived in many ways from certain values which, in the Bible, are grounded in divine revelation. When Miller adopts his heroic central figure— Poulet once, Derrida now—he speaks at first almost like John the Baptist. Whether the evangel is consciousness criticism or deconstruction, his initial tone tends to be evangelistic. But when the chips are down, Miller is very much a middle-of-the-road humanist who shares the central ethos of Western humanism. I think that's the post-theological heritage that the moral and other values of our civilization rest on, and I have the strongest confidence that Miller rests there, too.

In the earlier period of his enthusiasm for Derrida, I think that Miller tended to stress, and laud, some negative, countercultural implications of deconstruction. But it doesn't surprise me if he now moves to a more conservative or centrist position. In terms of the figure in my essay, of Derrida's tight-rope act, one might say that Miller now stresses the righthand side, in which Derrida affirms and uses the logocentric "effects" of a construable determinacy of meaning, of the existence of a canon of discrete and distinctive literary works, etc., where earlier Miller had stressed the lefthand side, whereby all such effects subvert, disseminate, and deconstruct themselves.

Question: In "What Is the Use of Theorizing . . . ?" you claim, with certain reservations, that all applied criticism presupposes a theory of criticism. Can you explain why your own self-proclaimed pluralism is not as limited by its presuppositions as the kinds of criticism you attack for their narrowness?

Answer: Yes, I did say, and do believe, that any set of critical observations by a practicing critic involves general, or theoretical, presuppositions, even though the critic may seem to eschew a general theory of literature. Matthew Arnold, for example, who always denigrated abstract theorizing about art, quite clearly presupposes certain premises which are distinctively Arnoldian premises about literature, very different from those of other critics, including many critics in his own time such as Oscar Wilde. And of course that generalization applies to my own preferred critical practice no less than to the practice of others. There's no way for any of us to escape the limitations of a particular set of presuppositions—what for short I call a "critical perspective"—because the very sharpness of focus that a perspectival view makes possible also blurs, or conceals, what lies outside its purview. When I proclaim myself a "pluralist" in criticism, I mean to affirm my belief in the usefulness—in fact, indispensability—of diverse sets of critical presuppositions or perspectives, if we are to see literature in the round, rather than in two-dimensional flatness.

Some of us critics are very reluctant to give up the idea that we can somehow invent *one* set of critical premises and procedures that will tell us the whole story about literature. Historically, that has never happened, nor do I think it possible. Anybody who tries to be eclectic and all-inclusive ends up mashing everything together—instead of an egg you get an egg salad. I don't think we should be nonplussed by the recognition that our preferred premises can never yield everything. Why should we want to believe that one set of theoretical presuppositions will suffice to reveal the whole story about something so richly textured, so complexly structured, so diverse in the human interests it can appeal to and in its relevance to matters of human concern, and so interinvolved in both its causes and effects with other cultural factors, as literature? I'm not bothered by thinking that whatever I myself have to say about literature is only one part of the story—of a story, in fact, which has no conclusion. From my preferred, broadly humanistic premises, I decry the radical exclusiveness of certain opposing views, and even mutter darkly about their implicit threats to the very fabric of our culture. But in a more genial humor I recollect my principles as a pluralist, and say that I welcome well-considered alternative viewpoints and often find that I can learn something of substantial value from them. And since I'm now speaking in my genial humor, I'll add that this statement applies to deconstruction.

Question: How would you characterize Northrop Frye's attempt to construct a single inclusive system of criticism?

Answer: I think it's an admirable synoptic enterprise, but in some sense futile. He has made a remarkably strong and persistent effort to show how everything valid that's been revealed about literature by alternative critical premises and analytic procedures is subsumable under his own archetypal theory. But the minute they are subsumed, they can no longer play the role they played in earlier theories. They're now playing a different, circumscribed role within his particular overview of literature.

It's an admirable overview, however. It places all individual literary works within a world of imagination, wherein human needs and desires project a realm of archetypes which reshape the experienced world, yet remain relevant both to ordinary life and ordinary human concerns. Frye traces his basic conceptions back to Blake, but they seem to me no less close to Shelley's views, in his *Defence of Poetry*, that all great works of literature reflect an enduring realm of neoplatonic archetypes.

But whatever his precursors, Frye's treatment of literature is remarkable both for its originality and for its comprehensiveness. When I reviewed *The Anatomy of Criticism* many years ago, I drew attention to its limitations as well as to its strengths. Let me affirm now my overall judgment that in that book, and in the many writings which have followed it, Frye has proved himself to be the most innovative, learned, and important literary theorist of my generation.

Nevertheless Frye's system can't achieve what it sets out to achieve. That is, it cannot, by assimilating them all, displace all alternatives. Take a basic premise of the New Criticism, that what matters in reading poetry is to come to terms with the autonomous and unique organization of an individual work in isolation. Frye's theory is antipodal, in that it moves from the individual back to the universal. The work is viewed as participating in an imaginative universal, or archetype, and that archetype is conceived as having its place in the total and enduring structure of the imaginative world, with its seasonal analogues and so on. Now, Frye is so flexible and acute a critic that I am sure that if he chooses to, he can operate to great effect as either a New Critic or an archetypal critic. But even Frye can't operate, coherently, as an archetypist in such a way as to achieve the critical results made possible by the special premises and methods of the New Criticism.

Question: Might it be possible that the presuppositions of your own views have biased your conclusions about Romanticism? Since your approach in *Natural Supernaturalism* seems to assume the values of Western religion, for example, is it any surprise that it ends up in the realm of the Romantic positives, which are transformations of those religious values?

Answer: As a matter of biographical fact, my thinking, of which *Natural Supernaturalism* was the published product, developed in the opposite direction: first I found what I call "the positives" (the chief moral and cultural values) that were assumed and affirmed by many Romantic poets, and only gradually did I come to see how deeply they were grounded in certain values of the religious tradition, of which they constitute, in part, a secularized translation. These values, of course, are in that aspect culture-bound, but many of them are not simply Hebraic-Christian values; they have equivalents in other major religions. Furthermore, we mustn't forget that the values of much Western theology are not simple derivatives from the Bible, but were biblical concepts as reinterpreted and expanded in terms of the philosophy of the Greeks and Romans. So that the primary Romantic values had a mixed origin; and they seem to me to remain central to a humane view of life and to be relevant among the criteria by which to judge literature—as T. S. Eliot put it, not to judge whether a work of literature is literature, but to judge whether a work of literature is great literature.

One other thing. There are numerous elements in the Western religious tradition which I find abhorrent and which have had disastrous implications in history—they have fostered fanaticism, tyranny, cruelty, internecine warfare. Radical antinomianism, for example, is a recurrent strain in that tradition. Another is a literal apocalypticism, or chiliasm, which in times of stress has led people to pin their fanatical loyalty to a messianic leader of what Rufus Jones has called "an apocalyptic relief expedition from the sky." So it is a question of which values from the inherited tradition you select. I think it a good thing that many major Romantic poets turned from their early faith in a chiliastic recovery of Eden by bloody violence to a belief in an imaginative transformation of the self that would make one see the old world in a new way, and to act accordingly. Some historians regard that change as no more than a weak retreat from political radicalism to political reaction. But I think it undeniable that some of the greatest Romantic poets, including Blake, Hölderlin, Wordsworth, Coleridge, Shelley, wrote their best poetry after abandoning their literal faith in an apocalypse by violence for a metaphorical faith in an apocalypse by imagination.

Question: Changes in theories of literature seem to change the shape of literary history. The New Criticism, for example, devalued Romanticism, while Frye's archetypal criticism makes Blake central to Romanticism and Romanticism central to literary history. Is deconstruction changing our view of Romanticism?

Answer: It's hard to see how it could do so without being unfaithful to its own premises, which make it radically ahistorical. It dissolves not only the boundaries between literature and nonliterature in any one period, but also the boundaries between one writer and another and between one period and another. Writing, that is, is always writing; its constitution is always the same play of differance, it always exhibits logocentrism, and it is always ultimately self-subversive. Of course, there is the conservative righthand side of Derrida's equilibrium, which acknowledges the standard distinction between distinct works, individual writers, and various periods on the level of logocentric "effects": but Derrida recognizes and uses such effects only "provisionally," or "strategically," as a stage toward disseminating them. Since a major thrust of deconstruction is to convert all antitheses into chiasmus, and to dissolve temporal as well as all other "boundaries," I don't see how any thoroughgoing follower of Derrida can have anything in particular to say about Blake, Romanticism, or any individual writer and any literary period. Except, of course, to the degree that a deconstructive critic forgets his own premises. Fortunately, all of us theorists sometimes escape from our premises long enough to say things which, however inconsistent, are insightful and important.

Question (continued): Under the influence of deconstruction, isn't it natural to value Blake more than Wordsworth? Complaints about Wordsworth seem to have increased sharply—it no longer seems undiplomatic to launch an outright attack on his self-contradictions—while I've heard it said more than once that Blake may have been the first deconstructionist. He seems so aware of the pitfalls of language and so playfully wily in confronting them. Wordsworth's linguistic earnestness makes him an easy target of deconstruction instead of a paradigm. How true is the generalization that literary history under deconstruction favors the writers who reflect its concerns with and attitudes toward language?

Answer (continued): You persuade me of the need to make a distinction between deconstructive procedures in reading that I neglected in my previous answer. Derrida clearly, in his readings, distinguishes his treatment of writers whom we may for convenience call "paradigmatic," from his treatment of other writers. Paradigmatic writers he construes as asserting, or at least implying, doctrines about language and metaphysics and central Western concepts which approximate his own views—even though I think he would not want to call his own views "truths." Among his paradigmatic writers are of course Nietzsche, and also Mallarmé—in fact, it is my impression that Derrida's typical essays on writers ordinarily called "literary" are not radically deconstructive, but stop at the stage of reading these writers paradigmatically or at tracing approvingly their way of playing with key metaphysical concepts and distinctions.

In his deconstructive essays, Hillis Miller seems to follow Derrida's differential way of treating paradigmatic and nonparadigmatic writers, but he applies the distinction within the literary realm as well as outside it. For Miller as for Derrida, Nietzsche is clearly and reiteratively paradigmatic. And within literature itself, Miller treats Wallace Stevens, for example, primarily as paradigmatic. That is, he for the most part stops at reading—in my sense of construing—selected textual passages from Stevens as anticipating what he presents as deconstructive truths about language and metaphysical concepts. His analysis of Wordsworth's "A Slumber," on the other hand, is devoted to showing how that poem, when read allegorically by an unmystified reader, can't help but manifest the deep truth of the death of the "logos," and thereby undoes itself despite itself. Which can, I think, be translated to say, in my terms, that its implicit allegorical meanings inadvertently but inescapably undo its construed meaning.

But to the thrust of your question: deconstructive critics indeed seem to set higher value on paradigmatic writers whom they can construe, and not simply allegorize, as anticipating their own revealing convictions about language. But there's another factor involved in their choice of writers to write critical essays about, and that is the challenge of taking a writer who seems canonical, straightforward, and resistant to deconstruction, and then showing how his texts unknowingly deconstruct themselves. I'm very dubious indeed that Blake, for all his controverting standard uses of language, can be read by a deconstructor as paradigmatic; beyond most poets, he is an essentialist who claims that his fundamental assertions disclose presence. Another major poetic text of the Romantic era, Byron's *Don Juan*, is of a more paradigmatic order. It is easy to show that in many passages in *Don Juan*, Byron can be construed as deliberately subverting not only the poem's own narrative premises, but also major concepts and oppositions in Western metaphysics—so easy, in fact, that it doesn't present much of a challenge. Wordsworth, in his seriousness of asseveration, presents a much more inviting challenge.

We find a parallel in the evolution of the New Criticism. Cleanth Brooks, like his colleagues, began by reading Donne as a paradigmatic exemplar of the major literary virtues of ambiguity, symbolic imagery, irony, and paradox, and used those criteria to derogate poets of the reigning canon—Milton, Romantic and Victorian poets—as writers who are defective because unironic, committed to forthright assertions, and unparadoxical. But as time went on, Brooks delighted in taking up the challenge of demonstrating that such canonical poems as Milton's "Lycidas," Wordsworth's "Intimations Ode," and Tennyson's "Tears, Idle Tears" can also be accounted great poems, insofar as they in fact embody features, overlooked both by critical precursors and by the poets themselves, of ambiguity, symbolic imagery, irony, and paradox.

Question: Do you think that the deconstructionist interpretation of a text has any cognitive value beyond correctly "construing," as you say, the primary meaning of the text? To put it another way, do you learn anything from the specifically deconstructionist moves involved in Miller's reading of Wordsworth's "A Slumber Did My Spirit Seal," or are you merely entertained by them?

Answer: I've already said that I have learned things I value both from the analytic procedures and verbal play of Derrida. (I find particularly notable the essay called "White Mythology.") I have also profited from the writings of de Man, Miller, Barbara Johnson, and other expert practitioners of the deconstructive craft. Some things I've learned are positive; others (no less valuable to me) are negative, in that they've forced me to redefine and defend my own critical stance, and led me to try to identify the moves which enable deconstructors to achieve their startling new readings.

Miller's essay on "A Slumber" I chose for commentary, as I have said, in part because it is so extreme an instance of radically deconstructive criticism. One of its inherent values consists in Miller's flair for language and the zest he communicates in his own ingenuity at finding in Wordsworth's little poem a galaxy of meanings that no one hitherto has in the least suspected. (I shudder to think what we may expect in a similar vein from deconstructive critics who lack Miller's talents, learning, flair, and, the *sine qua non*, his tact and sensitivity in reading a text on the primary level of construing.) But in this particular instance of the deconstructive, or "allegorical" phase of Miller's criticism, I can't say I've learned anything that I consider valid about the meaning of Wordsworth's poem, except insofar as his claims have driven me back to scrutinize the text itself.

It's worth noting that, according to its own frequently given account, poststructuralist literary criticism aims to be "productive" and autonomous rather than auxiliary, with a function no less creative and interesting than that of the literary work to which it ostensibly directs its attention. To the degree to which deconstructive criticism in fact accords with its own statement of its function, it is a mode of what Aristotle called epideictic rhetoric. That is, it belongs in the class of display oratory, of which the aim is to celebrate an occasion such as the Fourth of July. The orator doesn't really undertake to tell us anything we don't know already about his ostensible subject, the Fourth of July; instead, he sets out to show how well he can meet a ritual emergency which has evoked innumerable earlier orations and to display his own invention, verbal and rhetorical skills, and aplomb for the admiration and delight of his audience.

Question: Would you clarify the difference in the role that construing a text plays in more traditional criticism as against deconstructive criticism?

Answer: At the level of construing a text, the reader makes out what the sentences of a text signify, in the order in which those sentences occur. He does so on the supposition, for which we have convincing grounds in our experience in learning, using, and understanding a language, that he shares with the writer of the text certain conventions governing the practice of the language which enable him to understand what, on this primary level, the writer undertook to say.

All of us, including deconstructive critics, have to construe a text such as Wordsworth's "A Slumber," or else we're simply not reading English: and although no construal is ever capable, by reference to an infallible criterion (what Derrida calls "a transcendental referent") of being absolutely provable beyond any possibility of error, we are capable in most instances of achieving adequate assurance about its construed meaning, which is confirmed by substantial agreement with other competent construers. But construal of a poem merges, without sharp boundary, into what I have called "explication," which poses questions about the kind of poem it is, what is central to the poem, how it is structured, what effects its author undertook to achieve, etc. In this aspect of what we loosely call "interpreting" a poem, criticism begins to become variable, and by that fact, more interesting. You get, for example, the application to the construed poem of diverse critical perspectives, as well as favored value-concepts, such as the ambiguity, irony, and paradox of the New Criticism. (In "Five Types of *Lycidas*," an essay written decades before the emergence of deconstruction, I pointed out how radically different are the explications effected by applying to a single text diverse critical perspectives and criteria.) Here we find the area of critical disagreement widening, and a diminishing consensus about the criteria for deciding between alternative explications; I've always liked the formulation of F. R. Leavis that, in this aspect of his procedure, a critic who proposes an explication learns to expect from another critic at most the qualified agreement, "Yes, but. . . . " By and large, however, the mixed class of what Hillis Miller called traditional critics agree in keeping the text-as-construed a primary reference—that is, they would reject an explication which is patently out of keeping with the construal; a traditional critic will also agree that many of the reasons offered by another critic, even for a radically alternative explication, may be sound reasons, even though he regards them as falling short of being convincing reasons. The deconstructive critic, however, rejects both the reference to the construed text and the standard reasons for justifying an explication, as illusory "constraints" on reading which are overcome by an inherent force, or "surplus of meaning," which is beyond any possibility of control by either the writer or the reader of the poem.

171

(Let me interject, by the way, that although New Critics tended to regard the "interpretation"—constituted by the construal and the explication of a text—as the be-all and end-all of criticism, literary critics before, during, and since that era have fortunately continued to carry on the traditional enterprises of enhancing our understanding of individual works of literature by bringing them into various relations with other works, other genres, other modes of discourse, the life and times of the author, and the intellectual, social, and economic as well as literary history of the West.)

I have said that a standard move of the deconstructive critic, in establishing a requisite freedom of interpretive maneuver, is to make the text-as-initially-construed (and in part explicated) into a pre-text for interpretive over-reading—often this over-reading is labeled "allegorical" and is imposed entirely independently of any evidence that the author intended his work to be an allegory. This move has some, though only partial, parallels in more traditional critical procedures. Let's take a very simple case. A Freudian critic comes across Blake's gnomic lines:

> Can Wisdom be put in a silver rod?
> Or Love in a golden bowl?

Aha! A rod is convex and a bowl is concave; we all know what such shapes symbolize; we can now proceed to over-read what Blake meant according to Freudian mechanisms, independently of what Blake may have consciously undertaken to say. Notice that this interpretation begins by construing the determinate meanings of "rod" and "bowl," which become a pre-text for the over-reading, and that the Freudian critic would agree that if he has misconstrued the primary meanings of "rod" or "bowl," then his symbolic over-reading is also mistaken. Notice also that our postulated critic proposes that his symbolic over-readings of Blake's sentences constitute their determinately right, or deeper meanings, even though these meanings are supervenient on the construed meanings.

It is with this last claim that the deconstructive critic radically disagrees. His or her allegorical over-reading of the construed text "produces" a disseminative "overloading" (Derrida's terms)—an endless scatter of meanings which are "undecidable," rather than determinately multiplex, or "polysemantic." That is, the construed text, as over-read deconstructively, has no determinately right meaning, nor even a limited set of specific meanings; it disseminates, allegorically, into an indefinitely open set of inevitably contradictory possibilities.

(By the way, my intention is to use the term "over-reading" non-invidiously, for convenience of exposition. I would be glad to reverse the implicit diagrammatic polarity, and trade the metaphor of over-reading for the metaphor of under-reading. This change to under-reading is compatible with the deconstructive claim to *under*mine meaning and would also cancel the built-in implication of "over-reading" that to read deconstructively is to do something excessive. I must point out, however, that the change would also cancel the implication that deconstruction is a mode of higher criticism. I leave the choice between these directional metaphors to the deconstructive critics.)

Question (continued): When you say that deconstruction can produce traditionally acceptable or genuine readings in passing, do you mean that these insights occur despite the theory rather than because of it? Just what is it that you claim to have learned from a deconstructor such as Derrida?

Answer (continued): A deconstructive reader, even in his disseminative phase, establishes a mode of reading which (I quoted Derrida as saying in my essay) is relatively, but not entirely, free from the "legalities" that constrain the initial phase that I call construing. Furthermore, deconstruction is in principle a mode of double-dealing with texts, in which you can take or leave (rather, take-and-leave) such constraints. Both in principle and in practice, then, deconstruction can produce readings that are sound according to traditional criteria of interpretation.

Besides, there are things one can learn from what Derrida calls his "style." Some of his characteristic modes of verbal and rhetorical play are very infectious. I would not, for example, be prepared to avow that my own procedures in the present dialogue have in no instance been affected by Derrida's proclivity, rejecting the "logocentric" logic of either-or, to speak and write in a way which, instead of being either serious or nonserious, is at the same time *neither* serious nor nonserious and *both* serious and nonserious. I leave the decision to my auditors as to which of my assertions from this platform were intended to be taken as entirely serious. (Including, of course, what I've just asserted.)

Question: You distinguish between construing, explicating, and disseminating a literary text. How would you respond to Stanley Fish's claim that all aspects of interpreting a text are relative to a particular strategy, which is an arbitrary, or at least an optional, strategy? To Fish, even what you call "construing a text" deludedly thinks it finds shared meanings which are in fact projected on an empty text by members of an interpretive community who simply happen to share a certain strategy of interpretation.

Answer: Those issues are too complex to be fully discussed here. But

173

let me propose some crude headings for a response to Fish's claim. I have said in an essay ("How to Do Things with Texts," p. 587) that Fish seems to me right in his claims that the meanings of a text are relative to an interpretive strategy and that agreement about meanings depends on our joint membership in a community which shares an interpretive strategy. It's a question, however, of how extensive that community is and whether it includes the writer, as well as the reader, of a text. Take Milton's "Lycidas" as an example. In construing the sentences of Milton's text, we have excellent grounds for the assurance (based on reading Milton, Milton's contemporaries, and writers before and after Milton) that he belongs to our interpretive community, which is no less extensive than all those who speak, write, and understand English; that Milton used his inherited expertise in the conventional regularities of the English language to write texts (admittedly, on a high level of complexity) meant to be determinately construable by competent readers; hence that we, as members of Milton's community— making allowance for limited and largely discoverable historical shifts in the conventions of the language—by applying our shared expertise, are for the most part quite able to construe what Milton undertook to mean by the sentences he wrote.

It is our diversity of interpreting "Lycidas" on the level I have called "explication" that gives some plausibility to Fish's claim that there are an indefinite number of interpretive communities, each of which produces its own poem. (A fuller discussion would need to point out that the distinction between construing and explicating is not sharp-boundaried but nonetheless useful for exposition; also that even the phase of construal is to some degree responsive to a particular explication, yet recalcitrant to excessive explicative distortion.) In explicating "Lycidas" as a poem, for one thing, we have less grounds for assurance than we have in construing its component sentences as to just what poetic conventions Milton deployed, though we do have a number of sound clues to their nature. Also, as I pointed out in "Five Types of *Lycidas*," a number of critics have chosen to explicate "Lycidas" by applying a diversity of critical perspectives independently of any clues about Milton's own artistic intentions. You can, if you want to use Fish's concepts, say that the set of new-critical explicators of "Lycidas," the set of archetypal critics, the set of more or less Freudian critics, as well as the set of old-fashioned critics like myself who undertake to read "Lycidas" "with the same spirit that its author writ," each constitutes a distinct explicative community; that these communities have all been institutionalized in the Academy; that the diverse critical perspectives adopted by these communities produce what I have called diverse "types" of "Lycidas," with identifiable family resemblances among the instances of each type; and that individual critics within an explicative community are much more apt to agree with each other than with someone who applies a radically different critical perspective.

To bring an over-hasty discussion to a hasty conclusion: In construing Milton's text, we have no interpretive option except whether to resign from the ongoing community of speakers, writers, and readers of English into which we, like Milton, were born. In the phase of explicating a construed text, however, we can distinguish a variety of loosely constituted subcommunities; and in this aspect of critical interpretation, it makes sense to say that readers have a choice among available interpretive strategies.

Question: While you obviously believe that it is possible for an author to communicate a meaning and for a reader to get that meaning, you have on at least one occasion characterized metaphors as inherently inadequate:

> The human compulsion not only to say, do, and make but also to understand what we say, do, and make enforces a discourse about these processes and products of consciousness, intention, purpose, and design. This discourse unavoidably involves metaphors whose vehicles are natural or artificial objects, and since none of these objects runs on all fours with the human primitives it undertakes to define and take into account, each metaphor, however pertinent, remains inadequate. It is because a number of metaphorical vehicles are pertinent, yet no one is adequate, that the history I undertook to narrate [in *The Mirror and the Lamp*] displays the recurrent emergence, exploitation, displacement, and supplementation of constitutive metaphors; this historical process seems to me to be in the long run profitable to understanding, in that it provides . . . a vision in depth in place of the two-dimensional vision of the complex realities with which the metaphors engage.

Answer: Your quotation occurs in a context in which I was explaining why none of the "constitutive metaphors" that are applied to works of art, since their vehicles are natural or artificial objects, can equate exactly with the human, intentional, and purposive procedures by which a work of art is designed and produced. But the point can be generalized. I quote Coleridge as saying that "no simile runs on all four legs." That is, no figurative term squares exactly with whatever it is you're applying it to; otherwise, you wouldn't be able to recognize that it's figurative. So I agree with Derrida that we can't dispense with metaphors, and also that there's always a discrepancy, which he calls a "surplus," or "excess," between a metaphor and its application.

What I don't agree, however, is that this discrepancy, or excess, in the vehicle of a metaphor is uncontrollable by a user of the metaphor, or by the listener or reader who understands how he's applying it—that the excess, by an internal energy, runs wild and inescapably goes on to say what the user of the metaphor doesn't want to say. In *The Mirror and the Lamp* I explored, for example, the way in which later users explored the implications of discrepancies in organic metaphors, as applied to the production and internal organizations of works of art, which earlier users of such metaphors, in the contexts of their usage, overrode as unintended and irrelevant. But when I read a user of organic metaphors such as Coleridge, I recognize what he intended that metaphor to signify—I understand, what, in the context of Coleridge's *parole*, the metaphor means. At the same time, I recognize potentialities in the features of the organic vehicle of the metaphor that Coleridge did not call into play; and on investigation, I find that later writers did exploit these features in their *paroles*. The process of the surplus getting out of control, that is, is a historical process, which I discover by examining a sequence of textual *paroles* by a variety of writers. I don't find that process necessarily occurring, despite the writer's intention, in every *parole* by every user of an organic metaphor on every occasion of its use; nor do I see how such a conclusion follows from the fact that in no metaphoric vehicle do all the features equate exactly with its tenor—with what someone in a particular context uses it to say.

Question: J. Hillis Miller confessed his willingness to say that metaphors signify a finite set of meanings. If so, aren't you and he agreeing?

Answer: I'm not familiar with the statement of Miller's that you allude to. But insofar as he undertakes to describe or paraphrase what any text, or metaphoric segment of a text, signifies, he has no recourse except to list a number of determinate meanings, which he presents to be determinately understood by us, his readers. You cite him as saying that this set, or scatter, of determinate meanings is finite; but as his analysis of Wordsworth's "A Slumber" demonstrates, it's a very large set, and probably an open set; I feel quite certain that if Miller should return to the poem, he could, by the freedom of interpretive maneuver he permits himself, readily make new discoveries of signification. But whether it is finite or not, the important features of his set of meanings, on which Miller indubitably insists, is that the set is very large, inevitably includes aporias, and is undecidable—that is, there is no valid reason whatever for choosing between incompatible alternatives.

We know, both from the texts written by some authors and from what they say about their own writings, that some literary works are intentionally written to be read in precisely this way, so that we can't in fact be said properly to understand such works except if we read them as signifying an indefinite set of undecidable and mutually incompatible meanings; this is a literary genre energetically exploited by some writers of the present era. The novelty of the deconstructive claim is that all literary works are instances of this genre, no matter how lucid, determinate, and coherent are the meanings that an author undertook to express in a work. The model of writing that a deconstructive critic presupposes is that of a power struggle between what a writer tries to use language, in his *parole*, to mean and what language, by an internal compulsion which manifests itself by an "excess" in the *parole*, goes on willy-nilly to mean—a struggle in which language ineluctably overcomes all attempts by the writer to control its unruly differential energy. This model seems to me to be radically unapt for our actual linguistic practice; but it serves as an effective rationale for the surprising semantic discoveries of a determined deconstructive reader.

Question: You have described yourself as, among other things, a cultural historian. Can you use your distinction—the distinction between the level of construing and explicating a text, and the second level on which the text-as-construed is used as a pre-text—to compare your role as an interpreter with the role of deconstructive critics? For example, would it be fair to say that you, as a cultural historian, substitute "real world" for "text" in the distinction I have described? And if so, that you confine yourself to the level of construing and explicating the real world, whereas deconstructors and fiction writers begin with a text and move up to the level of using it merely as a pre-text for a supervenient allegory?

Answer: I do not, in *Natural Supernaturalism*, claim to be interpreting "the real world." The materials that I interpret are texts and passages from texts. I construe them and explicate them in a determinate way; and on the basis of identifying in these texts certain thematic similarities, and changes in those themes over time, I develop a complex narrative history not about reality, but about altering human views concerning the nature of reality—about (to mention only one of many such themes) the overall form of the past, the present condition, and the future of the human race. The soundness of the history I relate— as a pluralist I hold that it can be a sound history, even if it is only one of diverse possible histories—depends on the representativeness of the texts I choose, given the focus of my undertaking, and above all, on the validity of my determinate readings of those texts. I don't deny that there are meanings of the same texts which, since they fall outside my purview, I do not explore; my implicit claim is only that by and large, and whatever else they mean, the texts that I cite at least mean, determinately, what I interpret them to mean.

An added comment. I think that I recognize in the way you pose your question a widespread current assumption that, since we can say, sensibly enough, that we interpret the world and also that we interpret a text, then an interpretation of a text is subject to no more "constraints" than is an interpretation of the natural world. Where this parallel fails is in ignoring the fact that the language of a text is a medium specifically developed to convey meaning, and that the text was written by an author who undertook to say something determinate by his use of that medium. The constitution of reality, or the natural world, lacks those distinctive and essential features for the determination of meaning— except, of course, for a theologian who believes, as many have indeed believed, that the world is the great book of nature, whose true meanings can be interpreted by cracking the code which determines the significations that its divine Author intended it to convey.

Question: Most of your published work is about Romantic writers. Do you see any Romantic tendencies in yourself and your work?

Answer: I'm not sure by what criteria I'd qualify as a Romantic or a nonromantic. But I think that my writings about selected writers of the era between the French Revolution and the third or fourth decade of the nineteenth century manifest a strong sympathy with many of their characteristic enterprises. This applies above all to the great Romantic undertaking, in a time of social, cultural, and moral crisis and demoralization—many writers agreed with Wordsworth that it was without precedent a time of "dereliction and dismay"—to reconstitute the grounds of social, cultural, and moral values in the West by translating the earlier theological concepts into primarily secular terms. In *Natural Supernaturalism* I traced this enterprise, as variously, and sometimes explicitly, proposed by many writers, whether in poems, novels, philosophy, or history. This is a common feature, for example, in Romantic works otherwise as diverse as Wordsworth's *Prelude*, Hegel's *Phenomenology*, Hölderlin's prose romance *Hyperion*, and Shelley's *Prometheus Unbound*.

Question: J. Hillis Miller said in answer to a question about his reading of a poem by Yeats that a traditional historical reading of that poem would be an incompetent or wrong reading. Would you say that his reading of "A Slumber Did My Spirit Seal" is incompetent or wrong?

Answer: Competency or incompetency in reading are terms that apply within a particular frame of reference. When he operates within the limits of traditional construal and explication, Miller has shown himself to be a competent traditional reader; when he operates with the freedom established by deconstructive premises, he has shown himself to be a competent disseminative reader. I don't, as you know, subscribe to the premises that serve to justify such freedom of interpretive procedure. But no gong rings in heaven or hell to proclaim that the premises and practices of deconstruction are wrong or wicked; nor do I know of a knock-down argument guaranteed to convince critics of the deconstructive persuasion that they are on a hopelessly wrong track. I point out to deconstructionists, for example, how easy it is, given the requisite learning and wit, to produce sensationally novel readings when their elected premises permit them to operate with such minimal constraints. Deconstructionists counter that my inordinate constraints are illusions engendered by a logocentrism from which I can't possibly escape, and which prevent me from discovering in a text anything more interesting than the reflection of my own projected illusions.

Now, how am I to argue against that? It's of no rational or practical use to hurl epithets and call down anathema, as some conservative critics do. What I first try to do is to understand what it is that competent deconstructors are actually doing, on what premises, and what it is that makes it, to such obviously intelligent, learned, and sensitive critics, seem worth doing. Then (as in my essay and in this discussion) I point out what seem to me anomalies in the theory and extravagances in the practice of deconstruction. In doing that, I solicit my wit and marshal rhetorical resources such as irony and *reductio* to highlight and exaggerate such features. But as I suggested at the end of the essay, the choice between a radically deconstructive and a more traditional mode of reading is a choice between premises which can't be conclusively argued by logic alone, because it involves a choice between values—it is a matter, as I said in an earlier essay ("How to Do Things with Texts"), of "cultural cost-accounting." Even so, if I should say to Hillis Miller that ultimately such a choice entails whether or not to be a communicant in a society held together by our capability to say determinately what we mean and to understand (actually, and not merely as a provisional stage of illusionary effects to be noted and transcended) what someone else has said—well, I'm quite sure that Miller would produce reasons for denying that his own choice of a deconstructive mode of reading entails so drastic a consequence.

Question (continued): If Derrida or Miller shows that he can competently construe the text before deconstructing it, does that competence determine the competence of his deconstructive interpretation?

Answer (continued): If a deconstructive critic doesn't demonstrate competence at the primary aspect of reading that I called construing a text and explicating it in a way closely tied to that construal, he cannot be

M. H. ABRAMS

competent in what follows, because (as Derrida himself is careful to point out, in the passage I quoted in my essay) the effects of "classical exigencies" that constrain what he calls "traditional criticism" not only precede but, in ways that he leaves indefinite, continue to exert some kind of control over a second-order dissemination; otherwise the latter reading would, as he says, "authorize itself to say almost anything." Those classical exigencies, in my view, are grounded on solid evidence that authors largely share with their readers the regularities that govern the practice of a language and the evidence that most authors have in fact exploited their expertise in those conventional regularities to write texts designed to be determinately understandable by their readers.

In his disseminative commentary on Wordsworth's "A Slumber," Miller continues to rely, in however loose and tenuous a fashion, on some of the constraints that determine his initial construal. And even when he claims for his second-order deconstructive reading the feature that he regards as its special value, its openness "to the inexhaustible strangeness of literary texts," he uses "strangeness" in tacit opposition to the meanings we (and he) expect in the standard reading of a text; by what other criterion can he adjudge the disseminated meanings to be "strange"? So Miller's radically deconstructive reading is dependent upon standard reading not only in its initial phase, and (in undefined ways) in its disseminative phase, but also in his very attempt to argue the virtues of his deconstructive way of reading.

Question: You claimed that you have tried objectively to understand the premises, procedures, and reasons for the appeal of deconstructive criticism, and then went on to suggest that to choose it involves, in a final analysis, the choice whether or not to participate in a community for which the capability to communicate determinately constitutes an indispensable bond. But is that claim of objectivity sincere, and the alternatives that you suggest alternatives in which you genuinely believe? Might it not be the fact, as deconstructionists often assert, that your claim is a facade, and that your reasoning is in fact a rationalization of your nostalgia for a lost certainty of presence, involving a variety of rhetorical ploys that are motivated by anger (which is in turn a result of your terror) at the deconstructive demonstration that all our Western talking, writing, and thinking is suspended over an abyss by its reliance on a ground which deconstruction shows to be in fact groundless?

Answer: I am familiar with the charge by some deconstructionists that any attempt by a nondeconstructionist to understand their position objectively and to argue against it rationally can never be anything other than a rationalization for metaphysical nostalgia and cultural terror. That seems to me to be itself a rhetorical device to put all possible opponents in an untenable position. As a literary and intellectual historian, and as a theorist of language and of literary criticism, I have tried to emulate the procedure that J. S. Mill, in a great essay, attributed to Coleridge: When confronted with a position, posed by highly intelligent thinkers, which seems to me mistaken, I try to "look at it from within . . . to see it with the eyes of a believer in it; to discover by what apparent facts it was at first suggested, and by what appearances it has . . . been rendered . . . credible."

This is the third public occasion on which I have tried to come to terms with deconstructive theory and with radical deconstructive criticism. Each time, as the result of continued reading and reflection, I think that, in the Coleridgean sense, I understand it better and find in it, as I said, interesting and even profitable insights. But I nonetheless remain radically unpersuaded. So far as I am able to assess my motives, I remain unpersuaded on grounds of experience and reasoning and also (as I have said) of my commitment to certain social and cultural values; but not because of my nostalgia for a demolished ontological ground of absolute certainty in which I have never, in my maturity, invested any belief, nor of my abject terror at a conclusive demonstration that our culture is suspended by a network of illusions over a linguistic and intellectual *abîme*.

But I do confess to occasional fits of anger, or rather of irritation, at some deconstructive moves, such as the one you describe, designed proleptically to put out of play any possibility of validly reasoned grounds for opposing it. By way of conclusion, let me specify another such move. I have said that deconstructive theory proposes a model for the relation of a speaker or writer to language which seems to me to be very defective—the model, that is, of a power struggle between unequal antagonists in which the inherent differential energy of language ineluctably overcomes any effort by a user to master it, by disseminating what he says into an undecidable *suspens vibratoire* which includes significations that controvert what the user has undertaken to say. Some poststructuralists have translated the metaphor of power struggle into a metaphor of *Machtpolitik*, and have extended it from the relation between the writer and his linguistic medium to the relation between a written text and its interpreter. They assert that to interpret a text as signifying what its writer undertook to mean is nothing other than to succumb to the "author's" illegitimate claim to "authority," or "authoritarianism," over both his text and his reader. But to set ourselves to make out what someone has undertaken verbally to convey is simply to try to understand him or her, and the attempt to understand each other's utterances, whether spoken or written, seems to me indispensable to the maintenance of anything we can account a human community. I am thus irritated whenever I encounter this rhetorical move, by a play on words, to put anyone who tries to understand what someone else has tried to communicate into the humiliating posture of obsequiousness to an arrogated authoritarianism.

STANLEY CAVELL

In Quest of the Ordinary:
Texts of Recovery

When Morris Eaves and Michael Fischer first invited me to contribute to this enterprise, I naturally declined, on the ground that I did not know enough on the subject of Romanticism to be of use to others. They replied that what they expected from me might take the form of an account of why, in the concluding part, Part Four, of *The Claim of Reason*, Romantic texts and preoccupations keep putting in their appearances (some lines of Blake, "The Boy of Winander," Coleridge's Ode on Dejection, Thoreau on neighboring, or nextness). Put so, the question seemed too sympathetic to the work I had done for me to walk away from, however unprepared I felt for mastering it; indeed too congenial to paths I was already taking from the book.[1]

The first half of *The Claim of Reason* contains, along with some other things, an interpretation of Wittgenstein's *Philosophical Investigations* which focuses on its linked notions of criteria and of grammar and which argues that while Wittgenstein's work is written as a continuous response to the threat of skepticism, it does not, and is not meant to, constitute a refutation of philosophical skepticism. By skepticism I mean directly those radical doubts, or anxieties as expressed in Descartes and in Hume and in Kant's determination to transcend them, about whether

---

[1] In November 1982 I presented at Albuquerque a version of some of what is to follow here. By February 1983 that material had developed into good parts of the first three of the four lectures I gave at Berkeley as the Mrs. William Beckman Lectures, sponsored by the Department of English at the University of California, under the general title "In Quest of the Ordinary: Lines of Skepticism and Romanticism." This essay is roughly what became the third Beckman lecture, though I begin by sketching some of the ground covered in the first two. A version of the second lecture is printed in *Raritan*, 3 (Fall, 1983). *The Claim of Reason* was published by Oxford University Press in 1979.

we can know that the world exists, and I and others in it. The idea that the *Investigations* does, and was meant to, constitute such a refutation was, so far as I knew, the unchallenged, received wisdom of professional philosophy, motivating either a philosopher's liking or deploring of that book. My argument depends on coming to understand that this temptation to refutation itself constitutes skepticism's fundamental victory.

In the Introduction to the *Critique of Pure Reason*, Kant had identified skepticism—the denial that we can know objects "outside of us" (and Kant ought to have added, "subjects opposing us")—as a scandal to philosophy, and he dedicated his philosophical genius, that is, his Critical Philosophy, to ending the scandal. My thought is that if, as I take it, skepticism is a place, perhaps the central secular intellectual place, in which the drive to deny the conditions of human existence is enacted; then so long as that *denial* of the human is essential to what we think of *as* the human, skepticism cannot, or what I call the threat of skepticism must not, be denied. You might even take it as the mission of philosophy now to preserve rather than to turn aside the scandal of skepticism—as if this preservation is our access to the memory that we are, or meant to be, human, to live with stumbling.

This understands skepticism as internal to Nietzsche's problematic of nihilism, which he proposed overcoming in the way his precursor Emerson undertook to overcome skepticism, namely through what both call affirmation. They have been violently ridiculed for this proposal; but I understand it to be itself ridiculing, and suffering from what *others* call affirmation, from, let me say, the thing their tradition calls *consent* to the world. Their call for affirmation is a call for a world, or the possibility of a world, one can *want*. This is something that requires the overcoming of the human, as it stands. Only then would skepticism have found a historical end to match the fact of its historical beginning.

The way I work this out in relation to the *Investigations* starts from the thought that we share what Wittgenstein calls criteria by means of which we regulate our application of concepts to the world—means by which (in conjunction with what Wittgenstein calls grammar) we set up and follow out the shifting, advancing and retreating, conditions of intelligibility; in particular from the thought that the explanatory power of Wittgenstein's idea of a criterion depends on recognizing that, whatever their necessity for communication and for thinking, the criteria in which we are agreed are open to our repudiation, or dissatisfaction: our capacity for disappointment by them is essential to the way we possess language, our attunement with it, and at the same time it constitutes our capacity for skepticism. To take Wittgenstein's criteria as *refuting* skepticism is to take him as supplying or meaning to supply "logically sufficient" criteria for determining with certainty the truth of statements—say, such a statement as (to use perhaps his most famous example) that someone is now in pain. On my view—namely, that Wittgensteinian criteria reveal the kind of standing threat skepticism is—our capacity to be disappointed in them is our capacity to know from time to time our uncertainty whether, for example, the concept of pain applies *at all* to anything (other than myself); which means, to know our implication in withholding the concept, to know the possibility of that withholding, our denial of the world, of its things, and of the persons in it.

This brings me to Romanticism. When, in writing the last hundred and fifty pages or so of *The Claim of Reason*, I kept coming up with memories and quotations from various figures of Romantic inspiration, I found them unwelcome. I was not prepared, and did not feel prepared then to get prepared, to follow out the causes of these appearances, and yet they were endangering the end of my story, an end it had taken me twenty years, on and off, to find. On ending that story, however, I began thinking more purposefully about the question of Romanticism's appearances, especially in its American strain, and tracing out my sense that the sense of the ordinary that founds the philosophizing of the later Wittgenstein and of J. L. Austin is underwritten in the writings of Emerson and Thoreau, in their devotion to what they call the everyday, the common, the near, the low. The idea here is that the procedures of ordinary language philosophy do not (as some philosophers have from the beginning attacked and others defended these procedures for doing) defend ordinary or common beliefs, but rather take our words back, or take them on, let me say, to an intimacy with the world which exists before, or after, the expression of beliefs or propositions that may be true or false, certain or nearly certain or doubtful.[2] This idea eventuated in the title *In Quest of the Ordinary*, which names at once a quest and an inquest, as if what we call the ordinary, the thing we humans *can* adapt to as our habitat, is itself extraordinary, something like a monstrous parody of what we *might* call the ordinary, or home. (The extraordinariness of our ordinary lives is a dominating subject of my essay on Beckett's *Endgame*, "Ending the Waiting Game," in *Must We Mean What We Say?*)

A succeeding thought was that it was such an idea of the ordinary that guides Wordsworth's emphasis on the language of common men,

[2] I take up this connection first explicitly in "An Emerson Mood," added in the expanded edition of *The Senses of Walden* (Berkeley, 1981); and again in "Politics as Opposed to What?" in *The Politics of Interpretation* (Chicago, 1983).

on "the rustic and the low," when he dedicates his poetry (in the Preface to the *Lyrical Ballads*) to "making the incidents of common life interesting." This over-quoted and apparently genteel platitude hit me hard in this light, for two reasons. The first is, of course, its implication that the common world, the world common to us, is as it stands of no interest to us, that it is no longer ours, that we are as if bored quite to death, and that poetry has nominated itself to bring us back from this "torpor," presumably by means of its reviving therapeutic, or say redemptive, powers. (As often as I have heard it said that the word "poetry" comes from a word that means making, I do not know that I ever heard anyone say what it is that poets make, unless it was worth remarking that they make poems, that is, that poems do not grow on trees—at least not for non-poets. What Wordsworth is saying is that poetry, perhaps poetry alone now, makes something interesting to us, which, I guess, means makes us capable once again of taking an interest in what is happening to us.) The second reason is that to shift our "interest" is the guiding way that Thoreau and Austin and Wittgenstein name their philosophical demands on philosophy as it stands. Boredom and interest are terms in which Austin claims for his work revolutionary significance, and on the same ground Wittgenstein pictures what he has done as destroying what we have hitherto taken as philosophy.

Such thinkers perceive us as in a condition of intellectual boredom, which they regard as, among other things, a sign of intellectual suicide. So metaphysics would be seen as one more of the false excitements that boredom craves. (So may be the activities appealed to in refuting or replacing metaphysics—for example, logic or linguistic play.) This is what Wittgenstein has against metaphysics, not just that it produces meaningless propositions (that, even in the sense in which it is true, would be only a derivative of its trouble). His diagnosis is rather that metaphysics is empty, empty of interest, as though philosophy were there motivated by a will to emptiness. When Austin says of philosophical examples that they are "jejune," he is using a common-room word to name, with all due differences of sensibility and context, the Nietzschean void. (As if J. P. Morgan were to say of a business's collateral that it is jejune. What worse term of criticism does he have?)

I am not unaware that connections of the kind I am proposing here are not exactly habitual with professional philosophy, that reading texts of Wordsworth and Coleridge, for example, as though they are responding to the same problems philosophers have, even responding in something like the same way (a way that cannot be dissociated from thinking), is not how you would expect a philosopher from our English-speaking tradition and profession of philosophy to proceed. What I find more interesting, however, is that my connections and procedures here are not exactly foreign to that profession either.

Another word or two by way of indicating my path from *The Claim of Reason* to the lead of Romanticism. That book is heavily indebted to an idea I call acknowledgment, taking its significance to lie in its forming a key to the way I see both the problematic of skepticism and that of tragedy. This idea has been criticized on the ground, roughly, that in offering an alternative to the human goal of knowing, either it gives up the claim of philosophy to reason or else it is subject to the same doubts that knowing itself is. But I do not propose the idea of acknowledging as an alternative to knowing, but rather as an interpretation of it, as I take the word "acknowledge," containing "knowledge," itself to say (or perhaps it says that knowing is an interpretation of acknowledging). In an essay on *King Lear* I say, "For the point of forgoing knowledge is, of course, to know" (*Must We Mean What We Say?*, p. 325), as if what stands in the way of further knowledge is knowledge itself, as it stands, as it conceives of itself; something not unfamiliar in the history of knowledge as expressed in the history of science. Otherwise the concept of acknowledgment would not have its role in the progress of tragedy.

But it is not in this direction, I think I can say, that my concept of acknowledgment has mainly aroused suspicion, not in the claim that tragedy is the working out of skepticism; but in the reverse direction, that skepticism is the playing out of a tragedy, that accordingly our ordinary lives partake of tragedy in partaking of skepticism. This means that an apparently irreducible region of our unhappiness is natural to us but at the same time unnatural. So that the skeptic is as live in us as, let me say, the child.

Thoreau calls this everyday condition quiet desperation; Emerson says silent melancholy; Coleridge and Wordsworth are apt to say despondency or dejection; Heidegger speaks of it as our bedimmed averageness; Wittgenstein as our bewitchment; Austin both as a drunken profundity and as a lack of seriousness. To find what degrees of freedom we have in such a condition, to show that it is at once needless yet somehow, because of that, all but necessary, inescapable, to subject its presentation of necessity to diagnosis, in order to find truer necessities, is the Romantic quest I am happy to join. So I accept the traditional rebuke of such a quest, that it is childish, or adolescent, or, well, Romantic; that peculiarly maddening rebuke, which casts those who would diagnose our solemn, universal destructiveness, as themselves the gloomy malcontents. It is to be expected.

In my second Beckman lecture, I sketch out the ground for the more detailed reading of *The Rime of the Ancient Mariner* to be included here. This preparation consists of interpreting a few passages from Coleridge's *Biographia Literaria* which I take as declaring that his *Ancient Mariner* can be understood as a response to the *Critique of Pure Reason*. My purpose in this way of interpretation is to specify an example of the sense (I take it to be more or less uncontroversial) in which Romanticism bears some internal relation to the philosophical settlement worked out in Kant's Critical Philosophy. In particular, when Coleridge's "prose gloss" beside the poem speaks of the Mariner's ship drifting across a line and of its being guided back toward the line, the line in question is to be taken (among other ways, no doubt) as the line implied in the *Critique* "below" which or "beyond" which knowledge cannot penetrate. The effort to breach it creates, for example, skepticism and fanaticism, efforts to experience what cannot humanly be experienced. Coleridge's poem I take to show that Kant's lined-off region *can* be experienced and that the region below the line has a definite, call it a frozen, structure. This way of interpretation is not incompatible with interpretations of the poem as of the Fall; indeed I claim that it provides an interpretation of *that* interpretation.

As I take it that Kant's Critical Philosophy can itself be taken as an interpretation of the Fall. To declare as much is a way of understanding the extraordinarily interesting document Kant produced under the title "Conjectural Beginning of Human History." There he speaks (of the origin) of reason as (or in) a kind of "refusal," a power of opposition. You may take it as the ideology of Kant's "Conjectural Beginning" to make out that this opposition is not to God's law but to nature's, that is, to the rule of instinct. (This, however, would seem to make what happened in Eden a Rise, not a Fall. Kant does not gloss over a difficulty of this form at this point. The question of the direction in which the human is conceived to appear, as from above or below, is touched on in *The Claim of Reason* in an observation concerning Kant's concept of the human as the "animal rational" [p. 399].)

I would like to emphasize here an analogous implication of my thought that acknowledging is not an alternative to knowing but an interpretation of it. In incorporating, or inflecting, the concept of knowledge, the concept of acknowledgment is meant, in my use, to declare that what there is to be known philosophically remains unknown not through ignorance (for we cannot just not know what there is to be known philosophically, for example, that there is a world and I and others in it) but through a refusal of knowledge, a denial, or a repression of knowledge, say even a killing of it. The beginning of skepticism is the insinuation of absence, of a line, or limitation, hence the creation of want, or desire; the creation, as I have put it, of the interpretation of metaphysical finitude as intellectual lack. (So speaks serpentine infinity.)

In this connection it pleases me to cite, something one may take merely as a curiosity, a passing remark from Austin's essay "Other Minds," which constitutes perhaps his major version of an ordinary-language assault on skepticism. His assault involves, as one would expect of Austin, a tireless detailing of the errors, grammatical and semantical, in, among other things, the idea that there is a special class of empirical statements (unlike all the other classes of such statements) about which we can be certain, free of doubt; namely, so-called sense-statements, statements, that is, that confine themselves to the deliverances of our sensations, as opposed, say, to statements about material objects. In the passing remark I refer to, Austin momentarily turns aside from his work to observe: "It [viz., the view of an epistemologically favored class of sense-statements] is perhaps the original sin . . . by which the philosopher cast himself out from the garden of the world we live in."

While Austin would scarcely be interested in interpreting his little allegory of the garden very far (not, I take it, really believing in original sin, literally or allegorically) his unprecedented and unrepeated (so far as I recall) display of emotion toward the world here is a claim to his inheritance—even his—of English Romanticism. I mean by this that, as I read it, this display of emotion toward the garden of the world is not, indeed is meant to declare that it is not, a claim to his inheritance of English common sense, say in the form given it by G. E. Moore; it is not a claim to be defending common beliefs or common knowledge about the world, as if the world we live in were Eden because it *could* not overthrow our certainties. Austin can grant that the world is more than we can ever bargain for. The idea is rather that for all our human liability to error, the world is Eden enough, all the Eden there can be, and what is more, all the world there is: risks of error are inherent in the human, part of what we conceive human life to be, part of our unsurveyable responsibilities in speech and in evil (in, as Descartes put it, our being provided with free will); and this condemnation to an unsurveyable freedom is not well described by saying that we can never, or can only in a certain class of cases, be certain. If the earth opens and swallows me up, this need not prove that my trust in it was misplaced. What better place for my trust could there be? (The world *was* my certainty. Now my certainty is dead.) Of course there is a spirit in which you may feel like saying, "Trust nothing!" But would it express that spirit to say, "Take no further step on the earth!"? So there is a question about whether we can live our skepticism, and if we cannot, what kind of threat skepticism poses. Which is to say that there ought to be a question whether philosophy is the best place, or the only place, to consider the matter (philosophy as it stands).

The chief fault I find with Austin's parable of the world as Eden lies in the clause "the philosopher cast himself out from the garden of the world we live in." Gender identity aside, Austin is taking it that it is clear how philosophy is special in this casting of itself out, as though one can tell by looking, so to speak, which of us is and which of us is not philosophizing; as though it is clear how to end philosophy (to bring philosophy peace, Wittgenstein had said), hence how to tell whose life is found and whose lost by philosophy.

I continue in this essay to be guided by the thought of Romanticism as working out a crisis of knowledge, a crisis I have characterized as (or as something like, something interpretable as) a response at once to the threat of skepticism and to a disappointment with philosophy's answer to this threat, particularly as embodied in the achievement of Kant's philosophy—a disappointment most particularly with the way Kant balances the claims of knowledge of the world to be what you may call subjective and objective, or, say, the claims of knowledge to be dependent on or independent of the specific endowments—sensuous and intellectual—of the human being. And this in turn perhaps means: a disappointment in the idea of taking the success of science, or what makes science possible, as an answer to the threat of skepticism, rather than a further expression of it. Romanticism's work here interprets itself, so I have suggested, as the task of bringing the world back, as to life. This may, in turn, present itself as the quest for a return to the ordinary, or of it, a new creation of our habitat; or as the quest, away from that, for the creation of a new inhabitation: Wordsworth and Coleridge would represent the former alternative; Blake and Shelley, I believe, the latter. (Thoreau's notion of "revising Mythology" suggests that these alternatives may not be so different.) But Romanticism in either direction makes its own bargain with the concept of knowledge and the threat of skepticism, one which a philosopher may feel gives up the game, one that accepts something like animism, represented by what seems still to be called, when it is called, the Pathetic Fallacy.

This bargain seems simply to ignore Kant's companion effort, as determined as his effort to close off skepticism, to stave off dogmatism or superstition or fanaticism: his effort to make room for faith by, so to speak, limiting faith; to deny that you can experience the world as world, things as things, face to face as it were, call this the life of things.

About the victory Kant declared over skepticism by negotiating away the possibility of knowing the thing in itself, one will sometimes feel: Thanks for nothing. Yet someone with his or her Kantian conscience intact, if not unmodified—say, one's Enlightenment conscience—may feel precisely as strongly about this return of the thing in itself by negotiating for animism: Thanks for nothing (or more strictly: No thanks for everything).

Here is a clear place at which to pause to note a characteristic difficulty in the way I find myself setting out to think. A philosopher will ask me what exactly I mean by "experiencing things as things face to face," or someone will ask how I define "the life of things." The answer to the former question is: Nothing technical; the answer to the latter is: I don't. Such words mean nothing whatever, or I have no interest in their meaning anything, apart from their accuracy in wording an intuition—here my intuitions concerning something like a prohibition of knowledge, a limitation of it as from outside. This wording of intuitions is essential to what I mean by such words as "letting oneself be read by a text." The text in question here is some fragment like "the thing in itself is off the limits of human knowledge." This noting, of course, says nothing about why one desires to be read, or why one takes that for an intellectual virtue, or beginning, or where it will end. (If experiencing the life of things is another expression for a feeling for what Kant calls the unconditioned, then it is an experience, in Kant's terms, of the sublime. Then another open question for me— a companion to the question whether knowledge or consciousness is the more fundamental or useful emphasis in understanding Romanticism—is whether animism or sublimity is the more fundamental emphasis. While I am here following out the emphasis on knowledge as directed by the problematic of what I understand as skepticism, I assume that the alternatives in each question are inseparable.)

The price of animism is an aspect of the Romantic settlement in terms of which I proceed to the main business of this essay, the reading of four texts, the first and the last (*The Ancient Mariner* and Wordsworth's Intimations Ode) at greatest length, for they are the principal war horses—beyond Emerson and Thoreau—in whose terms or paces my statements about Romanticism here must find or lose support. The middle two texts, which I mostly glance at, are philosophical papers, one from each of the traditions of philosophy, the German and the English, whose mutual shunning—from the point of Kant's settlement and increasingly in this century (until perhaps a certain thaw of the past few years, in certain circles at any rate)—has helped to make satisfying public discussion of the issues most on my mind all but out of the question. The first of the philosophical papers is Heidegger's "Das Ding"; the second, entitled "Gods," is by John Wisdom, one of Wittgenstein's first disciples.

The matter of animism is not going to be simple to state, because it has seemed badly misconceived (though perhaps it no longer is) as something Romantics embrace—whereas Wordsworth's endlessly discussed remarks concerning poetic diction are in practice as much *against* the Pathetic Fallacy, against certain accessions to it, as in theory they are *for* the imitation of the rustic and the low, and perhaps the one because of the other. And in *The Ancient Mariner* the images of the animated, or rather reanimated, bodies I take as the equivalent in the realm of mind of what, in the realm of matter, or nature, the Pathetic Fallacy can accomplish. For an intellect such as Coleridge's, for which objects are now dead, they will not be enlivened by an infusion of some kind of animation from outside. (I think, further, of Coleridge's picture of animated bodies, the work in his poem of the figure of Life-in-Death, who has at that stage taken possession of the Mariner, as a parody of what a certain kind of philosopher, a person in a certain grip of thought, takes the human being, hence human society, to be. The Mariner says of his population, "We were a ghastly crew." I am thus reminded that in *The Concept of Mind*, less famous a book now than it was when I was in graduate school, when it represented what many took ordinary-language philosophy to be, Gilbert Ryle called something like this the myth of the Ghost in the Machine, and attributed the myth to Descartes. Ryle did not spell out his myth in remotely the detail Coleridge provides, but it is fairly clear that he meant something of the myth Descartes was at pains to *overcome* when, for example, he denied that the soul is in the body as the pilot is in the ship.)

The issue, or specter, of animism makes a momentary, somewhat disguised or frightened appearance in a late speculation in the final part of *The Claim of Reason*. That part keeps coming upon ways in which skepticism with respect to so-called material objects or to the so-called external world, and skepticism with respect to so-called other minds— or as I might say for short, skepticism and solipsism—are reciprocals or counters of one another, opposing one another in a lengthening set of features: for example, on the constitution in each of "a best case" of knowledge, on the consequences that befall me when a best case fails me, on the ideal of knowledge that each projects, on the role of the figure I call the Outsider in each, or whether these fates are equally to be lived, equally open to avoidance, and so on. The late speculation I have in mind now concerns whether one or the other route of skepticism is the more fundamental. It is meant, in context, to question the thought that solipsism may not be a genuine skepticism, that its grief stops short of world-denying doubt. The speculation is that the allegory (call it) I find of material-object skepticism in Othello's relation to Desdemona becomes, in turn, a further instance of that skepticism. I say in the book that this speculation anticipates further than my book actually goes (p. 451).

It is understandable that I shrank from that anticipation. It invites the thought that skeptical doubt is to be interpreted as jealousy and that our relation to the world that remains is as to something that has died at our hands. My new misgiving comes initially from the surmise consequent upon the surmise of jealousy, that we have killed the world, and specifically out of revenge.

Here there seems no shaking the sense that I have transformed the issue of skepticism into the issue of animism, exchanged one form of craziness for another. (As if this answer to skepticism has gone further than it meant to; as perhaps skepticism itself did.) Can this exchange be of intellectual profit? It may be intellectual profit enough if we come to see the idea of the jealousy of the world as bringing out an animism already implicit in the idea of doubting its existence—to the extent that the uncertainty created by this doubt is pictured less in terms of whether one's knowledge is well grounded (whether, for example, we can achieve assured knowledge of the world on the basis of the senses alone) than in terms of whether one's trust is well placed (whether we are well assured, for example, that we are not now dreaming that we are awake).

Turning to my first text, *The Rime of the Ancient Mariner*, I take the Mariner's shooting of the Albatross as the path I will follow through the poem, partly because that incident is in any case one that a fuller reading of the poem would be obliged to hazard, and partly because it confronts us, as I see it, almost immediately with the issue of animism, in the following way. Prominent candidates that critics have advanced as the Mariner's motive in the shooting have been a species of motiveless malignity and a kind of gratuitous violence meant to establish one's separate identity. It seems to me that the focus of the search for motive should be on the statement in the poem that "the bird . . . loved the man / Who shot him with his bow." Then the idea may be that the killing is to be understood as the denial of some claim upon him. In that case the moral of the poem is not well conceived as it is formulated by the Mariner himself: "He prayeth best who loveth best / All things both great and small," which generally leaves its readers somewhat dissatisfied. But why should the Mariner—who still wanders in penance at the end—have the moral straight, or full? I take what might be called the poem's moral in something like the reverse direction from his: to let yourself *be loved* by all things both great and small. This is of course not to deny the Mariner's formulation; it is meant as a practical or, say, Romantic interpretation of it.

Do we regard this as comprehensible advice? I suppose one answer to the question will depend on what we take the poem to say. I regard what I take it to say as testing that comprehensibility. It should speak to the question of why a false animism, some mindlike animation, is produced (as a kind of aberration of true poetry, or of true religion, in a self-derived place Coleridge calls, in Chapter IX of *Biographia Literaria*, a wilderness of doubt, "skirting the sandy deserts of unbelief"); and of how this is as much the enemy of genuine poetry (which resists it) as it is of science (which does not, since to science the difference between a false animation and the life of things is irrelevant).

On the account I have to give of it, the *centrality* of the killing of the Albatross is rather put in question, as if it were both asserted and denied, as if it is both fundamental and derivative. I know of no better discussion of the question of this act, and its motive, than Robert Penn Warren's of some four decades ago.

Taking "the fable, in broadest and simplest terms, [*as*] a story of crime and punishment and repentance and reconciliation"[3] Warren pertinently undertakes to characterize the nature of the crime ("the Mariner's transgression") that starts things, and he finds especially (and here I find myself most directly preceded by him) that the very feature of the shooting of the Albatross that other critics of the poem take as a failing (which they express by describing the killing as wanton, trivial, or unthinking) is on the contrary key to its success: "The lack of motivation, the perversity, . . . is exactly the significant thing about the Mariner's act. The act re-enacts the Fall, and the Fall has two qualities important here: it is a condition of will, as Coleridge says, 'out of time' and it is the result of no single human motive." If one bears in mind the idea that the Mariner's seascape is an image of the skeptic's temptation and progress past (what presents itself to him as) the merely conventional limits of knowledge, Warren's remarks fit my sense of the issue of skepticism as an issue of the human denial of the conditions of humanity for which there is no (single) motive. You might try understanding the motive as the horror of being human itself—but then the fate of denying this condition, hence denying the possession of such a motive, would be the point of this motive. Like Kant's Categorical Imperative and its basis of respect, respect for the human (that is, for the possessors of Reason, of which the horror of the human is

[3]*Selected Essays* (New York, n.d.), p. 222.

an opposite, a denial, or parody), the denial of the human signals not the absence of motive but the presence of a particular level of motive; Kant calls it formal.

But the concept of "perverseness" will not take us far enough in assessing the Mariner's state; or it will itself require as much, perhaps the same, investigation as the Mariner's state itself will. Perverseness brings to mind, in conjunction with the suggestion of motivelessness, Coleridge's characterization of Iago; whereas Othello is equally to the point. In the way I have set up my initial path through the poem, the initiating act of transgression—that which for me evokes the Fall—is the act of "crossing the line." It may be—so I am suggesting—that killing the bird is derivative from the ensuing drift into the cold country, along with the other events of that realm; derivative both in itself being a consequence of transgression rather than an original transgression on its own, and in its interpretation being determined, or determinable, in terms of the interpretation of the crossing of the line. In my second Beckman lecture, I indicate its interpretation in terms of Wittgenstein's idea of speaking or attempting to speak "outside language games," an idea that *The Claim of Reason* works from in altering the intuition of Kant's critical "line."

What is the matter with calling this crossing of the line—whatever actions that allegorical picture turns out to capture—perverseness? At a certain juncture in the skeptic's progress he may say such a thing as that we can never see *all* of any material object. One who finds that claim to be paradoxical may call it perverse. But one who finds the claim true may call the *denial* of it perverse. One side here will be expected to perceive the other as the loggerhead; but is either closer in touch with the facts? (I present a series of examples in *The Claim of Reason*, pp. 194–99, designed to show that both sides are out of touch— roughly, because the word "all" has been driven outside its ordinary language game[s], hence its occurrences are out of our control, or rather, take control of us.) Given my use of the skeptical problematic as my opening into Romanticism (and contrariwise), I am accordingly apt to be suspicious of the charge of perverseness. Applied to the Mariner, the charge seems to me in too great a hurry to declare him incomprehensible. Or is the claim on the contrary that the concept is exactly meant to make his conduct comprehensible? (The disputants about seeing *all* of something think they are explaining something too.) Then perhaps I should say: the application is in too great a hurry to declare the Mariner in some way different, in the grip of something special, a Jonah. That is, the charge would be more at home leveled by his fellow crew members, in a certain mood of their desperation.

The pang I feel in regard to this application may be made clearer if one considers that certain critics have objected to taking *The Ancient Mariner* as an interpretation of the Fall on the ground that it exhibits nothing to call disobedience. This would be decisively telling if the Fall must be imagined as, say, Milton imagined it. But what if the poem presents an alternative picture of the human outcastness from Eden, together with an alternative interpretation of succumbing to temptation, one in which it is a sense of going too far that produces a sense of prohibition, not the other way around?

In a section from the essay "Excuses" headed "Small distinctions, and big too," Austin cites as a result of failing to imagine ordinary cases (a consequence, he says here, of being "in the grip of thought") our subjection to a confusion he supposes Plato and after him Aristotle "fastened upon us," a confusion between succumbing to temptation and losing control of ourselves. (Wittgenstein's "language games" and Austin's "ordinary cases" do not coincide but they do overlap. Wittgenstein invents games that go beyond, in a sense, "what is said"; this is one sense in which he is not an ordinary-language philosopher, or not an ordinary one. But they do not go beyond what, in a sense, "can be said" [with ordinary language]. My view is that without seeing the internal connections here one will not know what Austin's cases are cases of.) Austin's example in the present instance goes as follows:

> I am very partial to ice cream, and a bombe is divided into segments corresponding one to one with the persons at High Table: I am tempted to help myself to two pieces and do so, thus succumbing to temptation. . . . But do I lose control of myself? Do I raven, do I snatch the morsels from the dish and wolf them down, impervious to the consternation of my colleagues? Not a bit of it. We often succumb to temptation with calm and even with finesse.

Call us casual. It is in taking the plot of *The Ancient Mariner*, in its "having passed the line," to illustrate a spiritual transgression in which the first step is casual, as if always already taken, that I see it as manifesting the idea of wishing to get outside language games, hence of tracing what Kant calls "dialectical illusions" (they may be taken as forms of spiritual derangement—Kant names them fanaticism, sorcery, superstition, and delusion). The idea of perverseness does not, to my mind, get at the condition of casualness. Apart from that condition, we are not considering the idea (fundamental to my chart of skepticism) that it is natural to the human being to wish to escape the human, if not from above then from below, toward the inhuman. The idea of perverseness here suggests defiance. It, so to speak, Romanticizes skepticism. This is no better, no purer an accounting, and maybe no worse, than skepticism's self-portrait, which tends to soberize, or respectify, or scientize itself, claiming, for example, greater precision or accuracy or intellectual scrupulousness than, for practical purposes, we are forced to practice in our ordinary lives. (To see in some detail how the claim of perverseness may be assessed in this connection, I take up in an Appendix certain of its classical locations in Edgar Allan Poe, from which Warren has assumed it.)

I have sometimes put the human effort to escape the human together with what I call our fear of inexpressiveness (something I take Wittgenstein's discussion of privacy to take on): "The wish underlying this fantasy [of necessary inexpressiveness] covers a wish that underlies skepticism, a wish for the connection between my claims of knowledge and the objects upon which the claims are to fall to occur without my intervention, apart from my agreements" (*Claim of Reason*, pp. 351–52). I find this thought pertinent to the familiar thought that the Mariner somehow also represents the *poète maudit*: Coleridge's curse, like the Mariner's, was not alone to know that his suffering could not be communicated, as if it were in fact incomprehensible to others (anyway, to others so far), but to know that he was more radically incommunicado, a state he describes or identifies as inexpressiveness in his Ode on Dejection. It presents itself to me as a state of incomprehensibility, the state Wittgenstein's fantasy of a private language is meant to capture. But if the Mariner is a poet, then his actions must be those of a poet. In particular, what has killing a bird got to do with what a poet does?

What is his act? The Mariner says "With my cross-bow / I shot the bird." He knows the consequence was deadly, but that may not have been what he intended. He may only have wanted at once to silence the bird's claim upon him and to establish a connection with it closer, as it were, than his caring for it: a connection beyond the force of his human responsibilities, whether conventional or personal, either of which can seem arbitrary. In dreaming his solution, to pierce it with his arrow, he split off the knowledge that the consequences of his act would be the death of nature, this piece of nature.

The dissatisfaction with one's human powers of expression produces a sense that words, to reveal the world, must carry more deeply than our agreements or attunements in criteria will negotiate. How we first deprive words of their communal possession and then magically and fearfully attempt by ourselves to overcome this deprivation of ourselves by ourselves, is a way of telling the story of skepticism I tell in *The*

Claim of Reason. I note here merely that being driven to deny my agreement or attunement in criteria is my lingo for being driven to deny my internal, or natural, connection with others, with the social as such. As if my reaction to the discovery of my separateness is to perpetuate it, radicalize it, interpreting finitude as a punishment, and converting the punishment into self-punishment.

The Mariner's shipmates, the remainder of the population of the ship of state, are dead to him before he shoots, as if just possibly the shooting should bring them back to life. If Coleridge's dream-poem were mine, had by me, I would take the shooting of the arrow to be a figuration for using words originally to name the world—winged words. Hence the poet may have cause to fear that his art is as fatal as science's; more fatal, because he had hoped to overcome (what has appeared to the likes of him as) science's or the intellect's murdering to dissect; whereas he now finds that he has murdered to connect, to stuff nature into his words, to make poems of it, which no further power can overcome, or nothing further in the way of power.

Then what is the crime in the act of shooting the bird? Warren says, at one point, that "the criminality is established" in such a way—namely through "a sacramental conception of the universe"—that "in the end we have . . . in the crime against nature a crime against God." Without denying Warren's findings here, let us take into consideration that the Mariner's acts in the cold country are self-absorbed, narcissistic, as if to parody that supposed self-reflection that some philosophers take to constitute one's possession of a mind. It would not be an allegory of skepticism otherwise, any recovery from which must—apparently—be made alone, in the absence of the assumption of others. Otherwise it is not skepticism you are recovering from. So there is nothing for the Mariner's act to be but self-absorbed. Most memorably, the Mariner sucks his own blood to free his thirst for speech and to enable himself to call to a ship for rescue. And I think it is roughly as clear that he identifies himself with the water-snakes, the loving and blessing of which precipitates the freeing of himself from the Albatross. This preparation depends on taking as a mark of identification the lines

> The many men, so beautiful!
> And they all dead did lie:
> And a thousand thousand slimy things
> Lived on; and so did I.

The gloss glosses (indicating a competition with, and in, the poetry): "He despiseth the creatures of the calm, And envieth that they should live, and so many lie dead." Then this for me means that he despises and envies his own being alive, as survivors may do. It is when, thereupon, he sees the snakes in a different light, in moonlight, that he accepts his participation as a being living with whatever is alive—accepts animals of the slime as also his others—that is, accepts the fact, or you may say the gift, of life. This begins his recovery from the death-in-life of inexpressible guilt. (My words just now imply that I take Warren successfully to have made his case for the relations between moonlight and sunlight in the poem, a case made substantially a few years earlier, it seems to me, by Kenneth Burke.)

Similarly, whatever else the Albatross may signify, to the Mariner it must present itself as a manifestation of himself. The gloss again glosses: "The shipmates, in their sore distress, would fain throw the whole guilt on the ancient Mariner; in sign whereof they hang the dead sea-bird round his neck." But the shipmates are no better, if no worse, at signs than sailors, and other blamers, may be. Their act of hanging guilt also realizes an idea of the Mariner's intimacy with the bird that my sense of his shooting wished for, and serves (especially if one takes it as physically impossible to hang in that place so large a bird) simply to identify them with one another—the bird (whose name alters, hence alludes to, a name for pelican) with the man (who bears his own kind of cross, or cross-bow), both of whom give their blood for the rescue of others. Then the shooting was a form of suicide, as the Crucifixion was.

The idea of suicide, further, combines with the idea of the breaking of attunement, the killing of one's connection with others, one's craving for exemption from human nature, to yield the crime of killing the humanity in oneself. It should seem to constitute its own punishment. Accordingly I do not see in the poem, as others wish to see, a reconciliation of the Mariner with society. Warren says that "it is by the Hermit . . . that the Mariner is received back into the world of men." But on what terms? He is not enabled to participate in that world on equal terms with others. To the extent that the Mariner is not recovered to the world of men, the country to which he returns (our world) *remains* dramatized, diagrammed, by the cold country he has survived. Otherwise, why would his penance be to proclaim to its inhabitants, ever and anon and from land to land, the identical moral he had to learn in order to survive his life-in-death? The difference in the countries is that above the line the inhabitants are able to conceal their rejection of the world, and for the most part or, say, for practical purposes, to adjust to their condition as if it were the ordinary condition of the world. To bring them back from their concealed life-in-death, accordingly, the Mariner has to break into their adjustments, to become a disturber of their peace, which is no peace. (He recognizes us as living our skepticism, or gives sense to that surmise.)

The Mariner entreats the Hermit to "shrieve" him, which is to say, to hear his confession and to prescribe his penance. The Hermit asks him to say what manner of man he is, whereupon an agony forces him to begin his tale, of which the Mariner says: "And then it left me free." The timely utterance of his tale gives him relief. And the penance prescribed by the Hermit (which the gloss wonderfully glosses as "the penance of life [falling] on him") seems to be exactly to repeat this encounter endlessly—to tell his ghastly tale in obedience to his agony, which therefore will endlessly return, and "at an uncertain hour," which keeps him wandering, looking into the faces of strangers to know who must hear him.

That the cursed poet, the skeptic turned believer, is shrived by the Hermit, the other figure of isolation in the poem, I take as a Coleridgean joke: to shrive is to prescribe something, that is, to write something (in advance), so the poet is shrived, prepared for redemption, by a writer, call him an unacknowledged legislator. Writing is accordingly a kind of self-redemption, which fits the fact that the Hermit's prescription is of a confession the very telling of which constitutes penance.

This is not complete enough to explain the punishment in this telling. Here what I have in mind turns upon the differences between the persons, first and last, to whom the Mariner is depicted telling his tale, at first the Wedding-Guest, and at last the Hermit. What I have now to do is to imitate the Mariner, I mean obey him, by drawing my own moral from his story. (I leave open whether this should count as continuing to read it. I mean continuing to give a reading of it.)

Coleridge makes dramatically clear the decisive importance of who speaks first. In neither case of telling his story does the Mariner speak first, exactly; I mean he does not tell what he has to say until he is asked a question. Hence, as in *Walden*'s sentence about attracting its inhabitants by sitting quietly, by owning silence, the poet is so far claiming the posture of a certain kind of philosopher, a certain kind of teacher, say therapist. But in each of his cases there is an ambiguity about who is first. The Mariner asks the Hermit, in effect, to ask him to speak; so his speaking first is only to ask authorization to speak. The Hermit complies perfectly, responding to his request with a question that allows him to tell his tale through; so far it is the Hermit who behaves like a philosopher. Or rather, since his question prescribes a penance, it *forces* the Mariner to the tale. The Hermit thereupon is absent, presumably because he has no further instruction for his interlocutor and because the ensuing tale has had no instruction for him.

From which it follows that he is not, after all, a philosopher. The Mariner is careful not to speak first to his initial interlocutor, the Wedding-Guest. He draws him aside from the round of life and thus prompts a question from him, but it is a question neither about himself nor about who or what the Mariner is, but only about why he has been interrupted. So again it is not an invitation to dialogue, and hence again philosophy is not present; the Mariner also is not that kind of teacher.

The Apostle, on the contrary, on Kierkegaard's view of him, does find himself drawn from the round of life to speak first, but he does not, like an old sailor, speak about himself. So the Mariner wanders between Apostleship and Sagehood, as though it is too late for religion, because nothing is any longer common to our gods, and too soon for philosophy, because human beings are not interested in their new lives. (No wonder the writer's explicit autobiography will be written in continuous digression.) He knows what he has to say and he sees to whom he is to say it. But he does not know why he speaks and does not know why his hearer needs to hear him. Without knowing the good of his teaching he can make no end of it. The gloss describes the Mariner as "having his will" of the Wedding-Guest. This is neither how apostles nor how philosophers teach; he is more a patient than a doctor, more a symptom than a cure.

The gloss dictates that the ancient Mariner "teach, by his own example, love and reverence to all things that God made and loveth." But how would his example show this, unless he holds his past life as a bad example? Or is he an example to teach that no one is beyond redemption? How does his example hold the promise of redemption? The examples by which the Mariner teaches, apart from the telling of his tale, are, I gather, these two: first to show that "To walk together to the kirk / And all together pray / While each to his great Father bends" is far "sweeter than the marriage-feast"; and specifically, second, to enforce the lesson by button-holing Wedding-Guests, preferably next of kin, and leaving them stunned, so that they too "[turn] from the bridegroom's door." Why? Even if one ceremony is sweeter than the other, it does not yet follow that they are incompatible, that we must choose between them. Why is the marriage deserted, that is, why are *all* and *each* found place for while *a pair* or *a couple* are not? Does God, among all the things he made and loves, not love, or no longer make, marriages? And shall there be no more marriages? How does the Mariner's tale compete with marriage?

It is, to be sure, a tale of loneliness so absolute "that God himself / Scarce seemed there to be." Moreover, the characterization of the

Wedding-Guest after the tale as like "one that hath been stunned" relates him to the Mariner's state as he successfully dreamed of rescue, when "The ship suddenly sinketh" and he was "stunned . . . like one that hath been seven days drowned." Being stunned is the state Socrates is described by Plato as having produced in those who have sought confrontation with him, but the Mariner *leaves* the Wedding-Guest in this state, without, so far as I can see, further rescue; permanently, one may say, awaiting redemption. No doubt this can be justified—say, as preparation for philosophy. But it is not philosophy's progress, and neither, I think, is it poetry's or religion's. So again I ask: Why is this preferable to marriage?

The way I figure the moral follows from the way I have been led to line up the issues, in which the Mariner takes his tale to compete with the prospect of a marriage, to prefer either aloneness or else society in its totality to the splitting or pairing contracted in marriage, and to have the power of stunning but not of further rescuing his interlocutor. And since, moreover, I am not one who takes Romanticism as the achievement of major celebrations of privacy, but rather, in these terms, as the achievement of the willingness for privacy, the survival of it until, if ever, genuine publicness is recognizably established, or reestablished, I figure this way:

However inviting the merry din of marriage, however essential to the hope of the social, it is no longer a sacrament, neither sponsored by God nor ratifiable by society as society stands, but is a new mystery to which outsiders, however close in kin, are irrelevant. Nor can the new bonds which must reconstitute a legitimate public, which means overcome our drifts into privacy, be secured by marriage as it stands. To marry now is to be willing to have a further adventure of aloneness, without solitude but also without society; as if marriage is a further investment of our narcissism, as children so typically are. If marriage is the name of our only present alternative to the desert-sea of skepticism, then for that very reason this intimacy cannot be celebrated, or sanctified; there is no outside to it. You may describe it as its lacking its poetry; as if intimacy itself, or the new pressure upon it, lacked expression. No wonder you cannot tell who is married.

Then the Mariner's may in this way be a message of Romanticism as such, that there is such an intimacy at large, and that poetry is responsible for giving it expression. (Then the question would arise: How did it get loose, as if disinvested? And why does not friendship demand it, as well as marriage? Or does it?) It is at all odds the Mariner's news for the Wedding-Guest that not only makes his tale more important than an outsider's attendance at a wedding-feast, but makes his news singularly pertinent to that position: namely, that such a position is unnecessary, even empty; that the expression of our intimicies now exists only in the *search* for expression, not in assurances of it. (If marriage is the emblem of intimacy it is equally the emblem of institutions. So friendship does have some institution, if it takes place within marriage.) If marriage so conceived, say, as letting yourself be loved devotedly and reciprocating the devotion (as if love were a ring), is the poem's hope against a false animation; if this is the poem's hope for and its recommendation of the intimacy with the world that poetry (or what is to become poetry) seeks; then it will not be expected that we can yet say whether this projects a new animism, a truer one, or whether the concept will fall away, as if outgrown. I would not call the poem an Antithalamion, but it is a fair enough warning about the stakes in play.

Since the stakes closely resemble those I find in the mysterious marriages, and their lacks of feasts, under observation in the best comedies of the Hollywood sound era, as well as the stakes in my preoccupations concerning skepticism, I can see that some may feel such results about Coleridge's poem are rather too good to be true. I hope that some will also try supposing otherwise.

The second of the sequence of four texts in which I propose to study the Kantian bargain with skepticism (buying back the knowledge of objects by giving up things in themselves) and Romanticism's bargain with the Kantian (buying back the thing in itself by taking on animism) is Heidegger's "The Thing," which I am taking as another effort, companion to Coleridge's, at the overcoming of the line in thinking, Kant's line to begin with.

Heidegger's essay gets us to Kant's question almost without our knowing it, over a Heideggerian path of questions that makes the Kantian seem simple in its familiarity. Heidegger's opening sentence is, "All distances in time and space are shrinking"; then further down the first page, "Yet the frantic abolition of all distances brings no nearness; for nearness does not consist in shortness of distance"; then on the next page, "How can we come to know . . . the nature [of nearness]? . . . Near to us are what we usually call things. But what is a thing?"; and on the third page, "What in the thing is thingly? What is the thing in itself? We shall not reach the thing in itself until our thinking has first reached the thing as a thing." This turns out to require "a step back" from the way we think to another way ("looking another way" Thoreau perhaps calls this). And close to the end the essay has: "Thinking in this way, we are called by the thing as the thing. In the strict sense of the German word *bedingt*, we are the be-thinged, the conditioned ones. We have left behind us the presumption of all unconditionedness."

What the essay is after is a return of human thinking around from Kant's turning of it upside down in his proud Copernican Revolution for philosophy: rather than saying that in order for there to be a world of objects of knowledge for us, a thing must satisfy the conditions— whatever they turn out under philosophical investigation to be—of human knowledge, Heidegger is saying that in order for us to recognize ourselves as mortals, in participation with earth and sky, we must satisfy the conditions of there being things of the world—whatever accordingly these turn out within philosophical thought to be. And this apparently means: The redemption of the things of the world is the redemption of human nature, and chiefly from its destructiveness of its own con- ditions of existence.

Is this a philosophy of Romanticism? If it systematizes something like the task of Romanticism in poetry, that is, if Romanticism believes, and it is right in its belief, that things need redemption from the way we human beings have come to think, and that this redemption can happen only poetically; then according to Heidegger's essay Roman- ticism would be right in believing that it is thereby a redemption of human nature from the grip of itself. And in that case the activity of poetry is the possibility of human life; so it is understandable that poetry takes itself, its own possibility, as its proper subject.

This, by the way, sketches out a response to one of the earliest and latest charges against the Romantics, to the effect that they prefer things to people, solitude to society. At a high level it is expressed in D'Alem- bert's rotten crack about Rousseau that he would not need so much to be by himself if he did not have something to hide. On a lower plane there is Irving Babbitt's Pastor Mandersish observation that "the hol- lowness of the Rousseauistic communion with nature" is one of Roman- ticism's "substitutes for genuine communion" (*Rousseau and Romanticism*, p. 235). And quite recently, in a review by Rosemary Jackson of some new books on the Romantics, Ruskin's views on the relation of political economy and "beautiful things" were linked with Wordsworth's, and he was characterized as one who, "while England was in the throes of Chartism and unemployment, was running around Italy collecting peb- bles and charting different colours of sky and stones."[4] Who would not prefer things to people who relate to oneself like that? They help to

---

[4]Rosemary Jackson, *Encounter*, June-July 1982, pp. 81–86.

make a desert and then blame us for being thirsty. They do not so much as treat us like things, things that think, great or small. (Perhaps Jackson is parodying the shrewish mocking that certain men attribute to their demanding wives when what the wives are demanding is simple equality.) It is almost enough, knowing what we know, to turn us into solipsists.

(I note that the years in which Heidegger was beginning to write his last essays, those after his so-called turn from *Being and Time*, were those in which John Crowe Ransom was writing *The World's Body*, another effort to link together the fate of poetry and of the experience of the world. From time to time I wonder [or wonder if it makes sense to wonder] what American intellectual life would have had to be for Ransom to have had a literary-philosophical culture comparable to Heidegger's within which to write. It was that culture, in Europe, that logical positivism had been formed to combat. When positivism was forced to America it had no natural enemies [it had in fact certain affinities with pragmatism], and the native intellectual culture had to take it on, as it were, single-handedly, hardly knowing what it was in for, as in the case of Ransom. I do not credit Heidegger with a better touch for literature than Ransom's, or Kenneth Burke's, or R. P. Blackmur's, or Paul Goodman's, but the Americans compose their theoretical works in a kind of scrip, good for exchanges at the company store but worth next to nothing on the international market. It may seem a kind of private language. [To say of the New Critics that they composed their theory privately or locally seems to me truer than to say, as I hear it said, that they composed no theory, or little. And then one might look more fruitfully for the cause of what theory they produced.] In bad moments it seems we have a choice only between this fate of privacy or that of fashion. But perhaps a better moral is a modification of the Mariner's: not everything is expressible in every country. [The case of England would of course be closer to that of America, though still quite distinct.])

Without lifting a finger now to lay out and to try to justify Heidegger's argument (roughly, that the recall of things is the recall, or calling on, of humanity), I point to the feature of it that poses to my mind, or let me say to the Enlightenment mind, the hardest barrier to this philosophical work, to our accepting this work as philosophy—its coming out with such propositions as the following:

The thing stays—gathers and unites—the fourfold. The thing things world.

That was published in 1950, when it would still have been fashionable for an analytical philosopher, had he (or just possibly, then, she) come across such propositions excerpted some place or other, to call them meaningless. More serious, or significant, for us now, I believe, is that we can see that such a term of criticism would have been offered with, or as, a kind of nervous laugh. I am confident enough that the older charge of meaninglessness, directed toward such propositions, has become quite quaint in its intellectual isolation: for not only can the meaning of those propositions readily be explained in the terms the essay, and its companions, set up; but the fact that apart from those terms—say, in what might be called cognitive terms—they would be meaningless is not only not a charge against the propositions, but the very heart of the teaching of which they are part. Those who teach them, or anyway say them, may be deluded; they may be frauds; but they are not speaking meaninglessly.

Yet I find that such propositions do project a barrier for me. It comes from my still not understanding the nervous laughter they still may at any time—to the post-Enlightenment mind—inspire. I interpret the nervousness as responding to another apparent exchange of knowledge for animism. But if Heidegger's idea of the thing as thing, gathering and uniting something or other, must be seen as expressive of animism, then what was presenting itself as a philosophy of Romanticism merely begs, it does not clarify, the questionable idea that keeps surfacing in Romantic texts, that there is a life and death of the world, dependent on what we make of it.

Have we arrived here at the bound of a hermeneutical circle, which we should undertake either to enjoy or to quit? Let us see if we can widen its horizons by glancing at the third of my sequence of four texts, the only writing I know within the Anglo-American analytical tradition that offers, even in passing, something like a rational justification of the idea of animism, John Wisdom's "Gods," published five or six years before "The Thing." Like Heidegger's, Wisdom's justification is led to propose a new view of, as it were, rational justification. Unlike Heidegger's work, Wisdom's, even at that period, would not have been treated by his tradition as laughable, yet by almost all the professional philosophers of my acquaintance then (or now, for all I know), also not, especially in its theistic open-mindedness, as much more than curious, or literary, possibilities, something for which as professionals they would have no serious *use*.

Wisdom investigates the idea of animism, or what he calls the hypothesis of minds in flowers and trees, by considering the question

"Do flowers feel?" He describes a context in which someone's treatment of flowers (one's caring for them, let us say) elicits from an observer the assertion, "You believe flowers feel." A year or two later Austin, in his much more influential essay "Other Minds," characterizes Wisdom's believer in the feelings of flowers as "holding a certain pointless belief"; it is one of Austin's few very drab moments in a superbly rich piece of writing. In "Gods," Wisdom claims that when the skeptic says to a man "You believe flowers feel," he feels that the man's treatment of flowers suggests an attitude inappropriate to them (though perhaps not to butterflies), even somewhat crazy, thus opening the question, I am sure deliberately, as to who is crazy. But why open it this way, by imagining it to be a liberal skeptic's description? It may be for just *that* reason that the man's treatment of the flowers is described in a way designed to invite, or incite, the suspicion of Pathetic Fallacy, because a skeptic can only imagine something like a projection of emotion in play, hence a suspicious projection, since *he* knows, so to speak, that flowers do *not* feel, or anyway that they are not animate, at least not as animals are, or not something.

Then let us hold off the explanatory hypothesis about believing that flowers feel (explanatory of what would make a certain way of treating them rational, anyway comprehensible) and instead imagine, if we can, someone's finding himself or herself struck by a treatment of flowers (a particularly nervous handling of them, or a special decorum in their presence, or a refusal to cut them, or perhaps a horror of cutting them, or a panic upon dropping them) in such a way that he is led to *consider* what flowers are, *what* it is he takes himself to know about what is and is not appropriate in our treatment of them. To consider, for example, that it is on the whole normal upon our meeting flowers to seek their odor; but on the whole not, with special exceptions, in the case of our meeting animals and persons; and on the whole not, it is worth adding, in the case of meeting stones and metals.

Wittgenstein says, in a famous passage, that if a lion could talk we could not understand him (*Investigations*, p. 223). Whatever one may wish to imagine about what a lion might, as it were, *say* if he talked, I take Wittgenstein's statement to mean that it is part of our understanding of human beings that (with understandable exceptions) they talk and part of our understanding of lions that (without exception) they do not, so that a lion's talking rather than roaring would not clarify for us, for example, why the lion is in discomfort. (It would, to say the least, perplex us in the extreme; in any case it would prevent our caring about his or her suffering then and there.) Recently an animal trainer and poet, Vicki Hearne, has published a remarkable account of some of her life with animals, "Talking with Animals,"[5] in which she alludes to my having said, in an early part of *The Claim of Reason*, that we can't talk to everyone about everything, and that we don't have to, but that there are some things we do have to talk about to everyone, if we are to talk to them at all. And then she goes further: "We have to talk to dogs about biting if we are to talk to them at all." Shall we say we are not really talking to the dog because the dog can give us no back talk? (Or can he? Let us grant for the moment that he cannot.) What else would you expect? If flowers could feel for us what we feel for them, we would not treat them as we treat flowers, for example, arrange them; not even lovingly.

In "Intimations of Immortality from Recollections of Early Childhood"—to turn to my final text—Wordsworth apparently claims to find not only that flowers feel but that they speak.

I preface what I can say about this poem here, dealing so briefly with so little of it, with three passages from Freud, as a kind of internal epigraph. I will say nothing about the relation of these passages to the poem's work, because either they will seem foreign material, in which case elaborating on them would make matters worse, or they will seem so native and pertinent that we could talk about them all night. The passages are from the case history, "Analysis of a Phobia in a Five-Year-Old Boy," which appears in Volume 10 of the Standard Edition.

> Surely there must be a possibility of observing in children at first hand and in all the freshness of life the sexual impulses and wishes which we dig out so laboriously in adults from among their own debris—especially as it is also our belief that they are the common property of all men, a part of the human constitution, and merely exaggerated or distorted in the case of neurotics. [P. 6]

> Any one who, in analysing adults, has become convinced of the invariable presence of the castration complex, will of course find difficulty in ascribing its origin to a chance threat . . . ; he will be driven to assume that children construct this danger for themselves out of the slightest hints, which will never be wanting. [P. 8, note 2]

> A few months ago—in the spring of 1922—a young man introduced himself to me and informed me that he was the "little Hans" whose infantile neurosis had been the subject of the paper which I published

[5]*Raritan*, 2 (Summer, 1982).

in 1909 . . . One piece of information given by little Hans struck me as particularly remarkable; nor do I venture to give any explanation of it. When he read his case history, he told me, the whole of it came to him as something unknown; he did not recognize himself; he could remember nothing; and it was only when he came upon the journey to Gmunden that there dawned on him a kind of glimmering recollection that it might have been he himself that it happened to. So the analysis had not preserved the events from amnesia, but had been overtaken by amnesia itself. [Pp. 148–49]

But I was about to speak of Wordsworth's listening to flowers.

Stanza IV of the ode ends as follows:

> But there's a Tree, of many, one,
> A single Field which I have looked upon,
> Both of them speak of something that is gone:
>   The pansy at my feet
>   Doth the same tale repeat:
> Whither is fled the visionary gleam?
> Where is it now, the glory and the dream?

(The speaking of the tree and the field and the pansy have, evidently, to do with their having been singled out from their kinds. That you cannot know individuals beyond the last of the species they belong to is a point of Aristotle's that may be pertinent here; I am not focusing on it.) And in the final stanza, XI, the poet is again present at their speaking. It opens:

> And O, ye Fountains, Meadows, Hills, and Groves,
> Forebode not any severing of our loves!

"Forebode" means foretell, or portend, so here speaking is interpreted as, let us say, bespeaking, forming an omen of something. And so the poet provides safer philosophical ground than we may have imagined for ourselves: it is easier for us—us English-speaking metaphysicians (to adapt the phrase Coleridge uses for himself)—to accept the idea of the earth as an omen, open to interpretation by us, than the idea, as in stanza IV, of the Earth as adorning herself, or, as in stanza VI, as filling her lap with pleasures of her own. Easier for an English-speaking poet as well, since this poem as a whole may be taken as a process of understanding and overcoming the unabashed Pathetic Fallacy that occurred in its opening stanzas, where the moon looks round her with delight, and land and sea give themselves up to jollity, and every beast keeps holiday. But in favor of what is this overcome, and why is it so hard? I mean, why is it, or why was it, when we were children, *natural* to us; an ordinariness which a new ordinariness must replace? (Or why does it, when we look back, present itself this way?) I note that the final stanza begins ("And O, ye Fountains . . . Groves . . . "), by for the first time in the poem speaking *to* preanimate nature.

Is this speaking to nature the replacement of taking nature to talk (back)? The idea should seem to us somewhat safer philosophically, I mean safer to take an interest in; but hardly perfectly safe, since our talking to nature ought to strike us as being nearly as crazy as being spoken to by it. Yet it seems to me worth trying philosophically to understand well, and to be the same as understanding what Wordsworth meant, in the Preface to the *Lyrical Ballads*, by "communicating with objects."

Coleridge will not allow Wordsworth to mean much, if anything, coherent by that phrase. In Volume II, Chapter XVII of the *Biographia* he says, criticizing Wordsworth's Preface: "If to communicate with an object implies such an acquaintance with it, as renders it capable of being discriminately reflected on; the distinct knowledge of an uneducated rustic would furnish a very scanty vocabulary." This willfully takes Wordsworth to be praising the rustic's knowledge, say, of the paths through his woods, as superior, *and in the same line*, as the knowledge that surveyors and cartographers could acquire of them. Not only does this refuse to interpret the preposition "with," as though what Wordsworth likes in his rustics is their ability to discourse in endless monologues about their belongings and neighborhood, as though they were veritable and boring Coleridges; but it perversely turns a deaf ear to Wordsworth's evident wish to speak of the kind of knowledge that is, let us say, wordless. Coleridge might have criticized Wordsworth for putting too much stock in such knowledge, or for aestheticizing, or we could say, Romanticizing it, but that is not what he does. When in his tremendous Chapter XXII he lists the "characteristic excellences" of Wordsworth's work, he cites "Fourth; the perfect truth of nature, as taken immediately from nature, and proving long and genial intimacy with the very spirit which gives the physionomic expression to all the works of nature." Here he has roughly glossed what Wordsworth, so far as I can judge, does mean by "communicating with objects," but instead of acknowledging this he persists in a view which takes Wordsworth, while having been granted by God an angel's capacity for singing, to have been allowed for theorizing the capacity of, let us say, a rustic. Coleridge thus romanticizes his own friend.

We might by now be able to think of the question of our communicating with objects as the question whether we and objects have access to one another; whether, perhaps like rooms that communicate with one another (or it may be caves), we are *near* one another, lead to one another, give ground.

A question for us becomes: Is there something we have to say to nature if we are to say some things at all? To say some poems, for example? I figure Wordsworth knows as much about such matters as anyone who ever wrote, and in concluding I indicate how I am approaching such writing, to ask it to speak again, to such a formulation.

In the line I cited in which the poet speaks to things, what he speaks to them about is their speaking, their foreboding. He commands them, or beseeches them, not to be omens of severing, presumably because he knows that severing is a reasonable thing for them to foretell; but the child ("Mighty Prophet! Seer blest!") may foresee another way. In the closing pair of lines the poet takes the communication further:

> To me the meanest flower that blows can give
> Thoughts that do often lie too deep for tears.

"Giving thoughts" is another formulation of bespeaking, and here what is foretold is something ambiguous about what can be expressed, or mourned for: are thoughts often deeper than grief, and would this mean as deep as joy? or do grief and joy have a depth that is inexpressible, or not fully expressible?

I will take in evidence mostly the single line: "Our birth is but a sleep and a forgetting." Since forgetting has to relate to the title idea of recollecting, which all will agree hearkens back to Plato's idea, or parable, of the preexistence, hence immortality, of the soul, let us take this statement philosophically, not (not merely, at any rate) as a description of a past event, indeed of the first event, in our biographies; but equally as a statement about the conditions of human birth, of the birth of the human, one that we, as we stand, might still suffer, sometimes called a second birth; a statement about the growth of the human mind after childhood. And let us put together with this the proposal that the child may take its life in terms of another major Platonic concept, buried in the sentimental stanza VII:

> The little Actor cons another part;
>
> . . .
>
> As if his whole vocation
> Were endless imitation.

Imitation, in Plato, refers to *participation*, of things in their forms, or, say, of time in eternity, as I imagine it does when we are asked to imitate Christ. In this poem, about recovering from the loss of childhood by recovering something of, or in, childhood (in particular, recovering its forms of recovery), we are to recover it, participate in it, by imitating it, as it imitated us (so imitating its endless readiness for imitation). This will mean participating in it by participating in what it participated in, for instance in remembering what it remembered, and in forgetting what it forgets (even perhaps in allowing it to forget); so imitating ourselves, or what we might become. In the line in question we are to participate in childhood's birth; which means to participate in our birth, in the fact, I would like to say, that we are natal, that we "[keep] watch o'er man's mortality" by recollecting his natality. If I call the poem Wordsworth's natality ode, this is to remind us, or to let Frances Ferguson's *Wordsworth: Language as Counter-Spirit* caution me, to go back to Milton's Nativity Ode. The connection, to my mind, is through the idea of the birth of the human, that it is the birth of a world, and that in the process old oracles are fled.

I take it amiss that Coleridge does not even try to determine why Wordsworth calls the child a philosopher. ("Thou best Philosopher, who yet dost keep / Thy heritage, . . . / Haunted for ever by the eternal mind.") I would like to answer in this way. The child is a philosopher because we are to learn from the fact of childhood, from the fact that we are the bearers of our childhood, Participation and Recollection; and initially by recollecting and participating in our own childhoods. These will be philosophical ways of letting childhood go, of bearing childhood as gone, as having become what we are, sharing our fate. It should be a productive way of putting aside childish things. It is the only path away from the sack of nostalgia, which we might think of, in opposition to remembering childhood, as the eternal reenactment of the past. (Its "acting-out." This concept of Freud's will come up again in the Appendix on Poe.) To thread through this difference between remembering and enactment I am taking as a task of Wordsworth's poem, call it a psychological task, or call it epistemological. It is a tract, or field, of instruction.

What we are instructed to recollect, to call back and to gather together, is a sleep and a forgetting. "Sleep" is characterized earlier as the region of fields from which the Winds come, which I take as pretty straight Romantic code for creative inspiration. And later the child's play is described as constituting "some fragment from his dream of human life." Hence in this respect to participate in the child's work, in his inspiration toward life, is to recollect the dream of life, as from fragments, as if the whole vocation of becoming human, of suffering birth, were endless participation in such a dream, that human life will come to pass. Only so can we recollect that we as we are are not yet the fulfillment of this dream.

"Our birth" occurs to me as a kind of abandonment: the clouds are of glory, but we only trail them; not in utter nakedness do we come, but not fully protected either. In which context "not in entire forgetfulness," as well as suggesting a past setting that was home, to my mind suggests, something other readers apparently do not share, a grudge, anger, at being deprived of this home for a sojourn on this earth. I suppose that *all* our feelings for childhood lost are feelings to be found intimated in childhood itself ("all that is at enmity with joy"), angers as well as griefs. Then merely to long for childhood is to ignore what the joys of childhood come from, its separations, its anxieties. To capture that braver joy, to have a new birth, requires a new sleep, a new forgetting.

"A forgetting" names not a thing forgotten but an activity, a process of some kind; not a lapse of memory but a success of forgoing, of giving something over. This is spiritually dangerous. Childish things can be put aside vengefully, which is not giving something over. The way recommended, so far as I have understood it, in the idea of a forgetting that constitutes a birth, lies in forgoing the grief and anger in abandonment, the one by God the Father, and the one by the Child who is father to the Man. (I do not mean to assume that this way is acceptable, as it stands, to the Child who is mother to the Woman; certainly not when following a poem about birth.) And the way lies in accepting relief such as timely utterance can give, lacking full depth, complete expression, as things of time will be lacking; and in willing nevertheless to say you are strong again, recovered as from an illness. In stanza X:

> We will grieve not, rather find
> Strength in what remains behind.

Among other things, grief suggests grievance, as relief suggests legal remedy. To get a remedy for a grievance is to receive some recompense. This has a strength, but not the strength of birth. To get relief from the thought of grief is to know that nothing can "bring back the hour / Of splendour in the grass," to let time lapse so that there can exist a "new-born Day," hence to "find / Strength in what remains behind." What remains should not compensate, but it may yet suffice. Suffice, perhaps, for more present angers. The twin of grief, which I just called grievance, fails to bring relief, release; it ties us to pastness because it is a modification of vengefulness: it makes getting even a condition of being the odd one one is, one's having that to recollect and to imitate that one has; so it is always pitching one's battles on alien ground.

We moderns are likely to imagine that the giving up of the ground of revenge is the *effect* of therapy. I take the Intimations Ode to be saying on the contrary that this forgoing is the *cause*, or say the condition, of change. We do not know where the inspiration to give up revenge comes from. Much of its poet's energy has to be spent in a kind of re-seduction (as do much of the energies of Heidegger, and of Wittgenstein, not to say Freud), because our powers of being drawn from elsewhere ("we come from afar"), of being interested, in heaven or in earth, are deadened. Otherwise we would not require birth, or poetry, or philosophy.

What remains of the "vision splendid" is that it "fades into the light of common day." Such is Wordsworth's construction of the ordinary. Shall we take this, as I suppose it commonly is taken, to be the same as a going out? But "fades into" does not *say* "fades out." It may propose some other mode of becoming, a happier disillusionment, so that the vision is preserved in the way in which it is forgone. Wordsworth's construction is to replace the ordinary in the light in which we live it, with its shades of the prison-house closing upon us young, and its custom lying upon us deep almost as life, a world of death, to which we are dead—replace it accordingly with freedom ("heaven-born freedom"); and with lively origination, or say birth; with interest. How far can the vision be preserved and lived? What remains of interest to us? What for us is remains? We must turn to that.

APPENDIX
POE'S IMP: SKEPTICISM AS PERVERSITY

Looking back at Robert Penn Warren's essay on *The Ancient Mariner*, I see I had forgotten that he adduces the following paragraph from Poe's "The Black Cat."

In the meantime the cat slowly recovered. The socket of the lost eye presented, it is true, a frightful appearance, but he no longer appeared to suffer any pain. He went about the house as usual, but, as might be expected, fled in extreme terror at my approach. I had so much of my old heart left, as to be at first grieved by this evident dislike on the part of a creature which had once so loved me. But this feeling soon gave place to irritation. And then came, as if to my final and irrevocable overthrow, the spirit of Perverseness. Of this spirit philosophy takes no account. Yet I am not more sure that my soul lives, than I am that perverseness is one of the primitive impulses of the human heart—one of the indivisible primary faculties, or sentiments, which give direction to the character of Man. Who has not, a hundred times, found himself committing a vile or a silly action, for no other reason than because he knows he should *not*? Have we not a perpetual inclination, in the teeth of our best judgment, to violate that which is *Law*, merely because we understand it to be such? This spirit of perverseness, I say, came to my final overthrow. It was this unfathomable longing of the soul *to vex itself*—to offer violence to its own nature—to do wrong for the wrong's sake only—that urged me to continue and finally to consummate the injury I had inflicted upon the unoffending brute. One morning, in cool blood, I slipped a noose about its neck and hung it to the limb of a tree;—hung it with the tears streaming from my eyes, and with the bitterest remorse at my heart;—hung it *because* I knew that in so doing I was committing a sin—a deadly sin that would so jeopardize my immortal soul as to place it—if such a thing were possible—even beyond the reach of the infinite mercy of the Most Merciful and Most Terrible God.

Some of this can indeed sound similar, should, to the view I have taken of the Mariner's killing of the bird. Poe's view and mine both assert some relation between the wish to be loved and the fear of it, and between this conflict and the sense that one's existence lies under some metaphysical suspicion. The views also seem opposite, since mine takes the moral to demand that one accept the claim of others as the price of knowing or having one's existence, whereas Poe—rather, Poe's narrator—asserts the denial or annihilation of the other as that price. I might try to fix the distance between these views by noting my having said (in the closing pages of *The Claim of Reason*) that Othello kills Desdemona not because she is faithless and disperses love but on the contrary because she is faithful, because the very reciprocity of the thing he has elicited from her is what makes him feel sullied; whereas Poe's words are, "hung it because I knew that it *had loved* me" (my emphasis), which, if this means that the love has now been withdrawn, however understandable the cause, would be a reasonably understandable case of rage and vengefulness.

But then again, are these views so different? Poe's (narrator's) revenge is still taken because he was loved, perhaps because he feels the love was too little, or because love is too little. Whereas to murder or abandon, as Othello does, because the love of you persists, is hardly an acceptable return of love, perhaps feeling that the love was too much, or because love is too much. The views seem closer and more distant than this makes out.

I have claimed that skepticism is our philosophical access to the human wish to deny the conditions of humanity, relating this, as well as to Kant's vision, both to Christianity's and to Nietzsche's hopes for the human to be overcome. Along this line we might understand Poe as asserting that skepticism itself is the best assurance of existence, as if skepticism's very will to emptiness should draw us to it. This apparently perverse account of skepticism (turning its effect into its cause) bears to familiar philosophical accounts of skepticism something like the relation Poe's paragraph from "The Black Cat," in its arrangement of sin and law and the Most Merciful and Most Terrible God, bears to St. Paul's account of such things. As if it reads Paul's saying that there were no sin but for the law to advise: break the law. One may take this as an insight into Christianity or as a parody of it.

What I am calling Poe's perverse account of skepticism does, I think, capture an essential perverseness in skepticism, at once bearing an insight into skepticism and enacting a parody of it. The insight is that skepticism, the thing I mean by skepticism, is, or becomes necessarily, paradoxical, the apparent denial of what is for all the world undeniable. I take skepticism not as the moral of a cautious science laboring to bring light into a superstitious, fanatical world, but as the expression of a demonic reason, irrationally thinking to dominate the earth. I take it to begin as a wish not to reject the world but rather to establish it. The parody is to deny this, to conceal the longing for assurance under an allegedly more original wish for self-vexation. This concealment is revealed at the end of the confessional stories, when the walls (inner or outer) are broken open and the repressed returns. But if the murder of the world (or the soul) will out, in these stories the end is as perverse as the beginning, or rather the perversity is still unmoved, still original, and tragedy and its recognition are still deflected into inscrutably multiplied ironies. (G. R. Thompson, in introducing his selection of Poe's short works speaks of Poe's writing "as the work of one of the greatest ironists of world literature."[6])

Poe's view, so characterized, is a materialization, no doubt ironic, of the most familiar understanding I used to hear of philosophical skepticism in school, and one that I believe retains a certain currency yet. It is the view, roughly, that skepticism's repudiation of knowledge is merely a function of having set the sights of knowledge too high: *of course* if you impose the idea of absolute certainty on knowledge, you will not find that we know anything (except perhaps mathematics, together with what, if anything, is given to the senses); *of course* if you

[6]*Great Short Works of Edgar Allan Poe* (New York, 1970).

try to turn induction into deduction, induction will seem wanting; *of course* if you demand that in order to see an object you have to see *all* of the object, then we can never really or directly or immediately *see* an object. (I give other examples of this pattern, especially with respect to the question whether a critical paraphrase, say of a metaphor, is really a paraphrase, in *Must We Mean What We Say?*, pp. 76–77.) So skepticism is just the cause of the disappointments of which it complains. People have said this about philosophy as a whole. And earlier, in the body of this essay, I alluded to a similar understanding of Romanticism, as wanting in its disappointments (say, in melancholy or withdrawal) exactly what cannot exist.

I did not understand how a philosopher could claim to be satisfied with such an understanding of skepticism, in the absence of an understanding of what, and how, a human being, call him or her a philosopher, would be drawn to "set the sights" so, drawn to just *this* form of self-defeat. Now, however, as a version of Poe's discrimination of perversity, it begins to make sense to me. What I am to conceive is that the self-defeat of skepticism is precisely the point of it. —But does this finally make sense to me? Or is its *not* exactly making sense something I should further regard as precisely its point?

I do not, as I said, object to the idea of perversity as a description of the skeptic's outcome; I accept it as a kind of translation of the paradoxicality which is an essential feature of the skepticism I mean. It is, as elsewhere, the attitude that rings false to me, or forced. (But does attitude much matter where what is at stake is the truth?) As I do not take the owner of Pluto—for that was the cat's name—to feel about the wife into whose head he buried an axe just the way Othello feels about the wife he suffocated, so I do not take the narrator committing and confessing his denials to be the Cartesian or the Humean or the Kantian thinker bringing himself back from, or giving himself up for, his deeds of doubt, back to the brink of the common world.

The attitude I am pointing to is one typically presented upon the promulgation of a paradox. When Pythagoras proved what has been called the incommensurability of the long side of a right triangle with the other (equal) sides, also called its measurement by an irrational number, some were frightened, some tried to keep the secret confined to an institution of intellectuals, some, I dare say right at the beginning, took it as a cosmic joke on humankind. Something similar will have happened in this century when Gödel's proof of formally undecidable propositions became known. So some seem to find these attitudes congenial toward the discovery that there are no marks or features by which to distinguish dreams from waking life, or fiction from fact, literature from life, as though this kind of indistinguishability made them identical—as though literature and life were known to be familiar objects and the issue remaining were to decide whether they are to be counted as one or as two. —Well, if not a sense of absurdity, or of ironic pleasure or pain, at the dashable hopes of humankind, what attitude would you recommend? —None.

I might describe the attitude I find myself resisting, the posture I would alter toward the events of horror in Poe's stories, as one in which the narrator is "acting-out" a fantasy or an unconscious impulse, as opposed (as Freud does typically oppose "acting-out," thus partially defining it) to remembering something, an opposite way of bringing the past into the present, a way that brings the promise of a freedom from the violence and the alienatedness of the impulsion to repeat.[7]

Since remembering is the organ of that way of philosophizing to which I am drawn, naturally I am distrustful of what would oppose it. Sometimes you could call this the merely literary, or impulsive playfulness, which may sometimes take the form of a technical and seemingly rigorous discourse. Far be it from me either to take it for granted that psychoanalysis has made sufficiently clear Freud's distinction between repeating and remembering, or to take Poe the writer as sufficiently like his narrator to be indistinguishable intellectually from him. But whether Poe (the name here, as will emerge, of a writer of two tales) is sufficiently unlike his narrator to draw on our (of course I mean my) philosophical interest, is a function of how interesting and convincing an account his discourse provides by way of grounding the notion of perversity; of, that is to say, accounting for the human temptation to deny the conditions of humanity, or in other words, the will to be monstrous.

I will sketch in a few lines one way I find this grounding can be made out for Poe's writing, looking at his "The Imp of the Perverse" (mostly, really, looking to derive its title) in a way he had predicted in "The Black Cat" that someone will want to look at what he does—thus impishly goading the unsuspecting, even the suspecting, into the attempt: "Hereafter, perhaps, some intellect may be found which will reduce my phantasm to the common-place—some intellect more calm, more logical, and far less excitable than my own, which will perceive, in the circumstances I detail with awe, nothing more than an ordinary succession of very natural causes and effects." I also take as my guide the opening sentences of that tale:

---

[7]See the entry under "Acting-out" in J. Laplanche and J.-B. Pontalis, *The Language of Psycho-Analysis*, trans. D. Nicholson-Smith (New York, 1973).

For the most wild, yet most homely narrative which I am about to pen, I neither expect nor solicit belief. Mad indeed would I be to expect it, in a case where my very senses reject their own evidence. Yet, mad am I not—and very surely do I not dream. But to-morrow I die, and to-day I would unburthen my soul. My immediate purpose is to place before the world, plainly, succinctly, and without comment, a series of mere household events. In their consequences, these events have terrified—have tortured—have destroyed me. Yet I will not attempt to expound them.

Here is the stock-in-trade of the opening of a skeptical investigation of the existence of the external world: the claim not to be mad, to reject the evidence of the senses, to consider and to reject the possibility of dreaming, and the orientation away from ordinary belief; we are given household events, ones we cannot, in a sense, fail to be familiar with, which will turn out, on consideration, to undermine what we have hitherto taken as our basis in existence. (I say we are "given" these events, thus at the outset dodging an issue dear to epistemologists, and perhaps to literary theorists. Poe's word for his act of production is "to pen," suggesting both "unburthening" [is this like singing a refrain, or refraining?] but suggesting also confining, like imprisoning or impounding. Then no wonder he says he will not "expound", i.e., let something go, de-pen it.)

"The Imp of the Perverse" is if anything more firmly, or stays longer, in an essayistic, or rather meditative, mode, before turning to (turning into) its story. It opens by claiming to have discovered an original motion of the mind hitherto overlooked by philosophy and religion, one that is itself unmoved, hence an unmoved mover in ourselves, which would, I guess, accordingly not only prove our existence but prove our immortality. It is no use saying that this claim to be philosophizing on this writer's part, even ontologizing, is meant ironically. You can as well say that the irony would be for the claim to be taken so. (Is it then Poe's peculiar brilliance to have discovered a sound, a sound, let us say, of intelligence, in which not the reader and not the writer knows whether he or she is philosophizing, or, say, seriously thinking, thinking, as it were, to some end? This can be an insight about philosophy, one shared by Socrates and Heidegger and Wittgenstein at least; namely, that it is as difficult to stop philosophizing as it is to start, to de-pen as to pen.)

The giveaway in "The Imp of the Perverse" (but beware of such writers bearing giveaways) is the series of what I will call imp-words that make an appearance throughout the sixteen paragraphs of the tale: there is impulse (several times), impels (several times), important, imperceptible, impossible, unimpressive, imprisoned, and, of course, Imp. Moreover, "imp.," is used as an abbreviation, according to the American Heritage Dictionary, for imperative, imperfect, imperial, import (and imported and importer), important and imprimatur; the Random House Dictionary adds impersonal, implement, in the first place, improper, improved, improvement. Let us add that "Imp.," is an abbreviation for Emperor and Empress. (Marc Shell tells me that he came across the abbreviation "Imp" endlessly in the days he was reading coins. Possibly it crossed Poe's mind that the phrase "the imp of Satan" can be taken to mean that Satan *is* Imp.)

If to speak of the imp of the perverse is in the first place to name the imp in English, namely as the initial sound(s) of a number of characteristically Poe-ish terms, then to speak of something called the perverse as containing this imp is to speak of language, specifically of English, as the perverse. But what is it about the imp of English that is perverse, hence presumably helping to produce as users of language, us imps?

It is, I hypothesize, the prefix "im-" that is in the first place felt as perverse. Then the "imp" would go on to specify the set of Poe-ish preoccupations, as with impulses and imprisonments or impoundings and with the improbable and the impossible and the impressive and the imperceptible, and also philosophical and religious preoccupations with imperatives and imperfections and imprimaturs and impieties and with implanting as a word leading back to ideas of coming into existence. What is perverse about the prefix "im-" is that, like the prefix "in-", it has opposite meanings. It is sometimes a negation or privative, as in immediate, immaculate, imperfect, imprecise, improper, implacable, impious, impecunious; and sometimes an affirmation or intensive, as in imprison, impinge, imbue, implant, impulse, implicate. (It is not impossible that per-verse, applied to language, should be also followed out as meaning poetic through and through.) In plain air we keep the privative and the intensive well enough apart no doubt, but in certain circumstances (say, in dreams, in which, according to Freud, logical operations like negation are not registerable or picturable, but are to be supplied later, by the dreamer's interpretation) we might grow confused as to whether, for example, immuring means putting something into a wall or letting something out of one; or whether impotence means powerlessness or a special power directed to something special; or whether implanting is the giving or the removing of life. And which is it in implacental? Suppose ourselves, at critical junctures, to fail to know the direction of any and all of the imp-words, so that we face perversity in our concepts of implication, imperative, imprecation, imprudent, impolite, impolitic, etc. Then we may know ourselves as the demons and children of the language, perhaps to be its Emperors—while we rule, say write. Here are the last sentences of the tale: "Today I wear these chains, and am *here*! Tomorrow I shall be fetterless!—*but where?*" (Fetterless; expounded.)

So the question as to the existence of myself, or creation of myself, is modeled by the existence of a writer, who exists simultaneously with the writing, only as it is being written, uttered. Users of language, humans are creatures of language, exist only from it, as equally it exists only from us. If one is perverse so is the other. If we cannot speak (if, e.g., we have something so horrible to say that it either cannot be said or cannot be believed) we are inhuman. If the responsibility for speech is suffocating, you might think to enact a deed so horrible that speech seems impossible; you might choose to become a monster. (Here it may be worth comparing Wittgenstein's speculation concerning what a private language would be.)

Such speculation may seem too much to be impelled to by an ordering of three letters. If it seems arbitrary, you might try to find a string of three others that have analogous properties. Whatever the fruits of such a search, the very possibility of it may be its most important feature. For word imps are not confined to a fixed sequence of letters; but, so it seems suggested to me, are constituted by any of the recurrent combinations of letters of which the words of a language are made. As with Cartesian skepticism, the nature of an example or two is everything. When the narrator of "The Imp of the Perverse" asks us to question our own soul in order to find undeniably "the entire radicalness of the propensity [viz., perverseness] in question," the example he thereupon appeals to is the torment "by an earnest desire to tantalize a listener by circumlocution," which is to say, the torment of the desire to tell stories, which is what becomes, as this tale manifests, even of the desire to write philosophy—thus using himself (who else would a skeptic invoke?) as the image or scapegoat of mankind. And he comments: "That single thought is enough." (I will not stop to make it plainer that the narrator, in saying "I am one of the many uncounted victims of the Imp of the Perverse," is declaring that his tale is about writing, about what penning convicts you of, or commits you to, and about who pens whom. But I cite just two sentences of the tale, without comment, for going over in the kind of light this writer sheds. "One day, whilst sauntering along the streets, I arrested myself in the act of murmuring. . . . " "I have said thus much, that in some measure I may answer your question [it is the first time we learn that we readers have a question], that I may explain to you why I am here, that I may assign to you something that shall have at least the faint aspect of a cause for my wearing these fetters.")

Words have their familiar looks and sounds, and their familiarity depends upon our normally not noticing the particles and their laws which constitute them, which is above all to say, their necessary recurrences. It is this necessity, the most familiar property there could be of language, that if there is to be language, words and their particles recur, that language is a system, in a word that words and their parts are impish, that ensures what we may think of as the self-referentiality of language. When we do notice these molecules, these little moles of language (perhaps in writing, perhaps in derangement) *what* we discover are the imps of language (however spelled), the initial movements, the implanted origins or constituents of words, staring back at us, leading lives of their own, their tongues wagging, giving us away, all the more alarming because they are in front of our eyes all the time. Like the Poe in poetry or in Poena or poenology; or even like the sinbearing thought in the phrase "single thought." Our perversity is no more original than our sin, if no less.

I mention even more briefly one further region of the unsayable in Poe's tale, a region that is not a function of the imps in language but of ourselves as its imp and image; our power of affirmation (without which there is no assertion), hence of denial.

Years after the narrator had committed a perfect crime, impossible to detect, the narrator's imp presented itself and made detection possible.

> I would perpetually catch myself pondering upon my security, and repeating, in a low undertone, the phrase, "I am safe." One day, whilst sauntering along the streets, I arrested myself in the act of murmuring, half aloud, these customary syllables. In a fit of petulance, I remodelled them thus:—"I am safe—I am safe—yes—if I be not fool enough to make open confession!"

That is, "I am safe" is true as long as it is not said; saying refutes it. More famous sayings whose saying refutes them are "This statement is not true" and "I do not exist." It may occur to you that (therefore) "I exist" is necessarily true, or undeniably true each time it is said, a reasonable interpretation of what Descartes says in proof of the Cogito. But you equally cannot safely say "I am not safe." (Hence this example is unlike other unsayables, like "I am not here" and "I am asleep." These are pleasantries, and their negations are, in certain circumstances, informative.) One's safety, or lack of it, is unknowable. What can be known is the fact of one's existence, and whatever follows from that.

222

Philosophers such as Descartes and Kant and Heidegger and Wittgenstein may agree on this point, and vary completely in what it is they find to follow. One may further try out the thought that the knowledge philosophers such as Marx and Kierkegaard and Nietzsche (and you may say Freud) begin from is that we do *not* exist, and vary in what they find follows from that.

It seems reasonably clear that Poe's (narrator's) search for a proof of his (her?) existence (in the confessional tales I was citing) is for a proof that he is alive, that he breathes. "I am not more certain that I breathe, than that the assurance of the wrong or error of any action is often the one unconquerable *force* which impels us, and alone impels us, to its prosecution." Assume that he is betraying here an uncertainty that he breathes; and then turn around his comparison of certainties. The imp of himself here apparently gives him to think that he is not *less* certain that he breathes than that there is the impulsion in question. So his certainty of breathing becomes dependent on his impulse to wrongdoing. In Descartes the capacity for "the wrong or error of any action" is the proof of the possession of free will. For Descartes it follows that we are responsible for our error because we are free not to refrain from it (in particular, free to judge beyond the knowable). For Poe we are responsible metaphysically for our errors exactly because we are not morally responsible for them. I *am* the one who cannot refrain. Some moralists are of the view that when I do what I am impelled to do, the action is not exactly mine. Poe's view seems to be that in such case the responsibility is never discharged—it sticks to me forever. Of course not all actions are of such a kind, but only ones that show what I have been calling the inhuman in the human, the monstrousness of it, ones that, I would like to say, come before and after morality: an example Poe gives of the former is the desire to tantalize in telling a good tale; examples of the latter are the more baroque Poe-behaviors, gouging out the eye of the cat, axing your wife, almost without provocation. The implication is that morality is stumped at certain points in judging human nature, a fact that should illuminate both. If there is a target of satire here, it is those who say they believe in determinism, who do not appreciate how free we are (capable of things it is hard to imagine) and how far from free (incapable of resisting this imagination).

"The Imp of the Perverse" opens with an explanation for our having overlooked perversity as a *primum mobile* of the human soul—all of us, the "phrenologists" and "all the moralists who have preceded them." The explanation is: "We saw no *need* for the impulse—for the propensity. We could not perceive its necessity. We could not understand, that is to say, we could not have understood, had the notion of this *primum mobile* ever obtruded itself;—we could not have understood in what manner it might be made to further the objects of humanity." And a little further on:

> It will be said, I am aware, that when we persist in acts because we feel we should *not* persist in them, our conduct springs from the *combativeness* of phrenologists. But combativeness is our safeguard against injury. Its principle regards our well-being. . . . It follows, that the desire to be well must be excited simultaneously with any principle which shall be a modification of combativeness, but in the case of that something which I term *perverseness*, the desire to be well is not only not aroused, but a strongly antagonistical sentiment exists.

Is this antagonistical sentiment a sentiment to be ill, which here must mean a desire to be injured? Say if you like (G. R. Thompson says it in the introduction to his edition of Poe cited earlier) that " 'The Imp of the Perverse' clearly spells out Poe's fundamental conception that it is man's fate to act against his own best interests." But I see no original desire for self-injury in the tale, however much self-injury results from the events. True, the imp may have to forfeit perverseness as a "safeguard against injury"; it will not be that kind of need that the evolution of perverseness can be understood to serve. But perhaps it is a safeguard against something else, something more original, even humanly more needful—a safeguard against annihilation, the loss of (the proof of) identity or existence altogether. (I am perhaps cagily masking the question as to what the proof of human life would primarily be directed to, to its existence or to its identity. To say both are in question is easy, if doubtless true. The question is as to priorities.) God's existence has been said to follow from God's identity. Human existence no more follows from its identity than the existence of a stone is assured from a description of a stone. But unlike a stone, a human identity is not assured, as certain existentialists used to like to say, from the fact that a human being exists. Romantics are brave in noting the possibility of life-in-death and of what you might call death-in-life. My favorite Romantics are the ones (I think the bravest ones) who do not attempt to escape these conditions by taking revenge on existence. But this means willing to continue to be born, to be natal, hence mortal.

One has to distinguish *what* condition it is that proofs of my existence are supposed to, or do, prove; what question it is one has to answer. Descartes's proof proves my existence as mind, it answers the question "Am I a mind or a body?" Psychoanalysis has distinguished the question "Am I a woman or am I a man?" from the question "Am I alive or dead?"—the former as the hysterical question, the latter as the obsessional. Obviously I am taking the latter as Poe's question. But I earlier complicated what this will mean by in effect giving him the question "Am I a human being or a monster?" (I have said a few words about these questions in "On Makavejev on Bergman,"[8] in relation to *The Claim of Reason*.)

The desire to be well is preceded by the desire to be. And against annihilation, ceasing to exist as the one I am, there is no safeguard, none suppliable by the individual, not even God's hand in our creation; its safeguard is the recognition of and by others. (So saying "I am safe" may save you after all.) If at the same time this recognition of and by others strikes you as threatening your life, you will be perplexed. I think we all more or less know of this perplexity. But to struggle with it by impulsively or obsessionally proposing that to gain proof you have to create (to be the author of) what there is to confess, as though there is nothing to acknowledge but in such confession, is trivial. It is trivial in comparison with the effort to acknowledge your unauthorized life as it is, taking an interest in it. Some will, I think, wish to say that there is no way one's life is; to me this betokens a refusal to try putting it into (provisional) words (a refusal to struggle for its authorship).

Poe's Perverseness may be seen as a parody of the vulnerability, the dropping of safeguard, in the placing of interest, in Poe's cases, the investment of love, the inevitable risks in its improbabilities. The truth of the parody is its measure of the pain these risks run, of how far our lives take on and maintain their forms by their need to ward off abandonment.

QUESTIONS AND ANSWERS

Question: In your quest for the ordinary, you seem to be using the term "ordinary" in a normative or value-laden sense. You speak, for example, of the accomplishment, the achievement, and, above all, the redemption of the ordinary. And you locate the ordinary not in popular culture but in such exceptional writers as Thoreau, Wittgenstein, and the English Romantics, writers whom most "ordinary" people find incomprehensible or maybe even fraudulent. Film is the single exception to your looking for the ordinary in high culture. You seem, in short, to oppose "the ordinary" to the popular or the common, or those things that are statistically or empirically ordinary, ordinary in the

[8]Reprinted in Stanley Cavell, *Themes out of School* (Berkeley, 1984).

sense of average or in the sense of falling within the experience of most people, like a Norman Rockwell painting. Instead of "the ordinary," then, why not use a more obviously honorific term like "the human" or "the natural" or "the real" or "the necessary"? I'm not asking you to comment on the disadvantages of these other terms but to defend the advantages of the term you have chosen. If "the ordinary" is so special, if, as Gus Blaisdell claims, it terminates in a vision of society in which every individual wills and respects the freedom of every other individual, then why call it "the ordinary"?

Answer: The quest for the ordinary is not usual—say, not popular. But it is also not the opposite of popular—say elite. For me it is philosophy, which is also not usual, but not because it has to be for experts. If it is for the few, that is not because it must refuse admittance but because the many will avoid its doors. I need my title—"In Quest of the Ordinary"—to be ambiguous. I need the ambiguity of quest and inquest to be there. In order to achieve the ordinary, there is going to have to be an autopsy on what we call the ordinary. As Thoreau saw, we are extraordinary creatures because of what we pick to be ordinary. I am in quest of the ordinary—and not, say, the "natural"—first of all because of my insistence on being faithful to the philosophy that I felt I wanted to inherit, the philosophy of J. L. Austin and Wittgenstein, for me two of the paradigmatic philosophers of this century. Their words for the thing they are after is what Austin calls ordinary language or Wittgenstein calls everyday language. Now there is, of course, an endless controversy about what that means, and my kind of study has been to find out what we mean by that. I first sensed that this pursuit was not an isolated or merely technical philosophical adventure on their part when I read Beckett's *Endgame*, a play that on the surface could not seem more remote from the way academic philosophy is taught. Beckett portrays a sense of ordinariness denied and, in particular, a sense of extraordinariness captured as ordinary, regarded as ordinary. Here was the first link that I saw between ordinary language philosophy and the modernist cultural movement. Thoreau, in the opening pages of *Walden* describing his fellow citizens' lives, also sees that what we call ordinary is extraordinary. His countrymen are torturing themselves, doing what mystics do when they blind themselves by staring at the sun or when they roast themselves over fires. "Quiet desperation" is also a description of what we call everyday life. But from what position is everyday life accepted? Our own dissatisfaction with the everyday is a pointer to the fact that "the ordinary," in my use of the word, is also the normal. Thoreau is writing to that dissatisfaction. The thing that we are to arrive at in Thoreau is another life to call ordinary, another thing that will be actuality for us, something neighboring or next to the world we call ordinary. This other life will not have despair in it, or business, self-laceration, and so on. Who knows what that would be like? Well, only William Blake, as far as I know, may know what that actually would look like. But the philosophers that I've been working with don't have such a picture, and it's extremely important that they don't. Heidegger, in his lesser moments, I think, tries to paint such a picture in *Being and Time*. Heidegger's word for the everyday is "averageness," and he in some sort of way loathes it the way Thoreau does, but the problem for me in reading Heidegger is that he doesn't understand it. He's incapable of describing it in even remotely the concrete way that Thoreau is. Heidegger, too, says that there is no way out of the everyday, no way to his famous idea "authenticity" but through a modification of life as it's lived. I can never believe in Heidegger's "authenticity" anymore, however, and partly because I can't believe in the description of the life of which "authenticity" is to be a modification. And all of this turns on the accurate description of what our lives are like; there is no other way to motivate this "quest for the ordinary."

Question: Why should philosophers in particular—Wittgenstein, for example, and Austin—be drawn to this quest for the ordinary?

Answer: What "the ordinary" meant for Austin and Wittgenstein above all was some effort to hold philosophy as traditionally conceived at bay, to resist the abstraction of philosophy, both because philosophy is itself natural to us, so at all moments has to be opposed, and because it invisibly approaches us, so you can't will yourself not to think philosophically. Philosophy is insidious. All creative philosophers as far as I can tell want to force philosophy as it stands to an end, to bring it into question. That becomes their dominating motive. In previous philosophers, Descartes, Locke, and Hume, for example, the ordinary is opposed to metaphysics. Opposition to metaphysics motivates philosophy in a tradition that culminates in a figure like Kant, who gives the critique of reason in such a way that we will always be able to spot reason's distortion of itself, or false philosophy and false religion. Put differently, skepticism is what all of these philosophers took as their way of bringing philosophy to an end. They had two tasks: to oppose skepticism and to oppose false answers to skepticism. This is above all why Kant is the major philosophical figure behind what I understand of Romanticism. He provides an answer to skepticism that brings us back to the world, but his answer at the same time removes the world.

Kant says it is a scandal to philosophy that there are skeptics who can deny that we know objects. But, for him the objects we know could not be objects for us without meeting the conditions of human knowledge as such. And, says Kant, by the way, there is indeed something we can never know, and I'm going to call that the thing in itself. Post-Kantians have been tortured by that solution ever since, feeling that what Kant gives up knowledge of is exactly what we wanted to know. And I'm regarding that response to Kant as already the tension in this quest for the ordinary. We live in this world, but the dissatisfaction with this world points not to an escape from it but to another way of living in it. And Kant called this definitively the requirement of the acceptance of limits or conditions in epistemology. And the minute somebody has said there are conditions and limits in human knowledge, immediately you have another name for the human dissatisfaction with the human condition. Who else but the human being could be described as just that creature dissatisfied with being human? The quest for the human is an internal, inescapable feature of being human.

Question: You mention that some philosophers, Wittgenstein and Austin, leave their picture of the ordinary blank, or fail to assign it any positive content, whereas Heidegger in his lesser moments unsuccessfully tries to picture it. Does the desire to picture "the ordinary" separate literature from philosophy?

Answer: I don't know. That is, if it is not the difference, it is certainly the border that any of these writings must cross and recross and cross again. It's one of the places where philosophy doesn't know if it's poetry, and poetry doesn't know if it's philosophy. I am not even saying that they are different, but only that this question of how can you describe "the ordinary" is at all times on my mind. How far can you envision it? I'm an ignoramus about Blake, but I think he may be the deepest of all, and exactly about these things. I feel Blake is just around the corner for me, but not yet. I'll say, however, this much about him: he has the vision in his bones that philosophical skeptics have to fight and toil for and don't know what to do with. In such a pair of lines as "How do you know but ev'ry Bird that cuts the airy way / Is an immense world of delight, clos'd by your senses five," Blake captures (at least) the skeptic's feeling that the world is not known to the senses. There is something about the senses themselves that won't allow us the right access to the world, and everybody who has learned from skepticism has said that, too. That's one thing that Blake pictures of which skepticism is a piece. But Blake proceeds to take a step that for me is essential to thinking about all these matters and that I think

Romantics generally take, and that no philosopher, I think, but Wittgenstein, and maybe Heidegger, has taken, which is to say that skepticism can be lived. Something that I mean by skepticism can be lived—the avoidance of the ordinary, whatever that is, the thing before the world comes back. And that's a life, an ordinary life, and what now has to happen is to describe that life in its various phases. That is, what you have to say is something like: for Blake, not just the mind, but the mind in all its phases and spirit makes a world. There's a world to build. Christians can say that, too. The religions say that sort of thing. I want philosophy to be able to say this sort of thing too. I want philosophy to be able to say there is a world made by the skeptics. Heidegger calls this world averageness, Thoreau calls it quiet desperation, Emerson calls it passive melancholy and Wittgenstein calls it the feeling of being bewitched. He says it politely. He says bewitched by the forms of ordinary language. But what he says is we are bewitched! The question is, does he use a poetic word like "bewitched" only to take a little academic vacation from propriety, or is he serious? In *The Claim of Reason*, I derive this world created by skepticism from our being driven to use words outside their ordinary language games. I say that you can do that, if you are driven to. That's a world. The ignoring of these questions, that is, the antiphilosophical effort to put aside these visions, also creates a world. It's a way to live. Cynicism about the folly of being human also makes a world. All these are postures that you can take. This is the message I'm getting from Blake. They are all ways you can live. The skeptic concludes that perhaps we don't know there is an external world and stops with that. I want to describe what that would look like if we lived it, as mostly we do live it. In short, describing what happens to the human spirit under the onslaught of that spiritual possibility called skepticism is worked out in what I know of Blake better than in any other poet I can think of. Presumably Hegel also takes you through every conceivable stage of the human spirit, but when I read Hegel I sometimes don't know whether he's captured a place I've been. But when I read Blake, often I have the feeling, yes, I know that's out there somewhere.

Question: I would like you to comment on your use of literary texts, in particular the English Romantic works that you cite in the last part of *The Claim of Reason*. Do literary texts simply illustrate or confirm what you have already learned from philosophy, or do they teach you something new?

Answer: I'm looking in these texts not for illustrations, but for allegories, experiments, conceptual investigations, a working out of this complex of issues, and I claim that that is what they are, that's what produces these texts. I am drawn, for example, to a phrase from the Preface to the *Lyrical Ballads* in which Wordsworth says what we set out to do in these seemingly simple poems is to make the incidents of common life interesting. Part of what I want to do is just talk about what a mouthful that is. Those words are the high point of practically all these studies I've looked at. I'm not simply going on the fact that Wordsworth happens to use the word "common," one of Emerson's favorite words, one that's an interpretation of the everyday. "Common" is an answer to skepticism, because it's an overcoming of isolation. What you feel in skepticism is that there is nothing common between you and anyone else. That's again a life. You can certainly lead that kind of life. And to a certain extent, many of us do, here and there in the shadows all the time: lives of narcissism, lives of hidden feelings of exceptionality which have to do not with the fact that you are unrealized but that you are better than somebody else. But the word in Wordsworth's statement that absolutely went through me was the word "interest." To interest. Whom are you saying that to? It's an immense word for Thoreau. It's an immense word in *The Senses of Walden*, this mild word, "interest." To interest people is to revive them from, another of Wordsworth's big words, "torpor." You could also call it spiritual death. And the answer to their torpor is to interest them. And all of that lies behind these Romantic war horses that I am looking at and is also meant to say why Austin and Wittgenstein were not just avoiding some little task in neglecting to say what they meant by the word "everyday." It's just as hard to say what they meant by that as it is hard to say what it is like to interest people who have run out of interest, who can no longer take an interest in their lives.

Question: In Wordsworth, the power that is going to allow him to do this is the imagination. Do you have any thoughts about the Romantic imagination?

Answer: "Imagination" in that context is another word for bringing words back. Just where Wittgenstein says bring words back, Austin says, "I want you to imagine an ordinary case in which. . . . " But I don't want to move from that practice to any known property of the imagination. I don't want to use the concept of imagination as a way of not having to think. Like many other people, I've learned a lot, I hope, from having read M. H. Abrams, Geoffrey Hartman, Paul de Man, and Harold Bloom on these topics. I'm not talking about some of their recent work so much as the work in the sixties and the early seventies when they lived and died with Romanticism, before the theoretical controversies that, you may say, either grew out of that work or allowed them not to think anymore about that work. But in them, the philosophical apparatus that they appealed to, virtually the only one you can appeal to, has to do with the problematic of consciousness, of self-consciousness, and with imagination, namely, the work of Kant and Hegel. That is where Coleridge also went in order to find out what it was he was doing. And in the course of trying to figure out Kant, and Hegel, and the imagination, Coleridge developed his own theory of the imagination, which is decisive for these later critics. And I say for me, philosophically, nothing more is going to come out of thinking too soon about that specific issue, the imagination. It's there. It's what there is to think about. But first one has to think about the practice that this word is supposed to explain. What Blake means by imagination, for example, is no simpler than Blake. You're not going to get that first and then try to figure out what Blake says. And you're not going to get imagination out of Coleridge without thinking out what Coleridge says. Now let's remember what sort of thing it is to look at the imagination in Coleridge. There are books, you know, libraries on Coleridge on the imagination, and nine tenths of the critics that I have looked at over the years go to Coleridge on the imagination and start trying to tease out from his work what he really means by "imagination," as if once you really found that out, then you'd know what all the Romantics are trying to do. Let me describe to you Coleridge's first volume of the *Biographia Literaria*, one of the strangest books known to me in the English language. One of the reasons I couldn't read it for ages was because of the despair in it and the hopelessness of its philosophical enterprise. He wanted to do nothing less than rewrite the history of human thought. Maybe everybody worth his or her intellectual salt wants to do something like that at some stage in life. And you may keep it in the back of your mind, but you don't let everything else in the world you want to do wait until you have done that. But Coleridge spends eight chapters in the *Biographia* rehearsing the history of philosophy. It is a hopeless history, hopelessly sketchy and private. Coleridge then makes his big turn, as we all do in these matters, to the German philosophers, whom he summarizes, quotes, and, people say, plagiarizes. If you or I crib a little something, that's plagiarism. But if Samuel Taylor Coleridge cribs stuff from Germany, don't you feel you need another word for it? Instead of picking out Coleridge on the imagination as a solution, then, I have a proposed alternative route, at least to stay afloat in thinking about these things. Instead of saying, with Bloom and others, that the dominating spiritual problem in Romanticism is the relation between consciousness and nature, I say my dominating spiritual issue is the relation between knowledge and the world, or between skepticism and the world. The problematic of knowledge and skepticism, the denial of knowledge, promises an access to the writing that we all care about, and it is a problematic over which I feel I have won some intellectual control.

Question: Can you explain why you haven't written much about Blake even though you admire him?

Answer: I feel seduced by Blake as well as threatened by him. If I ever leave the ordinary for his high prophecies and mythology—I am speaking here of the later Blake—I am not sure that I will ever find my way back.

Question: Are you trying to resolve the problem of skepticism by using the ordinary to form a bridge between the self and others?

Answer: I'm saying that skepticism wouldn't be threatening unless it deprived you of your ordinary, everyday world. It's that world, not some fancy world filled with atoms and molecules, that the skeptic says we don't know. If it were a fancier world, then we could say, "you can have that world." But it's tables and chairs and other people that are the stakes. The effort to arrive at the ordinary just is the problem posed by skepticism—the skepticism I care about.

Question: Could you comment on the politics of your quest for the ordinary? Does the recovery of the ordinary necessitate or lead to social change?

Answer: Skepticism is not a problem to be solved; accepting it (its threat, not its self-interpreted conclusion) is a further working out of human nature. Skepticism isolates you, it makes others inaccessible. I would not, however, translate the recovery of the ordinary as bringing the community back. We have lost nothing we ever *had*. Any politics I would claim for my quest is bound to utopian leanings. Skepticism is one name for the possibility of refusing our present historical condition as natural. And I do not imagine a future present at which this refusal will become unnecessary; which is to say that Utopia is not, as the word says it is not, a *place*. The community that would emerge if we got all that right we cannot get right beforehand. In fact, the only place I've ever even suggested that I have an image of such a community is in the book about movies you alluded to. No doubt that is as much a reason I write about movies as the fact that they are popular. These movies offer a quasi-utopian invention of what such an eventual community might look like. But even here this community is only enjoyed by two people.

Question: But what happens to these individuals if the rest of the society doesn't change with them?

Answer: They might become Romantics, and suffer the bad split, telling everyone else: "I know what the real world could be like. It's no different from this one. It's right at hand. Nothing to it. All you've got to do is simply be redeemed, and you'll have it. Slough the skin. No reason it doesn't exist. It's our madness that it does not."

Question: In the preface to the *Lyrical Ballads*, in addition to searching for ordinary subjects and ordinary styles of expression, Wordsworth also suggests that the only way he can materialize all this is by retreating into the study, recollecting emotion in tranquillity. Is that a different task from the search for the ordinary?

Answer: It's the impulse that you would have if you were to achieve it through art. If the thing we wanted to achieve was the life of the rustic and the low, then the two things you would have to do would be to recapture pleasure in your life and to have the thing Wordsworth calls communication with the most worthy objects. So you imagine saying to him, If that's what you want, why don't you just do that and not go off to your study to write about it? My answer to that partly is that Wordsworth is doomed to art. The world is such that he can only imitate being rustic and low. Then the wonder is that he *can*, which I say means he can participate in them. I'm particularly interested in Wordsworth's going to his study, because it's exactly the study that Hume says he is going to leave as a relief from these terrible thoughts of skepticism. Wordsworth's honesty as a poet depends on how he gets back to the study. And aren't there two possibilities? One is that he says to himself, I'm a poet and am going to go back to my study and recollect this, and then I'll publish the poem. Or he can say, the recollection is upon me. I'd better go find a place in which I can let it happen. Call that place the study. And then he gets this thing back and writes the poem. In that case, to go to the study to let the recollection flower is a kind of curse, a Romantic curse, if you like. But, if he's right, it's also a rebuke of the world. The world is such that the study is the place where I can now recollect some topics and not seem freakish and distracted and not have to answer to this or that. The oldest and the latest criticism of the Romantics is that they like things better than people, as when D'Alembert says to Rousseau, You wouldn't have to be alone so much if you didn't have something to hide. That is the most perfectly dirty remark you could ever make to Rousseau, or to any Romantic, the ones that I know. The answer of course is to ask, Why do I have to hide? What kind of world have you given me from which I want to hide?

Question: In your reading of Wordsworth's ode, you suggest that Wordsworth experiences a kind of skepticism at the beginning of the poem which he then overcomes as the poem progresses. Could you further explain the presumably antiskeptical affirmation that he comes to by the end of the poem?

Answer: There are two cautions about what you just said. The first caution is that I don't so much want to insist that he begins with a confession of skepticism as I want to offer that as some kind of interpretation of skepticism. The word "skepticism" I am being very cautious about, and I want to use it as closely as possible to the way the history of modern philosophy has used it. And until I started studying the Romantics, I had no idea that they used the word as often as they did. I had known that it was in Coleridge. He sometimes does, sometimes does not, seem to mean what Descartes, Hume, and Kant, say, mean by the word "skepticism"—and not just the word but the experience. I want to maintain that the tragedy of skepticism can be lived. I am, in effect, questioning whether skepticism is an on-and-off experience in which you are either in the study or else you have gone out and forgotten it. What I am looking for is the perseverance of that skeptical experience outside the study. Now you can say skepticism is adolescent. And, of course, there is something about skeptical philosophy that is adolescent, as perhaps there is about metaphysical speculation generally. Adolescence is the time when for many of us these doubts most readily scar you. When you get to be an adult, you don't *just* put aside all that. You do something with it, to it. I'm using the opening of the Wordsworth poem, as I am the image of the Ancient Mariner, to suggest that there is something about the problem of knowledge that is inherently tragic. And this tragedy has to do with my setting inquisitions on myself, say the inquisitions of acquiring knowledge of a certain kind, pictures of a certain kind, in Wittgenstein's language, that do not satisfy our real need. I want the Intimations Ode and the rest of the Romantic texts that I use not just to illustrate a prior philosophical problem of skepticism, but themselves to be interpretations of the same problem, to be as ground-floor, if that's the right metaphor, as philosophy itself. I start there, with Wordsworth's sense of something wrong, which is an interpretation of skepticism. Now, from that opening, I say there is no recovery in the poem. Take the line when he says we'll find strength in what remains behind, in the primal sympathy which having been must ever be. You read that one way and it sounds like pious, steady Wordsworth. But the way I'm reading it, the "must" is both a demand and a logical question mark. It *must* be. But *why*? *How*? That's the theme I want in this whole poem, a poem of faith, no doubt, but not of achieved convictions.

Question: But when Wordsworth suggests that the child's "first affections" are "yet the fountain-light of all our day," doesn't he claim to recapture the feeling of intimacy with nature that he is missing at the beginning of the poem?

Answer: But the only signs of there being such a fountain-light are "shadowy recollections." Say you can recapture those, but then what is it to recapture shadowy recollections? You recapture those shadowy recollections, which are a form of forgetting, by imitating childhood—in its forgetting. Plato's theory of recollection is unarguably in the poem, but I'm taking "imitation" as an equally Platonic word. It's as big a word in Plato as "recollection." What it means in Plato is the participation of objects in the forms or time in eternity. And that sense of imitation now means that what we're to do is not to imitate childhood by getting on the floor and playing with toys. As St. Paul tells us, we put aside those things. But we nevertheless participate in childhood by sharing its dream of human nature, its feeling ("high instinct") that we move about "in worlds not realized." Our birth, in other words, still lies ahead of us, and to be born we've got to imitate the thing in us that was already born, namely, ourselves as children. To do that we are instructed to sleep and to forget. To sleep is to be subject to the fields from which the wind comes. That's inspiration. To forget is to forget what childhood forgot—its home. We are to forget grief—"we will grieve not"—but also we are to forget the anger at abandonment. We're still grieving, but we *will* grieve not, rather find strength in what remains behind. You can look at that as wanting something made up for. But I'm saying nothing is going to be made up for. What remains may suffice, but we do not know that. That's where I think the poem ends, with the sense that our birth is but a sleep and a forgetting, and that you are not getting born until you are forgetting and that's a process. Forgetting is not a thing that you forgot. It's the process that you are accepting. I interpret the forgoing in forgetting as a forgoing of revenge. For us modern liberals, it looks as though forgetting our anger and grief is something that you get out of one or another form of therapy. My favorite form is psychoanalytic therapy. But there are lots of therapies. I mean we moderns are going to look upon redemption as some kind of therapeutic process. And certainly, the Romantics are involved in something like redemption. But this poem says the first thing you do is give up revenge. And then the therapeutic process can begin, has begun. There are even psychoanalysts who think that, too. I believe Sigmund Freud in invoking the death instinct was talking about this process. I gather nobody knows what inspires you to be willing to forgo justified grievances. We all are aggrieved. I'm still trying to see what it is that gets you to take that first step, the forgetting that has to happen first.

Question: You are saying, then, that the poem is urging us to forget the "high instincts"?

Answer: No, that the high instinct is a call to forget, to forgo the grievance you have against not being a child, the grievance the child already has in the discovery that it is a separate creature.

Question: Would faith be another name for this "high instinct"?

Answer: Rather than saying skepticism is resolved by faith, I would say that Wordsworth is declaring a faith that it can be resolved by forgoing these grievances in a birth which lies ahead of us. Natality is a problem for Wordsworth here the way mortality is a problem for any other philosopher. We can all say we are going to die, that is to say, that we are mortal. But then a good philosopher will say, Yes but that's the question. We don't know what it means to know that we are going to die. So, the comparable paradox with having been born is that we also don't know what that means and we are going to take that as having not yet happened. I'm taking the line, "Our birth is but sleep and a forgetting," not as a description of something that happened to us, but as a philosophical description of what a human life is. That is what it's like to get born.

Question: Could you contrast Wordsworth and Coleridge to the American Romantics you have been studying?

Answer: I think that the hope of Thoreau and Emerson, their commitment to the abandonment of despair, is absolutely what I'm talking about here in forgoing revenge. I would add that I also feel a special anguish toward Emerson and Thoreau that comes from their remaining unknown to the culture that they founded. Emerson and Thoreau are unshared by this culture. Of course, isolated bands of individuals know all about them. But they are not cultural possessions in remotely the way that in Germany Goethe and Schiller, for example, are cultural possessions. Emerson and Thoreau taught us the tongue, established American thinking—and they are repressed. Now that's already an extraordinary cultural position to be in. And I think they already knew that their words were not going to get through. That is a source of their anguish. Another source is that they want us to recognize ourselves as being on the road to something. They had this hope for America as such, not just for themselves, whereas in the Wordsworth poem, as far as I can see, this is not a hope for England. In the Intimations Ode at least, there is something like a reseduction of the individual, an invitation to go through an individual process. But the screaming going on in Emerson and Thoreau and the horsing around about whether I'm with you, or in front of you, or a mile away, are attitudes adopted to convert a nation.

Question: "Acknowledgment" is a crucial term in your quest for the ordinary as well as in your approach to skepticism. To clarify what you mean by "acknowledgment," can you give me a metaphor for acknowledgment, perhaps reaching out to something and grasping it?

Answer: "Acknowledgment" is important to me in marking the convergence between the continuous problematic of skepticism from the time of Descartes and the problematic in Shakespearean revenge tragedies. And that's, if you like, one of those discoveries that's no discovery. After I'd written an essay about *King Lear* in which I used the word "avoidance" as the opposite face of acknowledgment, I thought, What is news about that? All the Greek tragedies are about recognition, too. I next turned to *Walden*, the source of the deepest reflections on this issue that I know of. I take it that what is wrong with the gesture of trying to grasp something as a metaphor for acknowledgment is exactly the sense of possessiveness. Possessiveness and jealousy seem to me as good a way of interpreting skepticism as doubt is, ones I plan to work out. But *Walden* can be said to be all about possession, or owning, and owning in *Walden* is described not as grasping or holding, but as sitting. This is part of my view that you have to take Thoreau in *Walden* as a quasi-mythological character, each one of whose actions is to be interpreted partly as an allegory of writing, but also partly as an allegory of his journey, which is not finished in *Walden*. The last line of that book says that the sun is but a morning star. That means there are more days to dawn. We are only so far. But "morning" meaning "dawning" is also a pun on "mourning" meaning "grieving." I called *Walden* a book of losses, an accounting for the losses, adding up the losses, and so on. Now the first major place sitting occurs in *Walden* is, I believe, in the second chapter where Thoreau says that he used to sit down on all the farms in his neighborhood and live there, live there in a Thoreauvean way for an hour. Then he claims he owned all those farms by sitting there his way for an hour, and leaving. Now, that's Thoreau both horsing around and being in dead earnest. Track the notion of owning or possessing by sitting, and look at all the places he sits. You have to sit to write. Of course you have to sit to relieve yourself, too. He talks about that as well. He admires the religious treatises that can talk about that without any smirk on the face. That's human. Of course, we live in these bodies. What are you going to do about that—deny it? You've got it; you've got to put it someplace. You've got to hold it somewhere. You have to place it someplace. You've got to be in one posture or another. One of the great postures he talks about, then, is sitting—to read, to write, and to own. And, drawing on all these meanings, I say that one way of putting acknowledgment is owning, say owning up. It seems important to me to say that that conceptual development is not metaphorical.

Question: You illustrate your discussion with examples from "literature." How do you define "literature"?

Answer: I don't have an answer to that which seems to me worth sitting on. Practically everything I've done for years now addresses or glances at that question: What are the literary conditions of philosophy, What are the philosophical conditions or aspirations of literature? You say the texts that I pick are literature, but they don't come at me as literature. I don't care where the libraries file them, or in what departments the politics of universities put them. The fact of the matter is that it would be very hard to say what *Walden* is from my point of view. And it ought to be very hard to say what the *Biographia Literaria* is. I ask you. Is *Walden* literature or philosophy? And I hope you don't know. A big achievement for me would be that we as a culture, as a university culture, would agree that we didn't know. And that would make nicely for an upsetting state of affairs. *Walden* is taught in no philosophy department that I know of, except occasionally by an individual who happens to teach it on sufferance. In no literature department that I know of would someone be willing to lay it on the table as a work of philosophy. In the *Biographia Literaria* I see for the first time that I know the explicit questions, is it poetry? is it philosophy? is it religion? is it politics?, coming to the fore as the anguishing, central motivating topic of a great work of—what? I mean if the *Biographia* is about the redemption of these things by one another, what's the *Biographia*? If poetry and philosophy require redemption by one another, then the clear title to the book is the redemption of poetry and philosophy by one another. That's the topic. Is that a department in a university? The Department of Redeeming. That's what it should be. The Romantic quest that I want to join is the one that Coleridge lives.

Question: You have said that *Othello* could be read as the allegory of a philosophical problematic. Does that mean that you are simply expanding the uses that philosophy has always had for plots? When Austin talks about language or when Wittgenstein does, they often end up weaving little stories based on some word or other, and those often end up to be miniature plots. You also seem to make use of plots. Do you have a favorite affection for the plot of tragedy because of its association with skepticism?

Answer: Certainly I'm encouraged to look at these plots as expansions of philosophical problems by the examples of my masters. But these philosophers are in turn inspired to do that because of the way that thought can exist in storytelling. I want storytelling already to be thinking, so that "allegory" is an open word for me. I want to keep open my sense that these tragedies of revenge are things to think from, that revenge is a plot in all senses. It is not just my favorite, but I mean to be asking why revenge is something like the favorite plot of tragedy, and why the favorite plot of comedy is the overcoming of revenge. Of course, I'm being guided by various examples in my past, one of them being Nietzsche, who looks at the overcoming of revenge as the thing that will either redeem us or annihilate us. If I take skepticism as the favorite philosophical story, then I am trying to find a way to describe skepticism not so much as tragedy but as an interpretation of what tragedy itself interprets, life's dissatisfaction with itself.

Question: You have aligned comedy and tragedy on either side of skepticism. And you associate tragedy with dissatisfaction, comedy, I assume, with satisfaction of some sort. Do you see any uses for romance and irony?

Answer: I regard irony as a kind of tragedy, a deepening of dissatisfaction, and romance as the deepening of what comedy is laughing about.

Question: Would you say that the Romantics failed to overcome skepticism?

Answer: I don't think they did fail, either in imagination or in doing what humanly, individually, was to be done. I think they may in their later lives have failed to see where they got, but that's for personal, historical, all kinds of reasons. But I don't regard that as a personal failure. If that's a failure, it's a failure of the world. Coleridge may have felt that he failed to solve the problem of skepticism, but I don't regard that as his failure. I regard that as to his credit, because I regard him as being involved in the winds of that problem, in the deserts, the seascapes, and the frozen terrain of that problem. Coleridge is tortured by his own promise, his reputation as the most *promising* man. That's the myth of Coleridge. But Coleridge projected this myth onto Wordsworth and kept saying, you're withholding this from me, and Wordsworth labored and suffered under this accusation. So although I'm not going to say they failed at something, I will say that they felt that they had failed at something.

Question: I think I'm responding to your reading of Wordsworth, to your point about his not quite getting beyond skepticism.

Answer: There isn't any stable way to get beyond skepticism, I mean beyond its threat, or temptation.

Question: Would you say then that they did not accept that?

Answer: You want me to accuse them of something. I'm saying that one of the reasons that these poems are the great masterpieces and permanent treasures that they are is that they are instances of grasping, of living, this human tragedy, you may say comedy. These works do not deny either side, neither the terror nor the high questionings and aspiration. I am thankful for them.

Notes on Contributors

M. H. ABRAMS, Class of 1916 Professor of English Emeritus at Cornell University, is the author of *Natural Supernaturalism*.

STANLEY CAVELL, Walter M. Cabot Professor of Aesthetics and the General Theory of Value at Harvard University, is the author of *Themes out of School*.

MORRIS EAVES, Professor of English at the University of New Mexico, is coeditor of the journal *Blake/An Illustrated Quarterly* and author of *William Blake's Theory of Art*.

MICHAEL FISCHER, Associate Professor of English at the University of New Mexico, is the author of *Does Deconstruction Make Any Difference?*

NORTHROP FRYE, University Professor at the University of Toronto, is author of *The Great Code*.

J. HILLIS MILLER, Frederick W. Hilles Professor of English and Comparative Literature at Yale University, is the author of *Fiction and Repetition*.

W. J. T. MITCHELL, Professor of English and Art and Design at the University of Chicago, is editor of the journal *Critical Inquiry* and author of *Blake's Composite Art*.

Index

Abrams, M. H., 49, 87, 93, 94, 122, 123, 230; "Behaviorism and Deconstruction," 158, 163; "Construing and Deconstructing," 111–18; "Five Types of *Lycidas*," 171, 174; "How to Do Things with Texts," 162, 174, 179; *Mirror and the Lamp*, 175, 176; *Natural Supernaturalism*, 166–67, 177, 178; "What Is the Use of Theorizing. . .?," 164
Addison, Joseph, 32
Alter, Robert, 29
American Revolution, 25
Anderson, Donald M., 61n, 84n
Aristotle, 100, 127, 170, 196, 209
Arnold, Matthew, 96, 164
Aspinal, Arthur, 55n
Aucassin and Nicolette, 24
Auden, W. H., 25
Auerbach, Erich, 99
Austin, J. L., 93, 130, 185, 186, 187, 226, 228, 230, 238; Derrida's commentary on, 136–37; "Excuses," 196; "Other Minds," 189–90, 207

Babbitt, Irving, 204
Barthes, Roland, 160
Bate, Walter Jackson, 119, 124
Bateson, F. W., 145n
Beckett, Samuel, 185, 226
Benjamin, Walter, 104, 147
Berkeley, George, 47
Bible, 15, 16, 17, 31, 45, 59, 63, 88, 89, 163–64, 166–67

Blackmur, R. P., 205
Blaisdell, Gus, 226
Blake, William, 26, 29, 32, 37, 86–91, 93, 95, 165, 167, 168–69, 183, 190, 226, 228, 229, 231, 232; *All Religions Are One*, 59n, 84; *Book of Urizen*, 56–59, 83; "Can Wisdom be put in a silver rod?", 172; *Europe*, 71; *French Revolution*, 59n; *Illustrations to the Book of Job*, 65–69, 75–81; *Jerusalem*, 59n, 65–66, 71–72, 80, 84, 60–62; *Marriage of Heaven and Hell*, 59n, 71–75, 83–84; *Songs of Innocence and of Experience*, 55–56, 84; *There Is No Natural Religion*, 59n, 84; and writing, 46–86
Bloom, Harold, 39, 90, 91, 230, 231
Booth, Wayne, 98
Borges, J. L., 98, 120
Brooks, Cleanth, 119, 121, 145n, 169
Bruno, Giordano, 24, 40
Bruns, Gerald, 65
Burke, Edmund, 50, 52, 54, 56, 58, 59, 62
Burke, Kenneth, 93, 100, 119, 121, 199, 205
Butlin, Martin, 68n
Byron, George Gordon, Lord, 93, 169

Campion, Thomas, 18
Carlyle, Thomas, 52, 59
Cavell, Stanley, 91, 92, 94; Beckman lectures, 183, 187, 195; *Claim of Reason*, 183–87, 192–93, 195, 197–98, 208, 215, 225, 229; "In Quest of the Ordinary,"

Cavell, Stanley (*cont.*)
  226; *Must We Mean What We Say?*, 185,
  187, 217; "On Makavejev on Berman,"
  225; *Senses of Walden*, 230
Céline, Louis Ferdinand, 40, 41
Cézanne, Paul, 43
Champollion, Jean François, 83
Chandler, James, 93
Charles I (of England), 59
Chaucer, Geoffrey, 18, 24
Chester, Robert, 20
Christianity, 216. *See also* Bible
Coleridge, Samuel Taylor, 32, 33, 52, 59,
  60, 93, 167, 175–76, 181, 186, 187,
  190, 209, 226, 231, 234, 236, 239; *Bio-
  graphia Literaria*, 49, 53, 188, 194, 210,
  212, 231, 238; Dejection Ode, 183,
  197; *Lay Sermon*, 54; *Rime of the Ancient
  Mariner*, 188, 191, 192, 193–203, 214,
  215
Condillac, Étienne Bonnot de, 60, 83
Condorcet, Marie Jean Antoine Nicolas
  Caritat, Marquis de, 58, 59, 60
Cowley, Abraham, 21
Crabbe, George, 93
Cromwell, Oliver, 60
Cruden, Alexander, 46
Curtius, Ernst Robert, 64n

D'Alembert, Jean le Rond, 204, 233
Damon, S. Foster, 77
Dante Alighieri, 18, 22, 30, 37, 63, 64
Darwin, Charles, 24, 26
Davies, Hugh Sykes, 145n
De Man, Paul, 91, 104, 122, 126, 128,
  142, 146–47, 170, 230
Denck, Hans, 28
De Quincey, Thomas, 29, 30
Derrida, Jacques, 100, 115, 126, 172,
  173; Abrams's treatment of, 113; ahis-
  toricality of, 167–68; appeal of, 124,
  141–42, 161–62; as construer of texts,
  179–80; and Blake, 89, 90; and
  K. Burke, 119; *La carte postale*, 113;
  "Differance," 140; *Dissemination*, 132,
  142; "Freud and the Scene of Writing," 64; *Glas*, 120; and grammatology,
  48; and Hume, 128–40; "Living On:
  Border Lines," 136, 137–38, 142; on
  metaphors, 175–76; Miller's reliance
  on, 149, 151; and modern literature,
  160–61; *Of Grammatology*, 130, 138,
  140; pedagogical use of, 155–58; philosophers' reaction to, 161–62; politics
  of, 86–87; and reading, 114; and

Derrida, Jacques (*cont.*)
  Romantic poetics, 51; on Rousseau, 38,
  58, 116, 134–35, 138; "Signature Event
  Context," 133, 134, 136, 142; *Signe-
  ponge*, 113; "Structure, Sign, and Play,"
  123, 130, 131, 133, 134, 140; and tra-
  ditional literary criticism, 159; "White
  Mythology," 121; on writing, 88
Descartes, René, 95, 101, 183, 189, 192,
  217, 221, 222–23, 224, 226, 234, 237
Dewey, John, 92
Disraeli, Benjamin, 61
Donne, John, 20, 26, 169
Dryden, John, 37

Eaves, Morris, 56n
Eden, 167, 188–90, 194–95
Eisenstein, Elizabeth, 52
Eliot, George, 118, 123, 156
Eliot, T. S., 37, 38, 167
Emerson, Ralph Waldo, 185, 187, 191,
  229, 230, 236
Empson, William, 100, 119, 121
English Revolution, 59, 89
Erdman, David V., 56n, 58, 62n, 65, 74
Essick, Robert N., 82n, 91

Ferguson, Frances, 212
Fish, Stanley, 92, 98, 120, 173–75
Fletcher, Giles, 21, 25, 50, 51, 52, 53n,
  55, 58, 59, 88, 89, 178
Freud, Sigmund, 26, 64, 151, 172, 208–9,
  212, 214, 218, 220, 223, 235
Frye, Northrop, 90, 94, 99, 123, 158,
  165–66, 167; *Anatomy of Criticism*, 31,
  33, 34; *Critical Path*, 41; *Fearful Symmetry*, 86, 89; *Great Code*, 29, 31

Galileo, 24, 40
Gardner, Helen, 38
Gasché, Rodolphe, 124
Gay, Peter, 52
Gelby, I. J., 47n
Genet, Jean, 120
George III (of England), 56
God, 201, 202, 210, 213, 215, 216, 224
Gödel, Kurt, 217
Goethe, Johann Wolfgang von, 41, 236
Gombrich, Ernst, 46, 85
Goodman, Nelson, 92
Goodman, Paul, 205
Graff, Gerald, 124
Graves, Robert, 28
Gray, Thomas, 37
Greville, Fulke, 19

Hardy, Thomas, 26
Hartman, Geoffrey, 91, 128, 230
Hazlitt, William, 34, 52, 53n, 54, 88
Hearne, Vicki, 208
Hegel, G. W. F., 120, 123, 158–59, 178, 229–30
Heidegger, Martin, 113, 120, 187, 214, 219, 223, 226, 228–29; *Being and Time*, 205; "Das Ding," 192, 203–6; "Origin of the Work of Art," 104–5; *What Is a Thing?*, 105, 151–53
Hill, Christopher, 59n
Hilton, Nelson, 82n, 91
Hirsch, E. D., 94, 98, 145n
Hitler, Adolf, 41
Hölderlin, Friedrich, 28, 41, 122, 167, 178
Hulme, T. E., 38
Hume, David, 183, 217, 226, 233–34; and Derrida, 128–40; *Treatise of Human Nature*, 129–39
Husserl, Edmund, 113

Institute for Poetics and Semiotics, 99

Jackson, Rosemary, 204–5
James, Henry, 45
Jesus, 192, 212
Johnson, Barbara, 170
Johnson, Samuel, 32–33
Jones, Rufus, 167
Joyce, James, 27, 37
Jung, Carl Gustav, 123

Kant, Immanuel, 119, 126, 183, 190–91, 194–96, 203–4, 216–17, 223, 226, 228, 230–31, 234; "Conjectural Beginning of Human History," 188; *Critique of Pure Reason*, 184, 188
Keats, John, 49, 93, 95
Kierkegaard, Sören, 201, 223

La Belle, Jenijoy, 63n
Lamb, Charles, 45
Laplanche, J., 218
Lawrence, D. H., 25, 27, 37
Leavis, F. R., 37, 171
Lessing, Gotthold Ephraim, 50, 83n
Levine, Herbert, 29
Lévi-Strauss, Claude, 123
Locke, John, 226

McLuhan, Marshall, 87
Mallarmé, Stéphane, 123, 168
Marvell, Andrew, 19, 37

Marx, Karl, 24, 26, 43, 86, 89, 92, 95, 100, 124, 223
Meredith, George, 125
Michelangelo, 63, 74
Middle Ages, 43, 91
Mill, John Stuart, 128, 181
Miller, J. Hillis: "Function of Rhetorical Study at the Present Time," 120, 125, 163; *Linguistic Moment*, 121; "On Edge," 123, 126, 142–58, 162–64, 169–71, 176, 178–80
Milton, John, 17–18, 40, 53n, 63, 89–90, 120; *Areopagitica*, 41, 51, 59; "Lycidas," 169, 171, 174–75; Nativity Ode, 22, 212; *Paradise Lost*, 19, 22, 27, 196; *Paradise Regained*, 22
Mitchell, W. J. T.: *Blake's Composite Art*, 63n, 68n; *Iconology: Image, Text, Ideology*, 47n; "Politics of Genre: Time and Space in Lessing's *Laocoon*," 51n; "Spatial Form in Literature," 47n; "What Is an Image?", 47n
Moore, G. E., 189
Morris, William, 84n
Morton, A. L., 60n

Narcissus, 109
Nash, Ogden, 156
Neoclassicism, 33
New Critics, 99, 119, 121, 167, 171–72, 205; compared to followers of Derrida, 158–63; compared to Northrop Frye, 166; procedures of, 141; writers favored by, 169
Newton, Isaac, 25, 64, 68, 71
Nietzsche, Friedrich Wilhelm, 41, 110, 124–25, 139–40, 168, 184, 186, 216, 223, 238

Ovid, 17, 21

Paine, Thomas, 54, 59n
Paul, St., 216
Peckham, Morse, 163
Peirce, C. S., 92
Petrarch, 18
Pitt, William, the Younger, 56
Plato, 17, 31, 47, 88, 100, 105, 109, 113, 117, 123, 130, 196, 202, 211–12, 235
PMLA, 99, 128
Poe, Edgar Allan, 197, 212, 225; "Black Cat," 215–18; *Eureka*, 28; "Imp of the Perverse," 218–25
Pontalis, J. B., 218
Pope, Maurice, 82n

Poulet, Georges, 124, 164
Pound, Ezra, 25, 28, 38, 40
PTL, 99
Pythagoras, 217

Raimondi, Marcantonio, 84
Ransom, John Crowe, 205
Reynolds, Joshua, 46, 63
Rimbaud, Arthur, 41
Robespierre, Maximilien François Marie Isidore de, 58
Rockwell, Norman, 226
Rogers, Samuel, 93
Rorty, Richard, 92
Rousseau, Jean Jacques, 25–27, 38, 58–60, 62, 83, 90, 116, 134–35, 137–38, 204, 233
Ruskin, John, 204
Ryle, Gilbert, 192

Said, Edward, 93, 163
Sartre, Jean-Paul, 113
Satan, 220
Saussure, Ferdinand de, 131–32
Schopenhauer, Arthur, 26
Scott, Walter, 93
Searle, John, 124
Shakespeare, William, 16, 18, 32, 53n, 120; *Antony and Cleopatra*, 37; *Hamlet*, 36; *King Lear*, 17, 35, 37, 39, 187, 237; *Othello*, 193, 195, 215, 217; "The Phoenix and the Turtle," 20
Shell, Marc, 220
Shelley, Percy Bysshe, 26, 49, 92–93, 95, 120, 165–66, 178, 190
Sidney, Philip, 16–17
Socrates, 202, 219
Southey, Robert, 93
Spenser, Edmund, 16, 20, 120
Spitzer, Leo, 99
Stevens, Wallace, 119, 123, 168

Taine, Hippolyte, 99
Tasso, Torquato, 25

Tennyson, Alfred, 169
Thompson, Francis, 23
Thompson, G.R., 216, 224
Thoreau, Henry David, 183, 185–87, 190–91, 200, 203, 225–26, 229–30, 236–38
Tillich, Paul, 30

Valéry, Paul, 28
Vaughan, Henry, 21
Virgil, 17, 26
Voltaire, 59n, 90

Warburton, William, 46, 48, 60, 62, 82
Warren, Austin, 99
Warren, Robert Penn, 121, 194, 197–99, 214
Watson, Richard, 59n
Wellek, René, 99, 124
Wilberforce, William, 24
Wilde, Oscar, 164
Williams, Raymond, 93
Wind, Edgar, 74
Wisdom, John, 223; "Gods," 192, 206–8
Wittgenstein, Ludwig, 88, 92, 94–95, 186–87, 190, 196–97, 214, 221, 225–26, 228–30, 234, 238; *Philosophical Investigations*, 183–85, 207
Woolf, Virginia, 120
Wordsworth, Dorothy, 102, 106–7, 150
Wordsworth, William, 26, 51, 54, 55n, 60, 62, 86, 91, 93, 95–96, 167, 187, 190, 204, 226, 230, 239; "Boy of Winander," 103, 183; Intimations Ode, 169, 191, 208–14, 234, 236; Lucy poems, 143–44; "Nutting," 106; Preface to *Lyrical Ballads*, 185–86, 192, 210, 229, 233; *Prelude*, 49, 53, 105–6, 150, 178; "Ruined Cottage," 103; "A Slumber Did My Spirit Seal," 101–18, 122, 142–58, 168–69, 176; "Strange Fits of Passion," 109

Yeats, W. B., 25, 121–22, 124, 178

Library of Congress Cataloging-in-Publication Data
Main entry under title:

Romanticism and contemporary criticism.

Includes index.
1. Criticism—History—20th century.
2. Romanticism. 3. English literature—19th century—
History and criticism. I. Eaves, Morris, 1944–
II. Fischer, Michael, 1949-
PN94.R59 1986   801'.95'0904   85-19472
ISBN 0-8014-1795-3 (alk. paper)
ISBN 0-8014-9352-8 (pbk. : alk. paper)